*Caring Workplaces Inspire People
to Do Their Best*

QUALITY IN QUALITY OUT

NATELLA ISAZADA

Copyright © 2021 by Natella Isazada

All rights reserved. No part of this book may be reproduced or used in any manner without written permission of the copyright owner except for the use of quotations in a book review. For more information, address: info@natellaisazada.com.

FIRST EDITION

www.natellaisazada.com

I dedicate this book to my parents Oktay and Valida Isazada, who may have wished for me to become a doctor, but instead supported most wholeheartedly and relentlessly my determination in following my own path.

Editors: Ashara Love
Auz Berger
Book designer: Dragan Bilic

CONTENTS

INTRODUCTION 7
Quality In Quality Out – Caring Workplaces Inspire People To Do Their Best 7

CHAPTER 1 – Why Taking Care of Your Employees is Key to Your Company's Success 15

A. What is the Quality In Quality Out Concept About?.................................... 15
B. Choosing the Right People.. 19
C. Are You Looking After Your People Well Enough?.. 24
D. How Employee Satisfaction Impacts Your Bottom Line................................... 33
E. How to Tell if You Have Disengaged Employees... 36
F. How to Fully Engage Your Employees.. 43

CHAPTER 2 – Current Theories on Management: What Really Works and Why 50

A. One Size Does Not Fit All 50
B. Why We Should Pay Attention to Maslow & His Hierarchy of Needs............... 53
C. How Can You Help Your Talent Reach Their Maximum Potential................... 63
D. Make performance evaluations work for you 67
E. Set Expectations by Discussing Job Descriptions Up Front & Throughout a Person's Career 76

CHAPTER 3 – Mediocrity: A Sure-Fire Way to Turn Any Workplace into a Toxic Environment 79

A. How to Keep Dilbert and His Brand of Mediocrity Out of Your Workplace 79
B. Do Flat Organizations Really Work?.. 86
C. How to Develop & Promote the Right Person to Management 96
D. Train Your Managers to Be Inspiring Leaders... 104
E. The Importance of People Skills and Character in a Manager's Overall Skill Set 115

CHAPTER 4 – 'We Have Always Done Things This Way': Why Resisting Change Ensures that Companies Stay Less-Than-Great 124

A. What Resistance to Change Can Do to Your Company 124
B. Common Characteristics of QIQO Companies............................. 130

C. The Era of Disruptive Change 135
D. What Leaders Need to Know to Manage Change 140
E. 7 Steps of Change Management 145
F. Coaching Through Resistance... 157

CHAPTER 5 – Zero Follow Through:
The Flavor of the Month that Leaves a Bad Taste — 161

A. What is Flavor-of-the-Month Syndrome & Why It Never Catches On 161
B. Creating a Culture of Follow Up (and Follow Through) 168
C. How to Get the Most Out of Employee Suggestion Programs 173
D. Pros and Cons of Hiring Consultants... 178

CHAPTER 6 – Knowledge is Power:
Spread the Knowledge, Share the Power — 182

A. Why People Hog Information & Other Precious Resources........................... 182
B. Promote & Reward Sharing as a Company Best Practice............................. 186
C. Create a Knowledge Management System Accessible
to Anyone Needing Information 189
D. Create a Culture of Continuous Learning by Providing Paid Training 194

CHAPTER 7 – QIQO: Reaping What You Sow — 199

A. Counteracting GIGO with QIQO.. 199
B. How QIQO Helps to Overcome the Silo Mentality 202
C. Internal Customers are Just as Important as External Customers 207
D. How to Instill a Winning Culture — A Different Kind of Winning.................. 216

CHAPTER 8 – Creating Accountability in a No-Blame Environment — 222

A. How to Create an Environment of Accountability
Rather Than Assigning Blame 222
B. Understanding that Output Quality
or Other Problems Aren't Always People's Fault.. 228
C. How to Help Turn Around Under-Performers 232
D. Can Coaching Help with Toxic People? 236
E. Workplace Respect is a Two-Way Street... 240

CHAPTER 9 – The Benefits of Creating a Caring Workplace
– A Proud Legacy to Leave Behind — 244

A. Reinforce and Discuss Your Company's Why
and Its Values with Both Employees and Customers 244

B. Building a Culture of Social Responsibility
Where People are Proud of the Brand They Represent 252
C. Where Do We Go from Here, and How? 261
D. Conclusion 270

ACKNOWLEDGEMENTS	**274**
ABOUT THE AUTHOR	**276**
REFERENCES	**278**

INTRODUCTION

QUALITY IN QUALITY OUT – CARING WORKPLACES INSPIRE PEOPLE TO DO THEIR BEST

WHAT LED ME TO WRITE THIS BOOK

In my years of working in the corporate world, I had my ups and downs, and experienced my share of being unheard, invisible, and unrecognized in workplaces. I have witnessed my fellow employees lifelessly arrive at work, day in day out, with little to zero interest in what they do. I have met many resigned and uninspired people who work for the paycheck and the benefits only. No interest in what they do, no passion for how they do it, and no clue why they do what they do.

I understand that not everyone chooses an examined life and ponders the existential questions, but it truly bothered me to see how many people lived their lives in miserable or at best mediocre environments. It was painful to witness this, given that we spend a large percentage of our waking hours not at home, not with loved ones, not engaged in our hobbies, but at work.

There was a point in my life when I myself hit an absolute rock bottom of my unhappiness in a workplace when I went to Las Vegas for my birthday. I had planned an action-packed entertainment program there – but instead of enjoying myself, I couldn't allow my workplace issues to sit where they belonged, on a shelf, as I took what was planned as a short respite. I had a complete nervous breakdown during my trip. I suppose I finally stopped functioning, because instead of staying busy and covering everything up, I had time to actually THINK about what was going on at work.

At that moment, I realized that something was seriously wrong with my situation. If bothersome, intrusive, upsetting thoughts of work could not leave me alone even on a well-deserved vacation in what is considered the world's capital of entertainment, I recognized that I was in trouble. I knew there was a lot more to life than this mediocre, often miserable existence I was enduring. I had to take matters into my own hands.

I am a firm believer that we, humans are meant to be happy most of the time. We are not meant to spend our entire lives suffering. There is definitely suffering in the world. It's not always possible to avoid suffering in our life, but the only value I see in suffering is serving as a catalyst for change. It can certainly be useful to experience healthy doses of pain, so we can recognize what needs attention, and as a motivation to strive for Continual Improvement.

Making change happen is important, and possible, but… it has to be the right kind of change. Through my personal journey, I discovered that corporate miseries cannot be necessarily resolved by changing employers, even though, in certain cases it's strongly advisable. Safety first is always a good motto to follow. As many have no doubt found through regrettable experience, hopping from one job to another, in the hopes of finding an ideal workplace, can introduce new sets of problems and add to existing stress, anxiety, and frustration.

What I learned is a very important thing - it's nothing new or earth shattering, but it is essential to turning your life, your work, your efforts to successfully lead an organization, a team, a company, into meaningful and valuable labor. I think we all learn this when we are ready to grow into our best, most authentic selves. So here it is:

> *Any change starts from within. Without continual attention to your own personal growth, you cannot expect to change your surroundings for the better.*

As in any worthwhile effort to build satisfaction into our life's journey, if we are to step into business success, we need to find ways to become the kind of leader that is missing in people's lives. We need to become someone who sincerely cares about people and their wellbeing. As I have discovered, our best path to success involves creating opportunities for people's growth and development. This is not a solo exercise. It is a team process, and requires thoughtful implementation and leadership by example.

The corporate world has gotten a bad rap as a mechanical heartless machine that chews people up and spits them out. This perspective repeatedly underscores that there is no caring, there is no love in workplaces.

In fact, there is some truth to this perception: bringing up those concepts in a modern workplace sounds out of place, almost foreign, and is typically dismissed as having nothing to do with the business side of things. Things are often unfair from a personal perspective, but life is unfair. THAT is the commonly accepted response to anyone bold or strange enough to bring up concepts like love or caring in a business context.

MY PERSONAL EXPERIENCE

Life is unfair.

I never liked to hear this statement. It truly bugged me to hear it bandied about so commonly. Especially when this statement is made by those who could actually do something about the way things are. When we say life is unfair, I feel like we are hiding behind this axiom to deflect responsibility from ourselves.

Someone once said in front of me that there is a saying in their language: "Life is a mother to some of us and a stepmother to others". It stood out to me as a distasteful statement that failed to serve living, breathing people, especially those depending upon solid leadership, reinforcing in them the belief that they should just accept the fact that to so many people life will be unfair, and there is nothing that can be done about it.

Fairness and recognition are among my top values in life. They go hand in hand, to me. I have lived through years of being treated as invisible – when my ideas have been dismissed, or flat out taken out of my mouth and attributed to another person. When I spoke up about my concerns, they were not taken well or addressed respectfully. I often paid a price for speaking up.

I have witnessed my coworkers get publicly humiliated in meetings, or made feel stupid for asking their manager to clarify some of the job requirements. These people eventually learned to keep their mouth shut, at the expense of missing out on learning opportunities, advancement, and personal satisfaction.

They had their voice taken away from them. Often enough, despite the unfairness of the situation they were facing, many chose not to speak up at all. The feelings of fear, resignation, and hopelessness about the situation were so deeply rooted in them that many chose not to ruffle feathers. I was so sad to see that many chose to skip exit interviews instead of parting ways with some sense of resolution by getting things off their chest.

There were several circumstances in my life when I remained silent and invisible, dealing with my own "life is a stepmother" moments, but I found it much harder to sit there and do nothing when a fellow human being's self-worth was being trampled. I absolutely had to step in and speak on their behalf. This approach did not make me very popular in some workplaces. Mainstream corporate culture often fails to care for or pay attention to an individual person's feelings. It's the accepted approach to focus on "taking care of business" with no consideration of the people responsible for making the business happen.

The missing link here is that taking care of your people is the best way to take care of business.

To paraphrase Bill Marriot, we can say: Take care of your people, and they will take care of your bottom line for you. Well taken care of employees will be most motivated to look after things including the bottom line of the business.

HOW YOU WILL BENEFIT FROM THIS BOOK

I have written this book to provide a roadmap to improving corporate performance through the radical concept of providing a positive and supportive workplace for the employees who bring the results and success to the bottom line. We need to change the current negative perceptions by first acknowledging the limitations of living in a society where it is acceptable and accepted that corporations are seen and experienced as overpowering, uncaring, heartless monsters.

Lots of people put up with the way things are because they lost any hope for things to ever get better. Many don't speak up because they feel they are alone and that their voice is not enough to make a difference.

In this book, I have compiled the research and gathered resources so you will learn how to address the common distrust issues in the workplace. This effort is especially important to implement where there is a "they" and "us" mentality among disheartened and disappointed employees who feel that there is an ocean between them and those who hold higher power in organizations.

You will benefit from learning how to dismantle the isolation of noncommunication due to silo walls of corporate culture. Doing this helps establish a healthy environment, where your people can contribute their best, where teamwork is common, and where strong relationships are forged, based on trust and knowledge that management has their best interests in mind.

Without trust, you cannot expect the best output from your employees. People need to feel safe to venture out of their shells and speak up. No one who feels alone or too small thinks they have anything of value to offer; this overlooks a vast resource of ingenuity and willing contribution.

This book will show how, together, we can build Caring Workplaces, where people are not only comfortable being heard without fear of repercussion, but where they know they have opportunities to do what they love, what they are best at, to feel valued in contributing to the organizational success in the most wholehearted way, to realize their potential and be recognized for their gifts, knowledge, and contributions.

A truly Caring Workplace will assign the right people to do the right jobs, based on their strengths and passions. Allowing people to discover their **Why's** and discover how their *Why's* can align and support the company's purpose would be the ultimate match that allows your people to blossom and fulfill their purpose while benefiting the company in the most meaningful way.

Most people feel good knowing that they add value, and the recognition they want is not necessarily something monetary, something big or loud. If someone feels that their efforts are acknowledged and appreciated, it adds to their self-worth and encourages them to repeat the good behavior, to continue adding value through their contributions.

Positive reinforcement of achievements and contributions play an important role in encouraging people to do their best – for no other reason than because they are inspired to do so by the very environment they work in. This becomes a circle of growth, the opposite of a vicious cycle of failure and despair. By passing the goodness forward, we nurture and nourish a thriving work place, and the bottom line is guaranteed to show the value in doing so.

I have been fortunate to work with some truly excellent corporations, to learn the greatness of people empowerment, and to know, for a fact, what is possible to achieve if we set our minds on making a rewarding work experience for all our priority.

VISION

In today's society there is tendency to romanticize entrepreneurship at the expense of looking down on the concept of employment or being an employee. While working for corporations has gotten a bad rap (unfortunately, with some veracity to it), I believe it should not be mindlessly accepted or tolerated.

I have a dream. I dream of a world where people who work for a paycheck are happily employed by Caring Workplaces, where they are inspired to do their best every day. In my dream, even though these people are still called 'employees,' noone thinks of them as sad little beings with boring jobs, who live their lives devoid of fun and fulfillment. In my dream everyone's life is infused with joy, because every day they are adding value by using their talents to produce meaningful work, making an effort that is worth doing and personally rewarding.

As G. Shawn Hunter, author of *"Small Acts of Leadership"* said: "Some people have jobs, some have careers, and some have callings (Hunter, 2016). Jobs are a means to another end, such as supporting family and leisure time. Careers are driven not only by money but also by professional advancement. Often, when advancement stalls, alienation and disengagement set in. Yet a calling is a pursuit of something greater than oneself, and this is the path to the highest inspiration for others."

How can we help more people find happiness at work? Through creating workplaces where people can pursue activities with meaning, contributing to something bigger than themselves, growing and developing into the best versions of themselves. By fostering supportive workplaces and finding work that is meaningful and suitable to frontline employees, they get to work on something that they find inspiration in.

CHAPTER 1 – WHY TAKING CARE OF YOUR EMPLOYEES IS KEY TO YOUR COMPANY'S SUCCESS

A. WHAT IS THE QUALITY IN QUALITY OUT CONCEPT ABOUT?

What defines an organization and determines its success? This is not a novel question. Others have pondered this subject in depth and at great length. Is it the *excellent quality products and services* that we provide? Coming from a Quality Management background, I affirm that quality is extremely important – but, alas, it is more of an admission price than a guarantor of success. The secret to success is not simply having an inventory of excellent quality, highly salable products. A successful business giant such as Facebook creates no content of its own; Airbnb, a hugely popular hospitality marketplace, owns none of the rental accommodations it lists online; and Uber, a world-wide taxi company, utilizes driver-owned vehicles as convenient, flexible transportation for millions worldwide.

Do *state-of-the-art facilities* determine a company's success? Brick-and-mortar stores are disappearing, as more businesses are switching to virtual platforms. Furniture companies, like Wayfair and many others, have apps that allow their buyers to look at every piece of furniture or get entire room ideas that best suit their particular needs without touching it or seeing it in 'real life' before purchase.

Does a *strong mission statement* that unifies all of the organization's activities and efforts define lasting success? That is not always the case, as indicated by the history of one of the most successful American corporations, IBM. During World War II, this company's mission was to technologically support the WWII Holocaust in Germany, an undertaking that audaciously devoted itself to killing millions of people in Europe. Even though IBM pursued this mission with chilling success at the time, today, that is, most likely, a chapter in the company's history that they are not proud of (Black, 2000).

Is *technology that drastically transforms our lives and businesses* a key factor in driving organizational success? According to Jim Collins' research in his book **"Good to Great: Why Some Companies Make the Leap...And Others Don't,"** on why some companies successfully make the transition from good to great, technology and technology-driven changes were not the reason for profound transformation, nor was it noted as a root cause for a company's decline (Collins, 2001).

If these factors do not guarantee consistent positive business outcomes, what might be a more reliable indicator of success in an organization? Well, we often hear that *people are the greatest assets* of any organization. Of course, not just any people, but the right people. Having the right people on board must be the key to success, don't you think? Well, perhaps we need to delve a bit deeper.

As important as the people who work for you are, it doesn't take long to produce examples of companies that experienced a precipitous decline due to the mistakes and wrongdoings of their own people – in some cases, brought about by the very people who founded those companies in the first place. From Blackberry to Groupon to Enron – these companies faced business slowdowns, declines in stock prices, or even complete disintegration due to their founders' lack of innovation, unscrupulous accounting methods, or flat-out corporate fraud (McIntyre, et al., 2013).

If an organization's success is not determined by its product, technological capabilities, a mission statement, or its staff, then the important question still must be answered: What actually does serve as a key component to enduring stability and success?

As it turns out, the essential factor seems to be how people are led, inspired, and empowered to put forth their best effort, to persist, and to innovate. In turn, this enables companies to continually move forward, survive, and thrive through times of change. No company would be able to come up with a winning strategy for success without the knowledge and shared wisdom of its leaders. Many of these leaders are distinguished by a certain focus: fostering ongoing and stable corporate success outcomes by creating a productive and reliable work culture; in essence, that of a **Caring Organization**.

WHAT IS WORKPLACE CULTURE?

According to management consulting firm gothamCulture, *Organizational* or *Workplace Culture* is defined as the underlying beliefs, assumptions, values and ways of interacting that contribute to the unique social and psychological environment of an organization. It includes an organization's expectations, experiences, and philosophy that guides member behavior. It is expressed in member self image, inner workings, interactions with the outside world, and future expectations (Cancialosi, 2017). Workplace Culture is based on shared attitudes, customs, as well as written and — even more importantly — unwritten rules, developed and refined over time by regular application. An organization's culture is comprised of the shared values of individual people who work within that culture. Most importantly, those values are ideally supported by the leadership of the organization through daily decisions and actions.

Many layers of decision making contribute to the successfully built and sustained corporate culture of a truly *Caring Organization*. We will discuss the key components in greater detail throughout this book, but it's important to first understand the essential component of this culture: the **Quality In Quality Out (QIQO)** concept.

Visualize your life as a series of interrelated steps, where the connections may not always be noticeable upfront, but nevertheless, upon reflection, make sense later. The same is true within organizations, except with more pronounced, and often more immediate, cause-and-effect relationships. Every new step, in every new process, tends to impact the consequent, interconnected steps; some more directly, some less. The causal relationships between all parts of the system are always there, and the changes introduced by each new process upon the entire organization can be profound.

In systems thinking, the output of one process is, by default, the input of the next process. Here is a simple example: to fill a certain job opening in your company, the process usually begins by clearly defining the requirements of the job. If there is a lack of clarity about the necessary knowledge, skills, abilities, and crucial personal characteristics required for candidates to provide what the company is seeking, the hiring process typically produces questionable results. Originating in the field of computer science, the term **Garbage In, Garbage Out (GIGO)**, became a common cultural reference by describing the well-known mentality behind poor or mediocre performance, fueled by lack of attention to preparation, instruction, and requirements to get a project done properly. The term succinctly describes the culprit behind many workplace inefficiencies and nonconformities.

In my career, I observed a hopeless, helpless, rather passive attitude underlying this term. By placing blame on predecessors (Garbage In), one declares oneself a victim of circumstance forced to produce low quality outcome (Garbage Out). If you ask any informed quality auditor the definition of insanity, they will confirm that it's doing the same thing repeatedly and expecting different results. In other words, if a system repeatedly provides poor quality materials or unclear input, excellent results cannot be expected, unless we decide to give up the privilege of claiming ourselves sane.

To escape this vicious cycle, I propose making a commitment to once and for all abandon the tired GIGO concept and replace it in our minds, vocabulary, and actions with the more powerful *QIQO* model. Like its more pessimistic distant cousin GIGO, QIQO also raises the point that the value of the input will normally impact, if not dictate, the value of the output; what is drastically different about it is the shift toward taking full responsibility for the quality and value of one's own inputs.

By continually remaining aware of the needs of those who rely on our input for producing their output, and by making a conscious effort to consistently stand behind the quality of what comes out of our hands or our computers, all of us, as a team, share accountability for the final outcome of the process. This commitment sustains a chain reaction of consistent win-win outcomes, with the excellent side benefit of fostering an encouraging environment to develop a reliable team of empowered and accountable individuals. Leaders of successful Caring Organizations already think in terms of the QIQO concept. They may not use this terminology, but they definitely operate with a comprehensive understanding that the quality of our inputs determines the quality of our outputs.

B. CHOOSING THE RIGHT PEOPLE

Keeping the concept of QIQO in mind, the most important decision to make, in order to achieve quality results, is to select quality people to perform those jobs. Choosing the right people to fill crucial roles is also, undoubtedly, one of the most challenging skills that corporate leadership must nurture, develop, and sustain. It's quite common for employers to put more effort into hiring the right people for higher-level positions, as they are considered to have a higher impact on the results. While there is some truth to this, **Caring Leaders** know to place importance on hiring correctly for all positions, as the cost of hiring mistakes hurts the company in more than one way.

Google is an employer known to take pride in investing the same amount of time and energy to interview an entry-level software engineer position as they take to review a senior executive. With the goal of consistently hiring the best talent, they benchmark their process against the way it is typically done in academia. If one hiring manager makes a decision, they might not be inclined to hire someone smarter than them; human nature tends to get in the way. Universities are known for retaining their professors for longer-lasting tenures. Academic hiring relies on peer-based decisions rather than hierarchical hiring based solely on the choice or preference of a single hiring manager (Schmidt & Rosenberg, 2015).

Talented employees are not very easy to come across. The goal is to identify the talent you need for your organization's success, then attract it, bring it in, develop it further, and maintain a conducive work environment that will encourage the excellent quality talent to stay with your organization for a long time. What are the best methods for reliably locating good people? Many companies rely on recruiters, but that approach alone limits options, and can cost a great deal. If you already have great people on the team, they may know other great people they could recommend. While there is no guarantee that all of those internally recommended hires will work out, a high percentage do, as employees usually take care not to refer candidates with an array of issues.

One effective way to encourage great employees to recruit suitable candidates is to develop referral programs with attractive benefits for your employees, or to incorporate referrals as a part of the performance evaluation process, providing a basis for further incentives and rewards. Since the quality of our decisions determines the quality of the outputs we get, it is advisable to keep the hiring process merit based. To maintain the company's best interests, the decision-making power should reside with a hiring committee, thus avoiding a potential conflict of interest with friends hiring friends.

Often hiring managers anticipate the future success of the candidates based on past achievements, focusing heavily on the candidates' credentials. Of course, it's good to know that the person joining the team is capable of doing the job they are hired for, but an impressive resume could be hiding someone lacking other qualities crucial for the team's success. Another important consideration, in this era of rapid technological changes and scientific advancements, is hiring someone based solely on their specific technical skills, even though their technology-related skills and knowledge might be rendered obsolete in the near future. In many instances, a stronger approach is hiring candidates with potential for growth, such as lifelong learners whose passion for learning will continue encouraging them to improve their knowledge and skills.

While it's great to have a well-written job description for the position you are trying to fill, you risk overlooking some great candidates if you set out to find that ideal candidate with a proven record of doing 100% of what the role entails. A more realistic and practical approach is to hire candidates with 80% of what is required for the job, people who are willing and able to develop and acquire the remaining 20% of skills and knowledge once they have been hired. For most jobs, it's advisable to focus on their strength in dealing with people and being an effective part of the team.

A Canadian airport, a winner of multiple international awards, benefits from a hiring strategy that seeks more than just technical skills in their candidates. While the lead management team acknowledges that, for certain occupations such as finance, accounting, or engineering, the underlying technical expertise is a must, they believe that technical skills can be taught. They maintain that the most important quality is a cultural fit. Purely technically minded job seekers are not as valued as those who have the ability to get along with people, and who know how to build and maintain good relationships. An example of this hiring practice is a person with a sales and marketing background who served successfully in a position of Director of Maintenance, chosen due to her excellent leadership abilities and outstanding negotiation skills, which she had demonstrated both internally and outside of the organization.

How can the selection process ensure that the right things about the candidate are learned at the right time? Caring Organizations apply the QIQO principle during the selection process to get desirable results. For one thing, cookie-cutter questions yield cookie-cutter responses. The least helpful question of all is the one that is most frequently asked: "What are your biggest weaknesses?" It's no surprise that hiring managers get the most rehearsed answers to this all-too-common question. No one wants to discuss their weaknesses with a bunch of strangers, who also happen to be their prospective employer. That's why so often we come across the "overachieving perfectionists" who "tend to take too much upon themselves," are "guilty of working long hours" and are "harder on themselves than they should be." Job seekers are often advised to "cleverly" disguise one of their perceived strengths as a weakness in order to pass a job interview.

Instead of going through a tired script, Caring Organizations' leaders can focus on creating a safe environment conducive to a naturally flowing two-way conversation between the prospective employee and the prospective employer, where people authentically share everything relevant to the job at hand and organically highlight the candidate's ability to contribute meaningfully to the organization's goals. Instead of asking them to confess about their perceived weaknesses, it's far more effective to engage them in a detailed conversation about their past projects, with their high points and possible low points, what they would do better next time, and lessons learned. This allows you to learn about the candidate's thought process and get a better idea of how they might fit into the organization.

Some people are good interviewees, but do not work out in a new job afterward; the interview process should not be the only way to evaluate and select the best candidate. It's much more effective to apply a combination of methods, including personality and motivation tests. My father, who served in the military all his life, advancing from the rank of private to colonel, told me that new recruits were placed under stress to test the effectiveness of their problem-solving skills. In a civilian setting, employers may not have the luxury of seeing their candidates perform under real-life stress to the extent that's available to the military, but great tools such as personality or motivation tests can reveal candidates' working styles while under pressure.

Every organization has a unique culture. Define yours clearly, so that you and your team know what a cultural fit means to your organization, and can easily spot the preferred behaviors. Another common trend is to test the candidate's interpersonal skills in a free peer-to-peer setting outside of the walls of a boardroom. This can help determine if they are a good cultural fit for your organization. In service-focused organizations, QIQO requires greater care in employee selection, because of the direct and immediate interface between employees and customers. Employee attitude is capable of immediately affecting customers. Ensuring that employees are a strong cultural fit makes a significant impact on the company's success by cultivating positive customer experiences.

One example of a company that knows and embraces this concept is Zappos, an online shoe and clothing store, whose motto is to 'wow' their customers through service. To deliver the 'wow' experience, Zappos empowers its employees to create fun through using their imagination. They know that fun can only be created by those employees who are wholeheartedly engaged in their work and are enthusiastic about it. This employer is determined to retain only those employees who are the biggest fans of their company culture. Upon completion of initial training, everyone is offered a $2,000 bribe to leave the company. Those who are *not culturally fit will take the money and quit; those who remain tend to be keepers* (Robinson, 2018; Taylor, 2008).

The 2017 research by Waterstone Human Capital on *"Canada's Most Admired Employers"* concluded: "Cultural fit is king when finding, and keeping, talent." From this perspective, the Toronto-based retail technology company Flipp was selected as the winner. The recipient of two of *Canada's Most Admired* awards – *Best Workplace 2018* and *Best Managed Companies* awards – the management team at Flipp chose to focus on cultural fit as a key principle for long-term success, producing excellent results while reinventing their retail space (Waterstone Human Capital, 2017).

C. ARE YOU LOOKING AFTER YOUR PEOPLE WELL ENOUGH?

When asked what their most important asset is, most companies will tell you it is their people. Yet, most companies refer to their people using an ironic term: **Human Resources (HR)**. This notion compares people to any other resource such as raw materials, technology, or machinery. This term entered our vocabulary in the late 1880s, when a political economist from the United States, John R. Commons, first used it in his book, *"The Distribution of Wealth."* At the beginning, the role of *HR* was seen as a liaison, someone who could resolve misunderstandings between the employer and employees (Wikipedia). As the term was subsequently applied during the 20th century, it solidified the notion that workers could be viewed as a type of capital asset. Other similar terms such as: *manpower, labor, staff, headcount, personnel,* and *full-time equivalent, (FTE),* in the language of finance, took over the conversation, even though we could have simply referred to people as *people*.

Stating what should be quite obvious: there is a lot more to people than the mere function or title they hold on the organizational chart.

Personal ingenuity, imagination, and an acute mind are just the beginning of a list of attributes that might be important, but these qualities often get overlooked, inhibited, or discouraged. Treating people as mere manpower does not cultivate an inclination to capitalize on hidden talents, and prevents employees' true potential from being developed and enhanced.

In the 21st century, more and more organizations are moving away from using the term HR. Instead, they are selecting job titles such as Chief People Officer at Ceridian or World Vision Canada; Chief People Services Officer at Meridian Credit Union; VP of People Operations at Wealthsimple Financial; Head of Talent; Chief Talent Officer; and others that emphasize the personal nature of the employee/employer relationship. These companies' choices reflect an evolving culture change: from managing HR as a capital asset to engaging people, developing talent, and refocusing to become a people-centered Caring Organization.

WHAT IS DIFFERENT ABOUT CARING ORGANIZATIONS?

Caring Organizations do not make customers their only, or even primary, focus. They establish themselves in the marketplace by getting their internal affairs in good shape and by taking good care of, cultivating, and empowering their employees.

FedEx, the world's largest express transportation company, seems to have done something right about its internal affairs. Its 'People First' corporate philosophy is based on the premise that employees working in a positive environment will provide better service quality to customers, which would then lead to customers using more FedEx products and services. Managers are trained to treat all workers fairly and to promote respect company-wide. This culture has been integral to the company's success; FedEx is a recipient of multiple awards, such as recognizing it as one of the top 10 Best Employers in Aon Hewitt's Best Employers in

Korea five times, Best Employer for Young Generation in 2013, and the Best Employer for Women in 2011 (FedEx.com, 2016).

What are some of the cultural norms that keep our organizations from authentic excellence? Let's look at how our 'greatest asset' is actually treated in mainstream workplaces.

When I was growing up, I had a friend who worked as a lifeguard at a local swimming pool. One day, he convinced me to come to the pool so that he could teach me how to swim. When I showed up for our first lesson, ready to receive my instruction, without any preamble, he suddenly threw me into the middle of the pool on the deep end and left me on my own. Having never been in the deep waters before, I started drowning. I tried to take a breath but struggled to keep my head above the water. I was nauseated by the chlorine water I swallowed in the process. My arms flailing, my futile efforts to push myself against the water quickly drained my energy. Before completely exhausting myself, I managed to make my way to the side of the pool and grab onto the edge. My 'teacher' stood around and watched me the entire time as if nothing out of the ordinary was happening. As I slowly came back to my senses, he approached me. Seeing my distress up close, he apologized and informed me that the 'swim or die' technique usually worked, and he would have never let me drown. I felt that enough damage was done already, and I walked away from our swimming lessons and, eventually, from our friendship as well.

Later on, I learned how to swim through proper instruction and practice. The 'swim or die' technique never clicked with me. As I grew older and experienced different workplaces, I learned that this 'training' approach is actually quite common in the corporate world. Sometimes, the 'swim or die' culture is apparent from the beginning; an excellent candidate is recruited and hired for a suitable role, but after bringing them on board, literally nothing is done to help new hires get acclimatized to their new environment. This seems quite a waste of time and energy, but it is far from rare.

A design and manufacturing company in Washington State hired an out-of-state estimator. They did not provide the new hire with any type of orientation nor an office tour to introduce him to coworkers. The new hire began making their way through the premises, trying to meet people and to get to know the surrounding area, finding a location for lunch, etc. Another brand-new employee was left loitering around the office for two weeks without a designated desk or any direction on what projects she was supposed to work on. Any time this person approached the department manager with questions, she got excuses why the company email account was not set up yet, and she was flat out told to just go get busy. These bewildered new hires didn't last very long in their jobs.

In both cases, no one seemed interested in helping new team members start their employment on the right foot. When this happens, a new hire usually is left with two choices – to walk away, like I did from the swimming pool, or to blindly work through the corporate culture, finding their way through the intricacies of the job, managing unknown expectations, learning the politics, and trying to survive through trial and error, with a long, painful learning curve ahead of them. Clearly, this creates a problem for both parties: wasted time, money, the opportunity cost for the employer, and disillusionment and confusion for the employee.

The 'swim or die' technique can also be observed when shifting a person into a new role within the organization. Some companies consider this a fair way to test a candidate's ability to transition into a leadership position. Apparently without support or guidance, the employee is expected to demonstrate self-reliance and resourcefulness. However, this approach comes with a major opportunity cost for the organization. Instead of spending time treading rough waters in the dark, the fledgling leader could be providing a benefit to the organization by utilizing their natural strength in the most productive ways, while learning necessities for the new position, with proper coaching.

Other mistakes employers make, when it comes to how best to treat people, include time wasters such as falsely advertising vacancies, and doing a poor job of matching candidates to the jobs they are hired for. Companies that don't treat people right sometimes hide behind slogans such as 'Putting the human back in Human Resources' and 'Making everyone's life easier.' But there is nothing human in treating people merely as another capital resource, or even worse, in sacrificing time, energy, and self-confidence to suit the presumed efficiency of well-established production methods. This is exactly what is taking place at some of the world's most highly regarded corporations.

In 2006, a 45-year-old Toyota senior engineer was found dead by his daughter in his home in Toyota City, central Japan, where the company headquarters are located. This person's sudden death by ischemia, a shortage of blood to the heart, was attributed to more than 80 overtime hours a month, including systematic work on nights and weekends as well as frequent overseas trips to promote the hybrid Camry at an international car show in the U.S. Another Toyota employee died in 2002 after working about 106 hours of overtime in one month, until the day before his death. The 30-year-old Quality Controller collapsed due to heart failure at work.

According to medical professionals, high stress can lead to high blood pressure, which is a risk factor for heart disease and heart attack. Working for many years in the field of Quality Management in Manufacturing, I often witnessed great reverence for Toyota Production methods in terms of their reputation for a high level of efficiency, productivity, and commitment to *Continual Improvement (CI)*. No question, there is much to learn from these practices. Yet we don't hear nearly enough of the dire price of this efficiency and productivity – particularly with regard to the people literally worked to death. This is not only happening at Toyota.

In a more recent case, in 2014, a 27-year-old trainee at a casting company in central Japan died of heart failure in his firm's dormitory after his overly demanding work schedule finally took its toll. *This death was ruled to be directly related to the long hours of overtime he was forced to perform.* About 20% of the entire workforce in Japan are considered at risk of death from overwork. Statistics show that 10,000 workers a year drop dead after working 60 to 70-hour weeks. While in Japanese culture, a specific term – kiroshi – exists for death by overwork, workaholism is, in fact, a much wider problem. It deteriorates people's physical and mental health while it destroys families all over the world.

Here in North America, work-first culture is also quite common. According to a national study, approximately 43% of Canadian workers feel burned out. According to a Staples survey, more than half of U.S. employees feel overworked. There is a disturbing report from Oxfam America, called *"Lives on The Line: The Human Cost of Cheap Chicken,"* based on research conducted from 2013 to 2015 on the four companies reported to be responsible for the 60% of the U.S. poultry market: Tyson Foods Inc., Pilgrim's Pride Corp., Perdue Farms Inc., and Sanderson Farms Inc. (Oxfam America. 2015).

Oxfam America, a branch of a worldwide organization that works to address poverty and social injustice, reports that their staff traveled to three American states — Mississippi, North Carolina, and Arkansas — to conduct interviews with current and former workers, worker advocates, attorneys, medical experts, analysts, and others in the communities surrounding those poultry companies. The poultry processing plants, where 250,000 low-wage American workers are reportedly employed, were described as dark, cold, and foul smelling. According to the report, they have unusually high rates of workplace illness and injury, mainly musculoskeletal disorders caused by the repetitive motions of cutting, slicing and pulling over 20,000 times a day. In addition, the workers there have health complications caused by dehydration and minimized restroom breaks.

These conditions seem unimaginable in this day and age, in a highly-developed part of the world but, according to the senior advisor of Oxfam America Oliver Gottfried, it is more common than we realize. These poultry companies are trying to churn out as much product as they can, as quickly as they can. For many immigrant workers, this is a reality in the poultry industry. It leaves employees in physical distress, living in survival mode.

HOW DO OTHER EMPLOYERS TAKE CARE OF EMPLOYEES AND THEIR WELL-BEING?

Since people are supposedly a company's 'main asset,' why do so many employers overlook training and professional development? Some employers believe that people should only be trained for the skills they need to fulfill their current work duties. If they already know how to do their job, no further training is required. This perspective can be somewhat logical: "Why invest in someone's training, if that person is just going to leave to use their brand-new skills somewhere else?"

One tech company in California deliberately caps how much training their employees get. The company created a culture in which any knowledge sharing between coworkers was prohibited. Everyone was encouraged to stay secretive about their knowledge and skill levels. The result was narrow specialization and little to no teamwork among the staff. The owners' approach, controlling the workforce and preventing anyone from growing professionally, so that they could not go elsewhere with their knowledge, resulted in their top IT talent seeking jobs elsewhere. Eventually, the corporate environment deteriorated so much that a group of key employees left within a month of each other, and the company was left without much stability to sort things out.

Limiting training opportunities not only limits growth for the employees and the company they work for, it affects the entire marketplace and availability of trained talent in the overall pool of candidates eligible for employment.

Within 10 years, from 2005 to 2015, a staffing company called ManpowerGroup conducted its annual *"Talent Shortage Survey,"* asking employers how much difficulty they were experiencing filling jobs due to lack of available talent. The percentage of employers who reported a talent shortage fluctuated between 14% and 52% over the course of years, reaching its peak in the United States in 2011 and 2012, especially for tradespeople roles. Other jobs reported to be hard to fill were quite diverse, including drivers, nurses, teachers, administrative professionals, and more.

A high percentage of surveyed employers reported that lack of talent affected their ability to serve their customers' needs. At the same time, only 10% of employers reported that they are providing more training to their existing staff in order to prepare them to fill vacancies or to pursue other opportunities. *The Wall Street Journal* links this perceived inability to get the right candidates to the absence of support from those same employers toward solid employee training programs (Cappelli, 2011).

Caring Organizations know that while there is a risk of losing competent employees, the risk of incompetent employees staying is always higher. They also understand that employees who are naturally inclined toward learning will always be on the lookout for growth opportunities. They will appreciate their employer's support for their learning goals, and they can use their newly gained skills and knowledge, not necessarily for greener pastures elsewhere, but to become more versatile at work, moving to new functions within the organization. However, if they see no personal or professional growth available in their current positions, they will not tolerate stagnation for too long. Eventually, they will start looking for places with more opportunity for growth.

A 2012 study by **Harvard Business Review (HBR)** titled "*Why Top Young Managers are in Nonstop Job Hunt*" surveyed 1,200 young top performers internationally and found that "dissatisfaction with some employee-development efforts appears to fuel many early exits." Employers need to create well-balanced opportunities for supporting their employees' professional and personal growth, satisfying their need to learn without splurging on overly expensive training programs (Hamori, et al., 2012).

Sharing the cost between the employee and the employer can also be a good solution, depending on the situation. A manager taking a genuine interest in their employee's career goals and future aspirations can go a long way, along with the support they can provide, to fill in the gaps between where the employee wants to be and where they are currently at. During annual performance evaluations, employees are routinely asked where they see themselves in the future or what kind of training they would like to have. They share their aspirations and the desire to learn with their manager. How disheartening it must be for employees when, year after year, the manager just files away the paperwork, and lets another year go by without helping achieve those results.

Caring Organizations understand the value of treating their people right. For example, Stellar Solutions, a woman-owned small business that provides engineering services and management of commercial aerospace programs, set out their vision to satisfy their customers' critical needs while helping employees achieve their dream job. This philosophy allowed the company to consistently grow its revenues and profitability while enjoying the highest levels of customer satisfaction; 100% of its customers state their readiness to recommend Stellar Solutions to others. This approach led the company to receive multiple prestigious workplace awards including the *Best Medium*

Workplace, Best Workplace for Generation X, Best Workplace for Recent Grads, and most importantly, the *2017 Malcolm Baldridge National Quality Award,* granted to the most outstanding organizations in the U.S. by the **National Institute of Standards and Technology (NIST)**, the Department of Commerce, and the President of the United States. In the survey conducted by Great Places to Work, nearly 100% of Stellar's employees reported their company to be an excellent workplace, offering great challenges, atmosphere, bosses, communication, pride, and rewards.

D. HOW EMPLOYEE SATISFACTION IMPACTS YOUR BOTTOM LINE

Why do we care about customer satisfaction so much? Because we link it directly to our bottom line. Customer satisfaction or dissatisfaction with our services is potentially capable of making or breaking our business. We are clear on this. Throughout my career in corporate management, I have seen companies commonly set company objectives, vision, quality, and policy to focus quite specifically on customer satisfaction. I agree that customers' perception of the company's ability to meet their expectations, to create that *'wow'* effect, is vital to any organization's success. There are quite a few methods to monitor and measure customer satisfaction: investigating the slightest customer complaints, conducting **Root Cause Analysis (RCA)**, reporting back to the customers about **corrective actions** taken, and maintaining continual follow up until outstanding issues are resolved.

Root Cause Analysis defined:
Root Cause Analysis is a systematic process for identifying "root causes" of problems or events and developing an approach for responding to them. RCA is based on the basic idea that effective management requires more than merely "putting out fires" for

> problems that develop, but instead putting the focus on finding a way to prevent them.
>
> **Corrective Action** is the action taken to identify and eliminate the cause(s) of a problem, in order to prevent its recurrence.

Tracking the satisfaction levels of our employees is a far less common goal in businesses. The reason is that the direct link between employee job satisfaction and the bottom line is often missed. When organizations are entirely focused on tracking profits, they overlook processes that contribute to it and are integral to producing consistent positive results. The overlooked link is job performance. If treated as mere numbers or 'man-hour expenditures,' people cannot be expected to put extra effort into their work, exercise extra care when handling company property, or show initiative to improve the quality of the product they make.

A very important point is often missed: unmotivated employees do not necessarily decide to leave right away. They may remain in their place of employment for financial reasons or due to other obligations, at least until they feel secure enough to move on. In the meantime, they remain in positions that are unsuitable to them, affecting not just the job but the workplace, with attitudes of dissatisfaction, resignation, and apathy.

Here are just some of the statements I have heard in the course of my years working in corporations:

- "I'm paid by the hour here; I just do whatever it takes to get me through the day."
- "All I need to do is to show up, do whatever job I do, and stay out of trouble."
- "Why should I care to speak up if no one listens anyway?"

I have listened to mentally resigned supervisors who said, "I am just a cog in a mechanism, I am no one here," instead of taking charge of the success of the team entrusted to them. These statements are from people who've lost their spark, feel no excitement about coming to work each day, and only do so with a 9 am to 5 pm mentality. This defeated attitude is dangerous to the company as a whole, as it can infect the rest of the team. As a team member, employee, and manager, I saw how the company's bottom line suffered.

For a healthy bottom line, a company that encourages and empowers its employees' best efforts helps to build collective success. Typically, collective corporate success is defined by increased shareholder **Return On Investment (ROI)** through a company's strong financial performance. The definition of the bottom line is the net income left over after taxes and business expenses. You don't need this explained to you, but the missing piece that can all but guarantee a successful bottom line definitely needs to be highlighted.

Again, not rocket science: it has been proven that the more satisfied employees are, the better decision-makers and stronger problem-solvers they are. Studies of productivity show that organizations with more satisfied employees tend to be overall more effective than organizations with fewer employees who enjoy their work. Happy employees are also more likely to enhance the organization's image, by speaking positively about it both inside and outside the workplace. They go beyond their defined roles, and are more likely to help their coworkers; they do this because they want to re-create or amplify their own positive experiences.

In his HBR publication, Alex Edmans shares 28 years of data from the *"100 Best Companies to Work for in America,"* a study conducted by the Great Place to Work Institute. This study found that firms with high employee satisfaction outperform their peers by 2.3% to 3.8% per year in long-run stock returns – 89% to 184% cumulative. Moreover, the results suggest that it is employee satisfaction that causes good performance and not the other way around. When company performance in similar studies is measured by its profits, the correlation between satisfaction and profits is sometimes questioned. It becomes a chicken or egg argument – there is no easy way to determine which condition caused the other. That is why this particular study looked at stock prices over the long term as a way to determine the financial success of the company (Edmans, 2016).

A study by Kenexa, an IBM Company, that provides employment and retention services, confirmed the effect of employee satisfaction on the bottom line: it showed that the companies with the most engaged employees had five times higher total shareholder return over five years than those with the least engaged employees (Kruse, 2012).

Toronto-based Molson Coors Beverage Company found that engaged employees were five times less likely to have workforce safety incidents, and when the incidents did occur, they were significantly less serious in nature. Molson Coors published their average cost per incident numbers: $63 for engaged employees vs the average of $392 for non-engaged employees. This doesn't count increased worker's compensation insurance premium rates for time-loss incident costs due to worker-away-from-work time (Vance, 2006).

E. HOW TO TELL IF YOU HAVE DISENGAGED EMPLOYEES

Dissatisfied employees can go unrecognized and undetected in a workplace for any length of time. How can you tell if you have disengaged employees? Organizational behavior textbooks describe four usual ways employees express their dissatisfaction with the company they work for. Two of those approaches are positive and two are negative: *Voice and Loyalty,* and *Neglect and Exit.*

Employees' visible attempts to improve unsatisfactory work conditions include but certainly are not limited to: *Voice and Loyalty:*

- **Voice:** An active way to initiate change, intended to bring issues of concern to management's attention. If a dissatisfied employee is committed enough to remain employed despite poor working conditions, and if they have enough courage to raise these concerns, it is advisable for management to recognize and appreciate their effort, and listen to them, because these are the people who sincerely want to see the organization improve and succeed.

- **Loyalty:** A passive method, based on the belief that if they wait long enough, things might improve; this is an expression of trust that management will do the right thing. This method's positive outcome is not always guaranteed; simply waiting for change rarely leads to actual, needed change taking place.

On the other end of the spectrum are two negative methods for expressing dissatisfaction: *Neglect and Exit*. Employees tend to resort to those strategies after losing trust in management's ability and willingness to listen and to help.

- **Neglect:** In this strategy, employees do not exit, but choose to stay with the company for a variety of reasons. They stay (until they are ready to make a move), allowing their attention to their job duties to slide further and further. They have reached the point of resignation and cynicism. When they stop making any effort, they lower their productivity and may choose to spend time surfing the net or otherwise dealing with personal business, for example, researching on opportunities outside their current workplace.

- **Exit:** Employees typically use this strategy in one of two situations: (1) an appealing opportunity, even if unsolicited, presents itself from outside of the company and they cannot resist, or (2) they actively seek out a new job because they can no longer deal with the challenging realities of their current job. Even if there is less control over the employees wanting to explore new horizons, management can still pay close attention to growing dissatisfaction levels. How bad can it be, you may ask, when someone who's no longer interested leaves your company? The real question is – is it more of an exception or more of a trend? If your people are growing dissatisfied to the extent of leaving, it can really hurt the company. When your work environment creates a larger scale employee turnover, especially in a strong economy where there is no lack of employment opportunities, workplaces have to know what engages their employees and work on making their work environment attractive.

You can identify people who choose the *Neglect* strategy by their absenteeism records: they tend to take available sick time and personal days not only out of necessity but to gain some time — *any* time — away from work. Dissatisfied and disengaged employees are prone to producing non-conforming products and to experiencing more frequent workplace injuries because they stop paying attention or start taking short cuts, in order to get their tasks out of the way. After an occupational injury, they are also reluctant to return to work despite the employer's efforts to bring them back on modified duty. After mentally checking out of their job, they don't care if they are caught and disciplined for abusing the company's 'sick day' policy. Some may sabotage management initiatives by openly spreading their discontent among coworkers; others may appropriate company resources for their personal use, since they have convinced themselves that they are entitled to it, as the company has mistreated them for long enough. Depending on how 'creative' they are, dissatisfied employees can actually hide behind their desks and work in their resigned ways, getting paid merely for their presence at work and not for the results they produce.

Sooner or later, management is likely to become aware of the situation. How the situation is addressed can have long-term positive or negative outcomes. Instead of focusing on the symptoms of the problem by trying to address specific undesirable behaviors, it's important to understand the *root cause* behind the job dissatisfaction, by looking deeper into why your employees are absent.

What's keeping your team members away from work?

- Is it due to work-related stress?
- Do they have a sick relative to take care of?
- Do they have a health condition that may be stigmatized by society that they feel they must prevent disclosure in the workplace?

The more the employee remains absent, the easier it gets for them to develop chronic *absenteeism*. Unresolved health or other personal issues tend to seep into the rest of the person's activities, affecting their productivity, and remaining a distraction long after available 'sick' time has been used up.

Even if an employee chooses to return to work, unresolved health issues can lead to *presenteeism*, which is when employees are too distracted or fatigued to engage productively and contribute at work in any impactful way. Work-related stress, illness, allergies, etc., are frequent contributors to this phenomenon. *Presenteeism* is not about being lazy, avoiding responsibilities, or sabotaging the workplace. It's actually the opposite: people choose to tolerate pain or other issues for as long as possible, sometimes allowing their conditions to remain untreated because they feel it's against the company culture to spend the time on their well-being. Corporate wellness centers are often underutilized because employees do not want to give the impression of concentrating on the 'wrong' things.

Presenteeism is a less noticeable phenomenon than its opposing concept and may remain undetected for longer times, especially in larger corporations. Because of its latent nature, it causes extensive harm to all involved. In 2004, HBR cited a study, "*American Productivity*

Audit," by Dr. Walter F. Stewart, that covered 29,000 working adults over a period of a year and found the cost of presenteeism in the U.S. to be $150 billion per year (Hemp, 2004). HBR also confirms that the cost of lost productivity due to depression and pain is three times higher than the cost of being absent from work due to other illnesses.

Once you have a better understanding of the situation, what can you, as a manager and as a fellow human being, do to help your employee get through a rough patch in life? How can you find out about their levels of engagement early in the process, long before things get out of control?

Employee engagement originates from employee satisfaction and includes their involvement and enthusiasm about their particular job and overall workplace activities. To start evaluating your employees' engagement level, find out the following:

- If they feel their work is meaningful,
- If their interactions with coworkers and supervisors are rewarding,
- If they have access to sufficient resources,
- Whether they feel free to take advantage of opportunities to learn new skills.

It turns out, the more engaged employees are, the more passion they have for what they do, and the more deeply connected they feel to their company. If employees are in positions where they have direct interactions with customers, then their satisfaction makes an even bigger impact on the company — because the customers' satisfaction lies in their hands. That's why companies like Zappos rely so heavily on their employees to create that *'wow'* experience for their customers.

Sometimes, employee dissatisfaction is not even an issue of poor work conditions or anything else that management has control over. Sometimes it is due to intrinsic reasons. Two people can be in the same exact job; one might feel satisfied and involved with what they do, and the other may not. The difference it makes to the customer, or anyone who comes to use their products or services, is like day and night. This applies to any sector, industry, country, or organization type and size.

I remember there were two teachers in my high school who were polar opposites. They had the same responsibilities and the same students – yet with their drastically different approaches, they produced drastically different results. One was a chemistry teacher — let's call her Ms. Z — who hated her job so much that she made herself emotionally unavailable for us during class and could barely tolerate the lab activities. Once she was caught in the teachers' lounge near tears after a student simply said they didn't understand the course material and requested additional guidance from her. As a result of having this unhappy teacher, many of my classmates were alienated, which contributed to lower attendance; some dropped out of her class, and some lost interest in high school in general.

At the same time, we had a physics teacher — Ms. H — who was passionate about her job and inspiring to her students; she regularly demonstrated that she personally cared about each and every student's success. She met with students after-hours, in school, or in her own home — where she not only provided free private tutoring, but also greeted her students with homemade pies and a cup of tea. She was dedicated to helping students turn things around with their studies and their general outlook on life as well. One of my classmates had been at the end of his rope, not understanding the material taught in previous years. Frustrated and lacking confidence in his abilities to do well at school, he joined Ms. H's class to give physics one last chance. With her superb teaching skills, he was able to bring his grades up, but most importantly, he received a much-needed confidence boost, helping him successfully graduate from high school and ultimately pursue higher education.

Although this example is taken from the world of education, it is not much different from what happens in the business world. Students are similar to paying customers; they are entitled to high-quality education and customer service from the time of enrollment to graduation. This seems to be a given, but one important aspect of student satisfaction must be addressed: *educator satisfaction*. How do we know if educators are satisfied with their work? Do they love the art of teaching and have a sincere interest in their subject matter expertise? Do they enjoy the work environment? If the former must be identified during the hiring process, then the latter is what we need to be most concerned with – in all aspects of the work environment.

The best educators are not necessarily only engaged in one-way lecturing. They inspire and encourage their students to dig deeper, by sparking an interest to go further. They work together with their students in an environment of mutual satisfaction from the learning process. At the same time, they take a holistic approach to their students' lives and may even provide guidance in other aspects of their lives.

Let's return to the subject of the employee work environment. *Job satisfaction* directly influences our involvement, which then contributes to the quality of the work output that is required by the position we were hired to fill. When we talk about *job satisfaction*, my belief is that we don't need 100% of everything at work to be to our liking. If there is 80% satisfaction in a position, most will tolerate approximately 20% dissatisfaction. Management expert Peter Drucker noted that a level of employee dissatisfaction with certain aspects of their job may actually result in greater job engagement, if the employee is empowered to initiate action to improve the situation.

If you are a manager or owner, here are some questions about the kind of workplace you have:

- Are people in your workplace operating in an environment of trust, support, and understanding?
- Are they being judged or punished for making a mistake, or do they receive support to overcome or address those mistakes?

- Do people receive constructive feedback that allows them to grow and learn every day?
- Are your people empowered to take on more responsibility without fear of failure?
- Is training or support available if skills need to be expanded or strengthened to properly perform the job at hand?

F. HOW TO FULLY ENGAGE YOUR EMPLOYEES

Let's follow the journey of Toby L, an MBA graduate and a middle level professional. Toby took a job at a learning supplies manufacturer in a leadership role in their Quality Management and Compliance department. He couldn't wait to meet the challenges of the new role, to contribute to its success with newly minted business knowledge and existing skills. Arriving on the first day, eager to meet up with the new team, Toby was seated in a small waiting corridor with a few other new hires before entering the offices. When the door was unlocked and names were called, Toby was handed a timecard to fill out at the end of the day. A bit confused, he nevertheless took it. This turned out to be only the first in a series of surprises awaiting this new hire. He had been promised a salaried position in management that matched his skill set and experience level. Shortly after, it turned out that his job duties had been distorted: instead of a problem-solving, decision-making leadership role, the job he got only focused on mundane level Quality Control tasks.

Expressing concerns to the department director, Toby was assured that things would get better once a niche was created that would be just right for the specialized talents Toby possessed. Agreeing to wait, our new hire spent days in a tiny 4' x 4' soundproof test booth dropping toys from a certain height, picking them up, dropping them again, and counting the numbers of falls it took for the toy to break. A major demotivator was being reprimanded by a document control clerk for using a paper clip instead of a stapler or vice versa – confusingly, this was the area of focus for this employer.

Instead of receiving a transfer to the originally promised role, Toby was abruptly fired. The reason listed was "Did not perform up to expectations." At first, this appeared to be a paradox, given the unassuming nature of the task at hand. How hard could it have been for someone with Toby's skill level to manhandle toys and count the number of drops? The problem was not the job being too difficult or the work standards too high. The problem was that the job was neither stimulating nor challenging. During the exit interview, the HR manager admitted that the hiring decision had been made haphazardly. However, the person who replaced Toby did not stay with the company very long, either. The company continued losing (or firing) qualified employees shortly after hiring them.

Toby wasted no time job hunting, and his new job satisfied on all levels, as it required a much higher level of responsibility, more mental capacity, strong leadership, and outstanding organizational skills.

A good explanation for a phenomenon like this is offered by psychologist Dr. Charles Garfield, who worked with NASA during the launch of first astronauts to the Moon. As described in **"The Practical Drucker"**, Dr. Garfield observed that astronauts with moon-reaching performance levels tended to lapse into barely adequate levels of performance when the challenge was gone (Cohen, 2013).

What an amazing observation. The essential lesson is this: if high levels of performance are expected and we want people to continue to be successful, they need new challenges to engage with.

> *When people have an opportunity to do what they do best, in an environment of growth, development, and trust, their self-worth grows; that's when they contribute their best efforts and become more purposeful in their role in the organization.*

People with a positive view of themselves, who believe in their self-worth and trust their own competence levels, not only do well in challenging jobs, but are more inclined to take them in the first place. Those with a negative view of themselves and their talents do not set ambitious goals and are more likely to give up when they confront difficulties. This second group of people is more likely to gravitate toward jobs that may seem monotonous and boring to the others, possibly even to themselves.

So, how do leaders of modern workplaces maintain engagement for motivated people? It's important to understand that competitive pay and benefits packages are not enough. Most highly motivated people care about other things besides financial security.

In 2001, I conducted a study for my Master's dissertation that clearly confirmed this observation. I interviewed approximately 200 private and public sector employees holding both managerial and non-managerial positions in the city of Omaha, Nebraska. Monetary incentives were not listed as a top motivator in any of the categories. Interestingly, a high percentage of managers' responses showed that they incorrectly perceived the importance their employees placed on monetary incentives.

Of course, people expect to be adequately paid for their work. However, some of the top motivators they indicated were simple, non-monetary incentives that are relatively easy for the managers to put in place:

- Recognizing their efforts for engaging in meaningful work, in non-monetary ways; for example, a designated parking spot in their name.

- Ensuring fairness in the workplace: managers refraining from showing favoritism, and management defending people against unfair attitudes of coworkers and customers.

- Building trust in the workplace, where their work is not being micromanaged; being trusted to do a job that makes an impact on the organization.

Since my initial research, I have interviewed about 100 people from various sectors of employment, between the ages of 20 to 65 with various levels of seniority, about factors that influence staying engaged at work. Assuming that their pay rate is acceptable, these are the top answers:

- Getting satisfaction from doing meaningful and enjoyable work.
- Receiving recognition for their efforts.
- Having power to make changes in the workplace.
- Enjoying a low-stress job environment.
- Engaging in good relationships with coworkers and other people.

People want to know that the companies or corporations they work for care about them. With that confidence, they in turn care about their workplace, even including the profitability and financial health of the organization. Do they want to know how the company's success will translate to their personal success? In my research, I found that the language of employees boils down to: "What's in it for me?"

Employees want to be informed about what direction the company is moving in. Whether it's sales numbers, business growth, productivity, profitability – they need to have a good idea about how business is doing and how their role fits in the bigger picture.

To further connect employee performance with company expectations, it's quite helpful to agree on what **Key Performance Indicators (KPI)** the company is tracking. When sharing the *KPI* with employees, it's important to keep the following in mind:

- What do these numbers represent?

- Are they meaningful?
- Do they reflect the company's current aspirations and challenges?
- Do they support the company's mission, and will they help to achieve the clearly articulated corporate vision?
- Are they in line with the company's values? Are these numbers tied to any departmental or individual goals that the employees can identify with?

Metrics must have a tangible connection to the processes that employees have control over. For the health of your bottom line, make sure that any metrics you track are meaningful, support your company goals, and are clearly understood by your entire team. This perspective is highlighted by the deeply held sentiment of Dr. Edward Deming, one of the founding fathers of modern Quality Management. Dr. Deming taught us that companies must treat workers as associates, not hired hands. He blamed management if workers were not motivated to work well.

People have asked me in the past, if I liked my job. When I told them I did, they wanted to know if I loved it to the point of volunteering for my workplace, if money was not an issue. Hmm. Working for free for a privately-owned corporation? After some consideration, I thought, if I was to give the gift of my time, why choose a for-profit business? Why not focus on a nonprofit organization with a worthwhile cause that deeply resonates with me? So, the short answer would have been no; I would not volunteer for my job.

These days, when I think of that question, it takes on a whole new meaning for me. I do understand what it means to love your work or the company you are with to the extent of volunteering your time for it. The way I see it now, I believe all good employees are already volunteers in their companies. You may wonder how this would be true, if they get paid for their contributions? It's because good, happy, productive, engaged, and enthusiastic employees tend to go above and beyond the scope of work required of them, and they frequently put in more time than the hours they are actually paid for. That, to me, is the very definition of volunteering. Besides, good employees can leave the company at any moment to apply their talents elsewhere. Their willing loyalty is why they stay with their workplace.

What can we do to appreciate the loyalty of those employee-volunteers? Small things can go a long way towards deepening that bond. Sometimes, it's as simple as saying 'please' and 'thank you,' or 'I appreciate your help.' It could be asking them to do something as if you are asking for a favor, instead of giving a directive or 'telling' them what to do as they are 'expected' to do their job. Yes, everyone gets paid for their work, but they don't have to go the extra mile, answering urgent after-hours emails from you or staying late on Friday evening when your client in a different time zone urgently needs help.

Keeping employees engaged starts with choosing the right people for the right jobs in the first place, as discussed earlier in this chapter. This is equally important at the time of the initial assignment of the position and for any subsequent job promotions. Maintaining high job standards is another critical element of employee engagement. Employees need to have high but attainable job standards to strive for in order to stay interested in the job at hand. However, from that point on, there are no one-size-fits-all scenarios. What engages one person will not necessarily work for others. *Caring Leaders* understand that you can't speak the same language to everyone and expect them to respond to you in a similar manner. Some people are lifelong learners, and to keep them interested, the best you can do is to create opportunities for professional and personal growth at all levels of the organization, not only at the top.

A feeling of pride in what you do also contributes to employee engagement. Drucker suggests encouraging employees to acquire a managerial vision. Some employees thrive on managerial vision, which is useful for the times when management is not around, and workers have to make certain decisions on their own. Others are quite the opposite: they consider freedom of choice as a lack of guidance and therefore require more detailed instructions on addressing issues within their departments.

Caring Leaders keep in mind the way motivation works: it not only differs from one employee to another, but the same person at different points in time can be motivated by different things. For example, you may have a team member who is getting married and is interested in saving money for their upcoming celebration and honeymoon. This person is likely to take on every opportunity to work overtime to make extra income. Besides, they may be happy to keep busy in the evening hours in order to avoid the expense of going out. The next year the same employee might lose interest in overtime because their situation has changed: now they are married, maybe even have a baby, and look forward to finishing work on time and going home as soon as possible to spend more time with their family. Being aware of people's changing motivations helps with effective allocation of resources and management.

Caring Organizations develop the type of leadership that takes a situational approach to understand what gets people out of bed in the morning and what keeps them going throughout the day.

CHAPTER 2 – CURRENT THEORIES ON MANAGEMENT: WHAT REALLY WORKS AND WHY

A. ONE SIZE DOES NOT FIT ALL

Psychologists and management gurus have studied how motivation works and what motivates people to do a good job, seeking to identify the most effective approaches to leading people. Various theories have emerged through the years, and for the purposes of this book, it may be enlightening to review a few of them.

Let's start with an important inquiry into the motivation to be employed in the first place. Do people come to work because they love what they do and enjoy a sense of accomplishment from a job done well, or are they driven purely by their obligation to provide for themselves and their family financially? In the 1960s, American management professor and social psychologist Douglas McGregor introduced two theories that describe people's behavior and the managerial style suitable for each of those behaviors. *Theory X* assumes that employees are naturally unmotivated; they dislike working, and if things are left up to the workers, they will typically not get their job done. This theory calls for an authoritarian style of management with more intervention, closer control, and, if needed, even a threat in order to produce results.

An authoritarian style of management implies the burden of numerous layers of management and therefore, an inefficient supervisor-to-worker ratio. With a lack of employee empowerment, the main go-to is the *carrot and stick approach*. McGregor acknowledged that workers who view work as a burden and only get a job for survival do exist, but they are in the minority; yet, in larger companies specializing in mass production, *X-type management* may be the only way to go.

The same psychologist also developed the participative *Theory Y*, a polar opposite of the authoritarian *Theory X*. According to *Theory Y*, people are already motivated to work, take pride in doing a good job, and get satisfaction from seeing the results of their labor. With this approach, work is a part of life, workers use their creativity to solve problems, and even the most difficult jobs are seen as a challenge, not a burden. In *Theory Y*, management trusts workers, and their approach is not so hands-on; it resembles more of a coaching role. Management empowers employees to make decisions, take action and, in return provides opportunities for growth and development.

In **Making Grass Greener on Your Side** a former CEO of The Toro Company, Ken Melrose, describes their organizational culture. Created in support of *Theory Y*, the **Pride in Excellence (PIE)** culture is based on the belief that people want to do the right thing. "After fifteen years, I still believe this because I've seen proof of it time and time again," Melrose wrote. "I also believe that every employee – whether in the office, in the warehouse, or on the production line – wants to provide quality products and services in which they can take personal pride. I have seen many of our employees take on responsibilities that no one, including themselves, could have imagined when they began at Toro. Trust is the element that makes this possible." (Melrose, 1995).

Real-life *Theory X* managers are everywhere around us. We recognize them in the way they treat people. They micromanage, expect to be copied on every piece of correspondence, and demand to be involved in decision making at all levels including the most mundane tasks. One

X-style manager went so far as to require employees to conform to the exact seating arrangements she assigned during meetings, because she was convinced that they were 'not paying close enough attention.' Other X-style managers might be more toned down, but indicate in a variety of ways how little trust they have in their employees. Their training and coaching style is usually limited to telling people exactly what to do, as opposed to teaching them the underlying principles behind what is required around the workplace. Stephen Covey, in his book, **"Principle-Centered Leadership"**, describes the difference between the two styles as *teaching practices* versus *teaching principles* (Covey, 1991).

The risk of being strictly a *Theory X* manager is that over-management may push away good employees, and the remaining people are usually not inspired to do their best. They may simply continue working there out of necessity, only until they find a place to move on to. *Theory X* may be justified and needed when dealing with highly time-sensitive situations where immediate decision making and action is required of leadership without the flexibility of using the otherwise preferred *participative style*. It may also apply as a temporary measure in interactions with new and young team members who may require careful supervision while learning the task at hand, especially the safety aspects of it. As employees gain more knowledge and experience on the job, trust in their abilities should grow, and the control level should relax.

Theory Y leadership usually works better with mature individuals and professionals. Regardless of your preferred natural management style, in any given workplace, there will be times when a combination of both theory applications would work best. At times, workers themselves will indicate to you what works with them. A careful evaluation of your environment will help you to choose the most suitable style at the time, as opposed to just sticking with one. As compelling as the **Participative Management System** is, when used alone, it may lead to a lack of direction, unclear objectives, and frustration.

B. WHY WE SHOULD PAY ATTENTION TO MASLOW & HIS HIERARCHY OF NEEDS

'Man does not live by bread alone' is a Biblical expression that reminds us that there is more to life than only having our physical needs met. However, when there is no 'bread' for extended periods of time, it becomes the number one thought on our mind until our hunger is satiated. This is what Maslow's hierarchy of needs describes, in a nutshell.

After studying several exemplary people in 1940s, such as Albert Einstein and Eleanor Roosevelt, New York psychologist Abraham Maslow developed a theory to explain what drives people's behavior and why they do what they do. The theory outlines a progression of people's intrinsic needs, from the most basic to the most sophisticated. Even with some changes added, this concept has greatly contributed to the effort to better understand how human motivation works, how to enhance personal growth and development, as well as providing an excellent context for setting management training goals. All of these perspectives are necessary considerations when planning for organizational excellence.

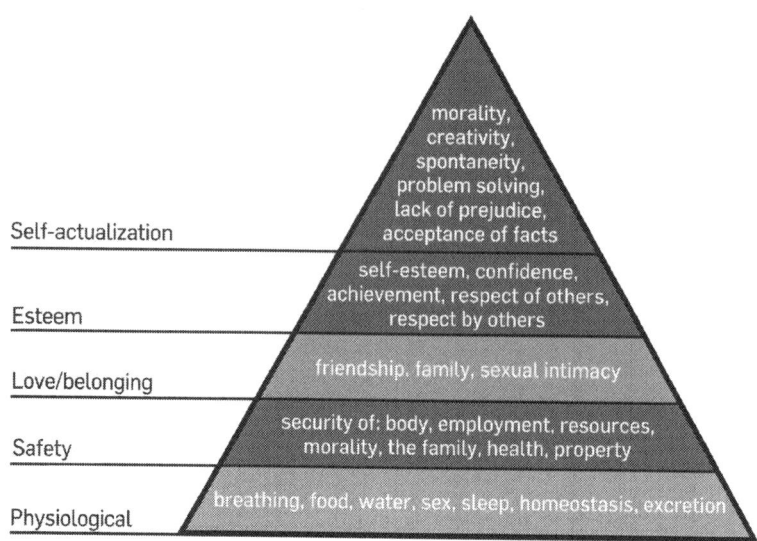

Picture 1. Maslow's original hierarchy of needs. - Wikipedia

Picture 1 illustrates the earlier and more commonly known version of Maslow's hierarchy of needs, identifying five levels of needs in the form of a pyramid.

1. Biological and Physiological needs: The ability to satisfy most basic needs such as hunger, thirst, breathing clean air, staying warm, and getting enough sleep. In a work environment, it means being paid enough to afford necessities.

2. Safety needs: Protection from elements, security, order, law, limits, stability, etc. At work, this means job stability and a suitable work environment, including safe work conditions.

3. Belongingness and Love needs: Family, affection, relationships. In work conditions, it means being liked by coworkers, belonging to a professional group, being included in social functions, etc.

4. Esteem needs: Self-esteem, achievements, mastery, independence, status and prestige. In work conditions, it means recognition, accomplishments, promotion, managerial responsibility, and for some people, competition and dominance.

5. **Self-Actualization needs:** Realizing personal potential, self-fulfillment, seeking personal growth, and peak experiences. At work, this means the ability to use skills to the fullest and exercise creativity.

According to the Maslow theory, the lower-level needs become a motivator for us when we lack them – these are referred to as deficiency motivators. The longer we go without such things as basic physical sustenance, the stronger our motivation to do something about it. However, once we have satisfied them, they no longer serve as a motivator. Instead, we move up to the next level of our needs. Psychologists refer to the higher-level needs as growth needs: the more these needs, for love, belonging, acceptance, trust, respect, and self-respect, are engaged, the stronger we feel them. A need for independence ultimately leads to self-actualization.

The lower-level, or deficiency needs must be met before the person can move up to the next level. It's not logical to expect a starving individual without basic shelter to care about attributes of prestige before satisfying hunger or putting a roof over their head. For example, students from unstable home environments, who spend their days in survival mode, often fall behind with their schoolwork and get lower grades than their classmates.

Safety and security needs in a workplace may mean that employees who believe their company has hit an economic low will start worrying about their own job security and most likely look for another job. Caring Organizations understand their peoples' need to have a stable place to work and an uninterrupted stream of income. Management shows leadership by addressing rumors proactively and sharing truthful information to the extent possible.

Every level of needs plays its own important role in workplaces. Let's take the need for *belonging*. As social creatures, all humans crave to be accepted by their surroundings and thrive when they feel they are a part of something bigger than themselves.

Lisa N, a middle level professional who formerly worked at a distribution center in Oregon, shared her workplace experience, which she calls traumatizing: "During the four months I was employed by the L.L. Inc. company, I saw a lot of cliquing and gossiping behind people's backs. I experienced constant exclusion from what the rest of my department was doing. It looked like they were purposely avoiding me. Once, during a trip to a local amusement park on a weekend, I ran into a coworker who occupied a cubicle right next to mine, someone with whom I thought I had established rapport. It was a surprise encounter and I was happy to say hello and connect for a moment. She barely acknowledged me and ran off. Another time, a different coworker refused to take the seat I saved for her at our company-sponsored MS Excel training class, which took place in an overfilled training facility. I caught a glimpse of her later, sitting at the back of the room. Coworkers openly planned parties and even work-related social events, passing out invitations in front of me, while never including me. There were a handful of us that seemed to be excluded from any events run by a large group. Management always looked the other way and pretended none of this was happening. I had enough. The day I gave my resignation letter, a coworker of mine who rarely talked to me otherwise, said she was planning her exit strategy as well."

In the workplace where Lisa found herself, the work environment did not foster inclusiveness and acceptance, and by turning a blind eye to the issues, management contributed to alienation. Cliquing is certainly not the same as belonging; it's quite the opposite, and it leads to loneliness and isolation. As G. Shawn Hunter describes in his 2016 book **"Small Acts of Leadership"**, loneliness can cause long-term harm: it may affect our health, lead to high blood pressure, increased risk of heart disease, and it is known to affect the quality of our sleep, which impairs cognition (Hunter, 2016). To save herself from long-term damage, Lisa made a wise choice to leave a workplace that did not foster a healthy team environment.

Connection and belonging include both deficiency and growth needs at the same time. Not only do we suffer when we lack companionship and have no one to turn to, we thrive when our need for belonging is fulfilled – when we feel accepted, loved, and connected. Since we spend so much of our waking hours at work, having a team to relate to and having a team environment to work in is indispensable. Allowing for that connection to build and grow can go a long way to filling the need described in Maslow's pyramid.

Connections and good relationships are also capable of undoing the damaging effects of stress. There are studies indicating that relationships lower cortisol levels in the brain. A study involved a monkey in a cage exposed to loud noises and flashing lights, which scared and stressed out the monkey. The researchers measured the cortisol level in its brain. Then the experiment was repeated with one change: they introduced another monkey to the cage, but all other stressful conditions were the same. This time, when the cortisol level was measured, it turned out to be half the value of what the lone monkey had been experiencing (Cloud, 2013).

Connection not only improves long-term health, it enhances people's capacity for performance by allowing them to put their minds together, exchange expertise more freely, expand their knowledge, and work together as a team in a way that is much stronger than each individual expert on his own. Caring Organizations foster a cooperative teamwork environment, which yields many benefits. It allows less experienced team members to learn from their more experienced coworkers, while the latter get to share their knowledge and establish themselves further as subject experts and coaches. Both sides gain more confidence and show better results in their performance. Teamwork offers far more of a benefit than simply making people feel better – it does so by accessing cumulative strengths and empowering people to be more creative, productive, and effective in their efforts.

Maslow's pyramid teaches us that we cannot inspire or motivate someone to perform to the best of their ability if they have unresolved issues on their minds. As a result of unmet needs, commitment to task and performance levels go down. An employee who is being evicted from his home (level 2 need, shelter) or taking care of an ill family member (level 3 need, belonging) may not be able to focus on the excellence of his work (level 4 need, esteem, achievement). People bogged down with family or personal problems require time to deal with those first, if possible; they may also need help with finding solutions, as appropriate. If you, as a manager, choose to turn a blind eye on your team member's personal, family, or health problems, those distractions will not go away. If you choose to discipline the team member for dealing with those issues, the outcome can be a drag on the employee's output, and therefore the benefit the employee typically offers the company will be lost.

Ignoring these issues will not only stall the solution to the problem, the company will have to cope with a seriously disengaged employee. If your organizational culture does not allow for opportunities to deal with family-related and other personal emergencies, your team members will pretty soon start searching for other employment opportunities. As hard as it might be to discuss personal issues, management still needs to open a two-way conversation while recognizing the need for confidentiality of sensitive matters. As a leader of a Caring Organization, you can create a safe space to talk, you can show understanding, possibly offer help to get through the rough patch, or guide the employee in the direction of getting needed professional help.

Workplace connections don't even have to be particularly deep to produce great results for job satisfaction and performance. Organizational psychologists point out that even brief moments of high-quality connections fuel openness, energy, and authenticity among coworkers, and in turn, generate measurable, tangible differences in performance. Shawn Achor, in his book *"The Happiness Advantage"*, talks about companies that grasped the importance of social investment. One particular study conducted at IBM by MIT researchers, followed 2,600 employees for an entire year, analyzing their social ties using mathematical formulas. The study produced quantifiable results showing that more socially connected employees contributed a better performance (Achor, 2018).

IBM used this information to strengthen their program of introducing new employees so that they could create connections. Providing an example for companies fostering the environment of *belonging and connections*, Google not only has an on-site day care center for its employees, but also encourages parents to check on their children during the day. Achor also highlights United Parcel Service (UPS), which — despite their focus on efficiency — allows their drivers to veer off their scheduled path and connect with other drivers over lunch to socialize and exchange stories. The company maintains that this social investment pays off in the long run, not only for the drivers but for the organization as a whole. Other companies mentioned in the book, such as Southwest Airlines, Domino's, and The Limited, set up programs that allowed people to donate money to their coworkers facing medical or other emergencies. This program showed positive results, growing social ties between their employees and overall improving their commitment to the organization.

People who feel their workplace cares about them will perform better. Unfortunately, in times of financial stress, social programs are one of the first things that companies cut or eliminate entirely. Maslow's hierarchy of needs highlights the importance of belonging and social investment for job satisfaction and overall performance, so it seems important to underline that everyone benefits when these needs are considered.

Once people make connections, once they find where they belong, once they feel accepted as a part of something larger than them, the next level of need motivates them to stand out from the crowd and to shine through their personal achievements. This is their need for *esteem*. *Esteem* involves recognition of achievements, competition, prestige, and the need for managerial responsibilities. Caring Organizations understand this need and create opportunities for people to do what they love, develop their skills, and grow personally and professionally. They recognize and celebrate the accomplishments of team members. Caring Leaders understand that when people come to work every day, they are facing a decision of how much effort to put in. The more people feel that their pay is fair, that their work is challenging and rewarding, that management and coworkers care about them, and that their accomplishments will not go unnoticed, the more effort they decide to put into their work.

When all of these needs have been met, humans reach a place where we are motivated by the next level of needs: *self-actualization*. *Self-actualization* is about reaching one's full potential, which I see not as an end goal, but as an ever-unfolding process. In a work environment, moving toward self-actualization means that people feel that they can achieve their personal and professional goals, and are given opportunities to engage in creative activities. The subject of self-actualization in the workplace opens up a conversation on those challenges and opportunities faced by employers when it comes to helping employees find their heart-centered meaning and purpose in life, an inquiry that goes beyond their work goals and duties.

Caring Leaders continually work on their own personal growth and development and encourage others to work on theirs. I had one of those managers at one point in my career, a busy person who was involved in volunteering at seminars and other events aimed at helping people grow and develop. This might have been representative of how

Abraham Maslow described self-actualizing people: they are "involved in a cause outside their own skin, in something outside of themselves."

In later decades, Maslow revisited the subject and introduced additional needs, among which, the highest of all, *transcendence*, was defined as the need to help others achieve their self-actualization. In workplaces, this can be witnessed through the leadership style of growth-oriented strategists, who continually inspire, motivate, and push people to better themselves in order to see all of their team members to reach their full potential.

Can anyone sincerely concerned for the best interests of their fellow humans be viewed as *transcendent*? With *transcendence* occupying the top of the pyramid, we would normally expect it from someone who has successfully fulfilled their needs at all previous levels. However, what do we say when a high level of social responsibility comes from someone who doesn't know where their next meal comes from? In May 2017, a bomb detonated during a concert at the Manchester Arena, killing 23 and wounding 139 people. Two homeless gentlemen spending the night near the concert hall heard the noise and courageously ran toward the blast zone to help those injured during the attack. Hailed as heroes by British media, both gentlemen maintained that they did not consider themselves heroes and were just doing what any 'normal citizen' would do (Bulman, 2017).

Based on what we learned from the media interviews with these two underprivileged Manchester gentlemen, (Watson, 2017), I could explain their selfless acts with their desire to be accepted by the society as 'normal citizens'" and not be judged by their life circumstances. This is, basically, the need for *belonging*. Driven by their motivation to save others, as a result, these two individuals ultimately received many benefits: acquiring financial security (fundraising accounts set up for them by the public); experiencing greater *belonging* (reconnecting with estranged family members and more acceptance from the general society); accruing *esteem* (spotlight on them for their actions); and, most remarkably, taking a big step towards *self-actualization*.

What this means for workplaces is that it might be beneficial to consider how changing the standard mindset around existing reward systems can bring good outcomes. The culture of our organizations, in general, is set up to reward motivation and behavior based on personal achievements. To create Caring Organizations, we could focus on encouraging people to reach out more and to help others succeed in achieving their goals. Helping each other realize their potential brings many benefits to all participants. It may help people boost their own self-esteem, make it easier to deal with their own less-than-favorable life circumstances, and help them find the energy and focus to improve and develop themselves. It can even help relieve depression, as psychologists suggest.

Seeing how different levels of Maslow's hierarchy of needs serve to motivate us, one after the other, it's important to recognize we don't need to be too rigid about the application of this theory. Life is not a perfect progression of events, and doesn't always work in a linear direction from lower to higher-level needs. There are examples of people 'skipping levels' — showing signs of being motivated by higher needs while their most basic human needs were at risk. One example is Van Gogh: living in extreme poverty, he was able to realize his potential through his creative work. Understanding the concept of *self-actualization* opens our eyes to this simple yet profound fact – seeking *self-actualization* and striving to realize one's full potential is a human need that every employee possesses, and it's not limited to a CEO level.

Maslow's hierarchy of needs is a good model for management training and personal development. Even though the hierarchy is not a prescriptive tool with exact answers for each situation, as a leader, you can still make good inferences about what drives people to do what they do. If someone on your team participates in sports and organized games, maybe they seek *esteem* through athletic accomplishments. If someone is motivated to volunteer time working with disadvantaged youth, they may have grown up in neglectful circumstances and are looking to fulfill a need for *belonging*. Someone who is into art might be seeking *self-actualization* through inspired creative work. Someone else, dedicated to teaching or conducting seminars to share acquired knowledge, might be on a path to *transcendence*, helping others realize their potential.

Studying Maslow's work allows employers to remain mindful of challenges and opportunities assisting people in their search for true meaning and purpose both at work and in their life as a whole. Caring Organizations do not simply sponsor work-related training, but also encourage employees on their path of personal growth toward self-actualization. They understand that the journey to success looks different for everyone. If someone wants to rise to a certain degree and not go any further, Caring Organizations would support their employees to grow and evolve to the degree they feel most comfortable.

C. HOW CAN YOU HELP YOUR TALENT REACH THEIR MAXIMUM POTENTIAL

During job interviews and performance evaluations, we often ask people where they see themselves in five years. Job applicants and employees learn to anticipate these questions, and often Google 'acceptable' answers upfront, but there is no winning in any case. 'Where do you see yourself in five years' is a double-edged sword. To show plans for growth, the candidate wants to appear ambitious, but cannot appear too ambitious. If they told the hiring manager the truth about wanting to head the department in five years, the answer would set them up for judgment or would even make them look like a potential threat. To manage a positive initial impression, the candidate may say they don't know what they want to do in five years. In that case, they risk appearing not ambitious enough. The question does not yield any useful information or insight. That's why I believe we should stop asking this question altogether.

Cookie-cutter answers to cookie-cutter questions do not determine the future of employees in a workplace. It's based on what people do best and what they love doing most. How do we begin to find what it is? This information comes from employee strength analysis, a subject that requires increasingly more attention in modern workplaces.

Workplace well-being teacher and author Michelle McQuaid, in her article *The 3 Mistakes Companies Make Focusing On People's Strengths,* refers to more than a decade of research suggesting that providing opportunities for people to build on what they do best every day can positively impact employee engagement and confidence at work (McQuaid, 2016). She points out that 51% of American employees reported that their organization is committed to building on their employees' strengths, and estimates that American companies spend $24 million annually to access *Gallup Strengths Finder* survey. Now we must ask: what do organizations do with the information obtained through those surveys? Through her experience teaching thousands of people throughout the world to put their strengths to work, McQuaid discovered three productive habits that organizations would be wise to adopt:

- Ongoing strength development; people who know their strengths and have established weekly strength development goals are reportedly three times as likely to be deeply engaged and energized at work.

- Embedding people's strengths into their job descriptions, performance plans, and weekly goals can make it easier for people to develop their strengths each day. Most people feel better working with the way their brains are wired to perform at their best.

- Meaningful strength-related conversations with their managers had the greatest impact on employees. Those meaningful discussions included how someone's strengths were being overplayed, underplayed, and used well at work. The conversations may also address potential weaknesses and set realistic goals for overcoming them.

While it's good to be aware of one's weaknesses, focus on this aspect should not nearly be as concentrated as that of intentional and consistent development of identified strengths. When it comes to strengths and weaknesses, I believe in paying the most attention, say 80%, to developing our strengths and allocating the remainder (20%) of the time, to working on our weaknesses. It's important that the focus should be on the weaknesses that stand between us and our ability to fully take advantage of our strengths. Employees who use their strengths every day are six times more likely to be engaged in their jobs and more than three times more likely to report having an excellent quality of life than those who don't, as 2015 research by Gallup shows. When people have the opportunity to develop their strengths, they expand belief in their abilities, they feel more respected and empowered, and their creativity levels surge. Team performance is maximized when the team can capitalize on each individual member's strengths (Flade, et al., 2015).

When managers focus on improving upon peoples' weaknesses, it's bad news for performance. Teams led by managers who focus on individual and team weaknesses are 26% less likely to be fully engaged than teams with managers who focus on their strengths. To help people maximize their potential, set specific goals based on their aspirations and in accordance with the performance level the company wants to see them at. Properly established performance goals promote self-improvement. If someone has an aspiration to grow into a management role, help them set goals that will allow them to obtain necessary management training and leadership skills. Options could include going back to school, obtaining professional certifications, or expanding knowledge of processes specific for the department of their interest. An important part of professional development comes from personal growth. You cannot maximize your potential without growing as a person.

Lululemon is one employer committed to supporting their employees' professional and personal growth. This company came to my attention many times when I proctored American Society for Quality certification exams, spoke at and organized professional conferences, and participated in the Landmark Curriculum for Living courses. In all of those roles, I would meet Lululemon employees sponsored by their employer to participate. I had the opportunity to interview several Lululemon employees who held both managerial and non-managerial roles. I learned that the company has a strong organizational culture driven by their core values. Despite some well-publicized controversy, the employer seems to be on the right path to figuring out the magic formula of success for people doing jobs they are good at and feeling very happy about.

For one thing, they allow employees flexibility to look around the company, explore other departments, talk to different managers, and see where their talents would fit best. One person I spoke to shared that in her five years with Lululemon, she changed positions four times, every time transitioning into a new role that was more in line with her interests. Along the way, she learned new skills that prepared her for increasingly higher levels of responsibility. Another employee happily stayed in the same exact role for over seven years. Managers strive to be coaches committed to each person's happiness – whether it's moving to new roles or staying where they are.

Everyone is required to come up with their own job-related goals; set their own measurements that support the company's annual business objectives. The employees are evaluated on their work goals. If interested in personal growth, programs are available for free, without making the participation mandatory or tying it to formal performance evaluations. However, if someone seems to become stagnant throughout the year, they are encouraged to reflect on that. A Caring Organizational culture that encourages personal and professional growth, with the ultimate goal of employee happiness and great performance in the role of their choice, is a solid model for facilitating progress on the path of fulfilling one's full potential.

D. MAKE PERFORMANCE EVALUATIONS WORK FOR YOU

We cannot manage what we cannot measure, Peter Drucker famously said; at least this quote has been attributed to him. To keep their finger on the pulse, companies utilize **Performance Management Systems**. Having performance markers in a workplace is useful for employees as well; it creates healthy competition and, if done properly, encourages them to strive for Continual Improvement of their performance. People seem to like having a way to track their performance; this is not surprising, given the growing popularity of fitness apps or step counting devices.

You might be wondering: Are current Performance Management Systems effective in leading to desired improvements? What are some common problems with the way they are set up?

I interviewed an HR consultant with over 20 years experience helping companies improve their **Performance Management Programs**. She shared with me that she has yet to walk into a company to find a program that is effective in leading employees to produce desirable performance improvements. I also interviewed about 100 professionals from the U.S., Canada, U.K., and Azerbaijan, asking for comments on the *performance management programs* in their workplaces. Responses from people on the receiving end of those evaluations, and those responsible for conducting them overwhelmingly tend to find the workplace Performance Management Systems ineffective. In many companies, managers are happy to move away from conducting employee performance evaluations. Employees do not find these evaluations useful either; they do not have much faith in either the process or the outcome. Specific reasons most commonly cited for ineffectiveness and inefficiency of Performance Management Systems included:

- Unclear Goals
- Lack of Follow Up
- Unfair

UNCLEAR GOALS:

Vague wording and little relevance to the job function are typically cited as the top problems with Performance Management Systems. It's confusing, to say the least, to have one set of goals on paper and another set of unrelated goals to work on throughout the year. To make any sense, performance goals must be linked to the processes that are actually important for the business and actually need improvement. To set up a clear and more relevant process, try having employees come up with their goals first, and ask them how they feel they can best contribute to the company's success. After reviewing those ideas together, collaborate to devise a plan that could best capitalize on the employees' existing strengths, providing growth opportunities while supporting departmental and organizational goals.

Another area that reportedly lacks clarity is the distinction between meeting and exceeding expectations. When the definition of excellent or outstanding performance is unclear, it leaves people frustrated about their inability to deliver high-level results, or even to break out of mediocrity. "If what I have to offer is never good enough to blow their mind away, then with time, I lose my interest in chasing that goal," admits Shawn B, a draftsman from a manufacturing company in Toronto area.

To inspire genuine effort and enthusiasm, set expectations that are clear, challenging, and attainable. Provide examples of 'exceeded expectations' that managers can use in their evaluations and for employees to use to benchmark best practices.

Steven M, a U.S. Air Force QA Inspector, shared in his interview with me that the way performance was tracked in his workplace was confusing. His first-line supervisor would not provide performance-related feedback. When Steven inquired how he was doing, he was told it was all great, with no details offered. The truth came out when Steven applied for a promotion but was rejected. The reason for the rejection was revealed when his personnel file was reviewed. He discovered his file was filled with consistently average scores of three out of five. To be competitive for promotions, he had to score higher. "That kept me from getting any promotions I applied for, and put me behind my peers. It took me years to catch up! If only there was clear communication in regards to what each number on the scale stood for, I would have taken timely action to improve on the areas where I needed it," said Steven. Things only improved for him when the workplace implemented a mandatory quarterly feedback system that provided a lot more clarity in regards to the department's expectations.

Caring Workplaces set their employees up for success. Clearly defined performance goals, and descriptive explanations on what it takes to produce average, good, and excellent performances, help to make the program fair.

LACK OF FOLLOW UP:

A fictional holiday, Festivus, was popularized by *Seinfeld*, an American sitcom that had a long successful run in the 1990s. The purpose of Festivus was to get together one day of the year to air grievances to, mostly, unsuspecting people in your life. In a way, many companies' Performance Management Systems remind me of this tradition: that dreaded day of the year when the manager gets to air grievances accumulated for the past six to twelve months. One difference is that, during performance reviews, those grievances might occasionally alternate with a couple of positive observations.

Usually, performance evaluation sessions are set up as annual events. By the year-end review, the employee has either met their goals or not – and that is what they are going to hear about from their manager. This is the reason why many fear these sessions; they never know what to expect. Some hope that having a good relationship with their manager will help get them through the process. Most of the time, the only people who like performance evaluations are those who believe they are the superstars of the workplace, but even for those used to praise and awards, the process can turn sour, if they receive a lower review than they had anticipated.

It seems to me that the best way to improve on overall outcome is to remove the element of surprise from the process. Specific performance results– good or poor – must be dealt with closer to the occurrence. If an employee did a good job, they would like to hear about it on the spot. If they were unable to meet the goals they were reaching for, it's even more important to address the issue and get the right help – before it's too late.

An effective performance evaluation process could still be conducted annually, but revisiting performance goals needs to be consistent throughout the year, to monitor progress, investigate any impediments, and provide resources necessary for completing goals and meeting agreed-upon targets. One way to make this a collaborative and effective process is to involve the employee in an RCA, to get to the bottom of the issue so as to prevent future recurrences. By seeking information together, employees are more likely to take the assessment as objective feedback even in those cases when your analysis shows that the issue originated from performance. This seems preferable to a once-a-year ambush review that takes the wind out of the sails of your eager and hardworking employees, while failing to provide sufficient guidance during the year for the ones who may be struggling without clear direction or a detailed enough roadmap to the intended destination.

Even the best performance evaluation becomes useless if the results are tucked away and only rarely reviewed. Information is only powerful if it's shared. When applied to work, it becomes knowledge that helps create positive change in the workplace. "Year after year, I score high on my performance evaluation, but nothing ever comes out of it," said Alvin A, a mechanical engineer with 15 years of professional experience, who currently works for a London-based research and development company. From his vantage point, lack of follow up erases meaning from the performance evaluation process. "It's nothing but paperwork. It is done once a year (on a good year), but once it's complete, the paper just gets set aside and forgotten," said Raul L, a designer from a manufacturing company in the Los Angeles area.

UNFAIR:

A sense of unfairness can infect the workplace when performance goals are based on outcomes employees have little control over. For example, if a person's job involves collecting debt, how fair is it to measure their performance by the amount of debt they have collected? Is it taken into consideration, for example, if the debtor filed for bankruptcy? Here is an example of performance evaluation done right: a newly hired collector with existing account files receives coaching from a current or past collector, who guides the new hire through the process of collecting bad debt. Training could include teaching the new employee to maintain customers. With this training approach, the new hire is learning different aspects of the job, and their evaluation will not be based on the success or failure with the numbers but based on what skills the employee is learning that are valuable for the company. This approach also ensures the strength of your succession planning, allowing both individuals to assume more responsibility and to grow into bigger roles as the company sustains and expands its success.

The concept of fairness in performance evaluations is also affected by the widespread use of the statistical concept of normal distribution, known as a ***Bell Curve.***

> **Bell Curve:**
> 1. A Bell Curve is a graph depicting normal distribution, which has a shape reminiscent of a bell.
> 2. The top of the curve shows the mean, mode, and median of the data collected.
> 3. Its standard deviation depicts the Bell Curve's relative width around the mean. Bell Curves (normal distributions) are used commonly in statistics, including analysis of economic and financial data (Bloomenthal, 2020).

The assumption behind the use of the *Bell Curve* is that a majority of employees will exhibit acceptable levels of performance; then, there will be *outliers* on either side: a small group of *weak performers* and a handful of *star performers*. Applying this concept allows us to encourage outstanding achievers to pursue advancement in the company, while giving the majority of employees motivation and focus to step up their game. Meanwhile, keying in on providing *weaker performers* with whatever support they may need, which might include more mentoring, training, or better placement, can happen in a focused way.

Using this method to analyze performance can also highlight particularities in management styles: the bell shape skewed to the left is usually a sign of overly strict ratings, which tend to score too many employees fairly low on performance; this might lead to lost hope and flagging enthusiasm. Alternatively, if the bell shape skews to the right, it might signify a management approach that is too lenient. This measurement tool usually works better in larger companies, there may not be enough people in smaller workplaces to fall into all three categories naturally.

Nevertheless, as a method for distributing available budget dollars, it seems to be expected that the two ends of the performance rating scale are identified as winners and losers, with everyone else placed in the middle of the curve. If managers don't follow this tool, they may be afraid to appear as lacking competence in differentiating between high and mediocre performance. Pressured to identify leading and lagging performers, they tend to force people into one gradient or another. There are so many opportunities for making an erroneous decision that it turns into the dreaded Curse of the Bell Curve. How do managers make sure they treat everyone fairly based on their actual, real world performance? How can proper management access true excellence while removing any possibility of bias?

When I was in elementary school, I was often teased by some classmates and had a hard time understanding what their motivation was. Years later, my old schoolmates admitted that they saw me as a teacher's pet, and it bothered them. Of course, I did not see it that way, since I could not recall receiving preferential treatment from teachers; I had to work hard for the good grades I got. However, the situation appeared quite differently to some of the children around me, and they took action. It doesn't make sense to me even today, but this is part of human nature. Whether perceived or real, the concept of the teacher's pet exists. So does the concept of manager's favorites in the workplace. Whether it's a conscious choice or not, the reality is, most managers do have their favorites among employees. Yes, the favorites, too, are (usually) expected to work hard and produce quality results, but there is typically an element of subjectivity when it comes to judging their performance.

Someone with firsthand experience on both ends of the spectrum, Laura S, was a young administrative professional when she enjoyed being a favorite at work. As her manager's pet, she always got five out of five on all aspects of her performance evaluations, and she was paid well. However, after getting those 'outstanding' evaluations time after time, she knew deep inside that she did not quite deserve every word of the praise and every dollar of the raise. As a result, Laura stopped taking those evaluations seriously, as well as any other feedback she received from her manager. At a later point in her career, in an entirely different setting, Laura found herself in the opposite situation; her manager consistently rated her at two out of five. In this job, she felt that there was nothing she could do right in order to approach reaching her performance goals. The whole experience was deflating and did not help her improve. She saw those ratings as biased and not reflective of her performance. She found out later, she got those low ratings because her manager thought she was abrasive!

Nearly every workplace has employees with good technical skills, who are not always personable or likable. As much as I am opposed to putting the so-called brilliant jerks on a pedestal, or even keeping them on board, punishing them through low ratings on their unrelated performance goals does not help to address their unacceptable behavior. It is much better to revitalize the evaluation criteria to include behavior consistent with values and principles the company wants to promote. A Caring Organization uses a Performance Management System to encourage and instill the right values throughout the company and foster a team environment, instead of solely rewarding individual achievements at any expense.

Managers who make specific decisions may allow their emotions and personal preferences to get in the way of objective performance evaluations. If they have a favorite in the workplace, they may find it difficult to tell this person they are failing. The consequence of using a program like this affects employee morale and the dynamic in the workplace. One of two things can happen to employees who feel they were not treated fairly: they either start working on their exit strategy or they stay with the company but are now resentful. Either way, this approach is likely to cost the employer money due to lower performance or loss of experienced staff.

Another factor that may influence the objectivity of performance evaluations is when the employer knows that personnel cuts are imminent. Management has to decide who stays and who must go. Those who are slated to be let go will have to be assigned a low-performance score to justify the decision to fire them. Since the performance evaluation process is usually linked to salary, the higher salary will command the higher severance payment. Companies need to plan for salary increases and need to know upfront who will be getting raises in the following year.

As a manager, you should do everything in your power to provide the person with the right tools, training, and guidance they need to do their job well. If you have decided they don't meet your expectations, do not punish them by refusing to give them a raise. Once you have done what you can, including additional training, and nothing has worked to improve their performance, just set the person free. It's not fair to anyone to keep them captive to satisfy the existing performance evaluation system and keep up the Bell Curve's shape.

Since every position is usually set up with the pay range of $10,000, employees who do their job adequately should be paid what the job is worth, and those with better performance results can get paid a higher salary within the range. With an annual raise of 3%, companies may hit the top of the range too quickly. In that case, outstanding performances can be rewarded in other ways: giving out bonuses, rewarding people on the spot! Experience shows that employees view bonuses as something extra and not as an expected entitlement of their job, such as benefits.

Certain positions come with a built-in performance evaluation, such as sales jobs. Sales personnel mostly work on a base plus commission; for them, there is no gray area in this process, no room for subjectivity. A sales rep understands that their pay every month is based on sales numbers. The same concept can be translated to any other job. You can benchmark any job. You can guide employees to work according to that established and mutually agreed-upon benchmark, instead of surprising them with unexpected criticism and punishment for non-performance once a year.

E. SET EXPECTATIONS BY DISCUSSING JOB DESCRIPTIONS UP FRONT & THROUGHOUT A PERSON'S CAREER

Thoughtfully designed job descriptions help in many ways right from the start, reducing expensive advertising and recruiting costs, while attracting the right candidates for the position. I have come across many companies that had a hard time finding the right candidate to join their team because of poor formulation of the skills and abilities needed for specific positions.

Adam K, a Supply Chain manager, applied for a leadership role within a manufacturing company based on the ad placed online. At the time of the interview, he found out that the hiring team was referring to a job description different from what he applied for; obviously, this created confusion. The HR manager explained that the position had changed since they first advertised it. The candidate decided to go along with the new development. In the second round of the interviews, another interviewing director introduced the third version of the same job description. It turned out that this was not the first time this company had made numerous changes to the job description throughout their hiring process. The situation they created became the main reason they lost their top candidate to a competitor and discouraged many other applicants from pursuing employment with them.

In another case, the outcome was even worse, as the candidate didn't notice the red flags until after the offer was accepted.

A mechanical engineer with a master's degree and nearly 20 years of experience found himself employed by a company that assigned him responsibilities that had nothing to do with the role he had been supposedly hired for. When he realized he ended up with lower-level responsibilities, this person, as he explained to me, 'gradually left' that job. When asked to elaborate on the meaning of 'gradual' departure, he said the whole process took him about three months; and he had mentally checked out of his job well before he was physically ready to leave. He turned in his resignation after landing another job that was much better suited to his skill level and professional interests. I'm not sure how long it took the employer to catch on to what was happening with this employee, but they definitely lost on productivity while he was there, in addition to incurring the cost of rehiring.

It's simply essential for job descriptions to accurately represent the scope of the job and the level of the responsibility required. It is equally important to faithfully represent the culture and values of the company, so the right people are attracted and retained. The right people, from the start, are more likely to fit in your culture and share your values. As previously mentioned, the cultural component is too often overlooked by workplaces, and the only culture that the job descriptions represent is the culture of the person who wrote it. This leads to loss of trust when candidates for employment encounter a discrepancy between the written job description and the organizational culture they discover after joining the company. One good thing about job descriptions is that they are not written in stone. They are living, breathing, dynamic documents that are best kept fresh by being reviewed, ideally once a year, as roles evolve, organizational structure changes, and new responsibilities get added.

Sometimes, being in a certain job for an extended period of time creates complacency and loss of visibility for employees and their actual performance. *I once knew a Technical Product Specialist whose role changed on numerous occasions as the company kept going through restructuring and changing reporting channels. The role was changed so many times that, in the end, it was no longer clear what his duties were and who exactly he reported to. Anytime someone at work approached him with a request, he kept saying he was busy. Once challenged on what was keeping him so busy, the specialist referred to the important Product Specification he was writing. This project remained on the 'work in progress' status for almost a year and a half, and no one ever saw it come to completion; everyone thought someone else was managing this person's performance.*

You don't want your people sitting there overcome by inertia, shielded by their computer screens, hiding behind some vaguely stated projects. This will not happen if the Performance Management process also includes a periodic review of job descriptions for accuracy and adequacy.

CHAPTER 3 – MEDIOCRITY: A SURE-FIRE WAY TO TURN ANY WORKPLACE INTO A TOXIC ENVIRONMENT

A. HOW TO KEEP DILBERT AND HIS BRAND OF MEDIOCRITY OUT OF YOUR WORKPLACE

Floating around the Internet, there is the tale of three cannibals who got hired by a large corporation for a variety of positions at the head office. On their first day, the HR manager said to the cannibals: "You are a part of our team now. You get all the usual benefits, and you can have your lunch at the cafeteria, but don't eat any of our staff."

The cannibals promised they would not eat the employees. Four weeks later, they were called to the HR office: "All of you are working very hard, and we are quite satisfied with your efforts. However, one of our janitors has disappeared. Do any of you know what happened to her?"

The cannibals all shook their heads no. As soon as they stepped out, the pack leader asked the others, " "Which one of you morons ate the janitor?" As one of the cannibals started hesitantly admitting his fault, the leader continued, "You fool!!! For four weeks we've been eating all kinds of managers and regional directors, without anyone taking notice, but nooooooooooo, you had to screw it up by eating someone important!"

Wait a minute! Cannibals don't exist in corporations, you might object. That's ok. This story isn't about cannibals anyway. It's a reminder on useless members of management who hide behind their important-sounding titles, add no value, and go unquestioned for years in corporations that lack effective performance management. These types of managers give the category of corporate management a bad reputation; mediocrity is their middle name. Many jokes and parodies in popular culture highlight how impractical, redundant, and flat out dumb some management practices are. Among the best representations of this insanity are a TV show *The Office*, the movie *Office Space*, the popular 90s sitcom *Seinfeld*, and many more.

One of the most widely celebrated caricatures of corporate culture and poor management practices is *Dilbert*, a cartoon that has been around for 30 years, appeared in 65 countries, and was translated in 25 languages. In fact, it hit the peak of its popularity after the setting was moved from the main character's home to his workplace. The much-discussed main topics included office politics, red tape, and the culture of praising tedious busywork over accomplishing real results. The manager in the cartoon is left unnamed specifically so that people could give him any name and imagine him to be their boss (Wikipedia, 2020).

How many of the following wasteful practices sound familiar to you:

- Failure to reward success or penalize laziness.
- Blaming employees for management mistakes.
- Micromanagement.
- Lowering employee morale by making demands that are impossible to meet.
- Failure to communicate clear, reachable objectives.
- Excessive, stifling corporate bureaucracy.

Below are a few common types of mediocre managers I observed in real life; these individuals feed the stereotypes and fuel the material adapted by writers to create familiar screen characters. Unfortunately, the damage they do in work places can be severe.

Go With The Flow managers: This type of manager takes the concept of 'picking their battles' too far; they show no backbone whatsoever. They take any direction from higher-ups with zero filtering, allowing themselves to get swayed from one course to another without standing for anything. Having no backbone, they frequently allow their direct reports to run the show by bullying their way with unaccountable insubordination. GWTF managers refuse to 'get their hands dirty' in any serious workplace issue and prefer to sweep awkward situations and problems under the rug, in an effort to preserve the all-too-mediocre status quo. When presented with a pressing but potentially unpleasant issue, they are not interested in systemic or long-term solutions. Instead, they prefer cosmetic fixes, similar to putting a band-aid on a gaping wound.

The GWTF manager's strong suit is following policies or procedures, even when they don't fully understand the logic and intention behind it. The procedure may outline conventional methods even though circumstances may clearly call for a more resourceful and innovative problem-solving approach. This type expects to be handed a policy that covers every scenario so that they don't have to think of any creative solutions. Some of these mediocre managers serve as a reminder of why one day, their jobs will be replaced by machines, and no one will notice their absence – just as the parable of the three cannibals in the workplace illustrated.

Dodgeball Player managers: This type of manager is an expert in one thing, and they do it perfectly: deflecting. More than anything, this type is concerned with dodging responsibility for any workplace projects. The DP manager type avoids responsibility skillfully right at the moment when the situation is first brought to their attention, such as a finding from a workplace inspection or an issue arising at a staff meeting. If called out by coworkers for lack of action, they seem easily threatened and go into a highly irritable, defensive mode. They go out of their way to make sure that no accountability is ever assigned to them.

If something determined by senior management to logically fall under their department's area of focus does miraculously make its way to the DP manager's desk, whether it's assessing new equipment needs, conducting staff training, or analyzing the safety of a work process, the DP manager will relentlessly search for a reason why they should not be in charge of the issue. Once they are able to successfully locate that one reason why another department should be assigned the task at hand, the DP manager's world comes to rest again, and they become their low-key selves again. As much as they love to dodge responsibilities, this type of manager is typically active at generously assigning tasks outside of their department at any hour of the day and night, expecting others to complete them in a more than timely manner. They love to play the avoidance game, and they are so good at it! Give these Dodgeball Players an AWARD!

My Way or The Highway managers: These managers are used to getting things their way. Sometimes they adopt this style because deep inside, they are threatened by a brighter, maybe lower-ranking team member. They are afraid of any promising talent, especially those with leadership or innovation skills; their preferred approach to dealing with this challenge is to nip all of it in the bud. They are always ready to squash any idea that did not originate from them, without evaluating the merits. *One company I know of made a corporate habit out of this attitude. Workers knew that presenting an idea through the company suggestion program was a fruitless effort: all suggestions would be passed on to the pertinent department heads, who had the ultimate authority to say 'yea' or 'nay.'*

Suggestions dropped on the MWOTH manager's desk for review inevitably disappear into oblivion. When questioned, the typical feedback is that the idea was impracticable, impossible to implement, or not worthwhile. Sometimes, the MWOTH manager pretends it was never submitted in the first place. Employees called that manager's desk a Bermuda triangle where innovation disappeared. Eventually, they stopped making suggestions altogether.

Occasionally, when the MWOTH managers can't deny the tremendous *ROI* and other benefits of implementing an employee's idea, they still don't want to give any recognition to the innovative thinker. Instead, they appropriate the idea and the credit that comes with it. Morale Destruction 101: Don't celebrate good ideas, steal the best ones for personal gain, and never ever give credit where it's due.

Depending on the organization's size and the number of bureaucratic layers in its structure, this kind of backward mentality can be widespread and deeply entrenched. Why does this unprofitable and unhelpful approach persist? Either these methods are used too subtly, with a skill perfected over the years, which makes them difficult to spot, or unspoken agreements are active between the layers of management. These highly popular hush agreements, exemplified by the time-honored 'You scratch my back and I'll scratch yours' approach, make it harder to call out these unethical practices. As a result, employee trust in management goes into the gutter, sinking productivity and work quality.

Politically Correct managers: While a healthy portion of political correctness can be a good thing, extreme devotion to this concept, in my opinion, can turn a quality environment into a mediocre backwater and then into a toxic swamp. In toxic workplaces, the PC culture does not allow for calling things by their true names, and a heavily political climate is more conducive to a conformist approach.

For example, a bully cannot be called a 'bully' because it might hurt their feelings. People witnessing less-than-desirable workplace behaviors choose to keep quiet for fear of receiving even poorer treatment or losing their jobs altogether. In this type of situation, independent thinkers often find it difficult to fit in and to thrive. While the best talent tends to feel unwelcome and leave, mediocrity is allowed and even encouraged. Tiptoeing around workplace bullies, failing to address their behavior, and enabling their disruptive methods in order to maintain the status quo, PC managers inaction can damage the team's morale and the organization's bottom line. When PC managers believe that maintaining a politically correct climate is the highest virtue of all and are afraid to tell a workplace 'superstar' that they are suffocating others, things do not improve on their own. The longer the undesirable practice is allowed to continue, the deeper it gets rooted. At some point, it becomes too late to deal with through coaching and behavior correction. The only remaining option is to part ways with the perpetrator.

I knew a mediocre PC manager who cared, more than anything else, about equalizing all of his subordinates. To remain equally popular with all of his staff, he made it his main focus to always make sure they got equal shares of everything that was available through the organization, regardless of individual employees' needs or contributions. For example, if one team member won a workplace award, then another would have to 'win' the exact same award; if one was sent to a training session, the other one had to attend the exact same training even though it was not needed for his position – just for the sake of continually keeping things even between coworkers.

Any time one employee received praise or constructive criticism, the others in his department expected to receive the exact same treatment automatically, without necessarily earning or deserving it. He ignored the fact that the people's contributions were drastically different, and his approach created nothing but unfairness. As a result, his obsession with keeping this 'equal' status, at the expense of everything else, alienated his staff and caused people to lose trust in his judgment.

When managers fail to take action out of fear of being disliked by their team members, it is counterproductive. The involved employee needs to know exactly how their behavior affects others in the organization while they can still change it. Besides, managers too get worn out by tolerating prolonged bouts of poor performance from their staff:

no matter how it shows up – attendance issues, lack of commitment, or poor work quality. When a PC manager is spread too thin, trying to sort out unworkable situations and cover for their staff's shortcomings instead of addressing them head-on, this by itself contributes to a vicious cycle of mediocrity, which only continues to breed more mediocrity.

PREVENTING WORKPLACE MEDIOCRITY

What are some of the most effective ways to prevent workplace mediocrity and promote excellence among management and, therefore, the rest of the teams?

> *It is well-accepted knowledge that employees don't leave companies. They leave managers.*

Having a supportive and knowledgeable manager not only may become a deciding factor in staying with the workplace, but it can also affect how engaged the employee is and how passionate they feel to be a part of the team.

Leadership needs to work hard to create a culture in which relationships are fostered and work itself is meaningful, a culture where human common sense dominates over robotic practices, and policies and procedures are in place to serve people by helping them turn their intentions into reality. A cultural breakthrough would move the organization toward creating more transparency of methods, personal accountability, follow up, and follow through systems. The old managerial style of top-down information transfer on a need-to-know basis does not work with younger generations, particularly so with Millennials and Generation Z. They have not been raised within strict hierarchical structures and often don't understand the traditional concept of a 'boss.' Not knowing how their work fits in the overall organizational picture makes the execution of their tasks less meaningful.

Younger workers don't want to blindly follow orders. They need to know the logic behind their tasks – otherwise, they feel out of the loop and disengaged from their work and the workplace. Effective managers need to understand the intricacies of working with newer generations and earn the respect of younger workers by assuming (possibly unfamiliar) roles as mentors and coaches. It's essential to keep this generation of workforce in the loop on everything pertinent to how their work fits the overall business goals. Some helpful guidelines might include:

- Holding periodic team meetings to explain what is coming down the pipe.
- Showing how their contributions add to the company's success.
- Sharing information visually.

More proactive and inclusive communication methods can help to celebrate success and to encourage personal accountability for working closer to established company targets, especially if team members were involved in setting those targets to support organizational goals. Take into account younger peoples' natural strengths, including their inclination to stay in touch with a larger number of people via social media, which tends to strengthen their sense of community with their direct team, within the organization at large, and with the profession they represent.

B. DO FLAT ORGANIZATIONS REALLY WORK?

Traditionally, management roles in organizations were established to oversee daily operations and the work of the team. If anyone on the team stumbled, managers would help make an informed decision on how to proceed. Ultimately, they would be responsible for the cost, quality, and timeliness of the service or product provided by the organization. This system has been reinforced through decades, if not centuries, and is backed up by many management theories. What happens as the team is empowered to grow, gain more knowledge, and learn to make decisions? What if the team takes control into its own hands, without having anyone manage their work? Does that diminish the leadership role, or does it enhance it by freeing up the leaders' time to focus on expanding an organizations' horizons? After all, we have seen significant success with process improvement, wherein teams of workers have shown themselves capable of improving their own processes and making good spending decisions within given budgets.

Organizations have traveled quite a long way along this path: in search of more efficient methods of operation, they moved away from traditional hierarchical structures and, in a grand experiment, some companies removed multiple management layers and chose, instead, nontraditional organizational models such as *flat organization models* and **Holacracy**.

FLAT ORGANIZATION MODEL

In the *flat organizational model*, layers of management are significantly reduced if not entirely eliminated. Responsibility for quality of work and authority to make decisions are shared among employees. One organization that implemented a 'flat' structure is a Washington-based computer game company, Valve Software, that proudly claims on their website to be 'Boss-free since 1996.' They claim their recruiting process allows hiring and retaining innovative, intelligent, and talented people who do not need to be managed and are empowered "to steer the company away from the risks and toward the opportunities." Even the company president is no one's manager. In their words, the flatness of the company's landscape allows the customer to be the de facto 'boss' and removes every organizational barrier between the person working on what the customer needs and the customer who enjoys the results of that work.

HOLACRACY

Another method of decentralizing management is *Holacracy*, trademarked by HolacracyOne LLC, a U.S. company founded in 2007. In this model, decision-making authority is given to self-organizing teams, comprised not of employees with job titles, but of legal partners with specific assigned roles, governed by the organization's by-laws. Roles related to the same purpose are united into *circles*. As described by the company, Holacracy does not remove the structure from the organization. Instead, it offers a new structure – an explicit and lightweight set of rules that establishes clear expectations and ensures the transparency of the decision-making authority at all levels.

According to HolacracyOne, the company has a nontraditional way of conducting performance reviews as well – through short, one-month cycles of evaluation to ensure that the team structure is optimized on an ongoing basis. Holacracy was created with the idea that "nothing should get in the way of the work." Other organizations looking to decentralize their management structure have adopted either Holacracy or the flat model, finding varying levels of success.

One proponent of the flat model, the California-based tomato plant grower, Morning Star, claims that this approach made their organization more 'effective and deeply human.' In the HBR article First Let's Fire All Managers, Gary Hamel claims that mainstream management structures add to the overhead and slow down decision making. They also discovered that decisions made at higher management levels prove impractical at the ground level. Finally, management has come to be viewed as an embodiment of 'tyranny,' leaving little to no power to the lower-level employees. The problem is described as going way beyond 'an occasional control freak' (Hamel, 2011).

While I could certainly see legitimate concerns with the complexity that mainstream management brings, I was interested in exploring whether the best method of governing an organization requires removing management entirely? Based on the experiences of some organizations, adoption of the flat organization model did not provide a structure that lasted very long.

A high-tech start-up in Vancouver, B.C., Canada, was built by a team that had worked together in a previous company where they had issues with management and HR; the founders did not believe in administration, and they were tired of hierarchies. Excited to leap away from the red tape, they built their new organization on the concept of 'if you want to do something, go do it.' In their new structure, they assigned heads of four key business functions who reported directly to the CEO, and each had their own team of employee-owners. Without the extra layers of management, decisions were made by a consensus, or relying on meritocracy, instead of involving a complicated bureaucracy. Any issue could be discussed and resolved among the colleagues; anyone could easily talk to the CEO as well.

In the twelve years since their inception, the company grew from a handful of people to the staff of 130. In the process, they learned a lot more about the flat organization model. As the organization grew in size, the team witnessed how every advantage of the flat system eventually turned into a weakness.

Here are some of the **problems** they ran into and some of the **solutions** they came up with:

PROBLEM	SOLUTION
Having no extra paperwork might be a good thing, but in a regulated industry, it becomes an issue when you cannot produce a paper trail to back up your process or product.	To offset this, the company invested in staff members such as risk experts and Quality Management specialists who would ensure that regulatory requirements were addressed.
When an issue arose with products and services, setting priorities became a problem for the team, because a large number of people had an equal say in the matter. Meritocracy is a great concept, but it can get awkward when there are too many voices to listen to.	The team agreed that the product or service that is already commercial (as opposed to R&D stages) takes priority and requires instant attention and response.
Checkpoints that require review and approval can become a bottleneck if ten or more people of equal expertise level are involved.	One solution is to automate as many checkpoints as possible, especially with the software checking and error proofing those points, instead of relying on people to do the job.
Software can make decisions on black and white matters, but some gray areas are not so easy to automate. It became important to figure out how to move forward with the right decision when opinions of involved team players not only differ but also contradict each other.	The company has specified key stakeholders and their responsibilities for each process. Others may also be involved in the review, but their approval signature is not required to move forward. For example, Quality can be important for every project, but it's not necessarily the determinant for every project. Risk Engineering is assigned overriding power.

PROBLEM	SOLUTION
Sometimes a search for efficiencies can lead to taking shortcuts and looking for scientific ways to justify those shortcuts.	The company found that the key is to have a balanced team of people with essential skill sets, specialists who know what you can and cannot do as an organization. Plus, someone with a background in Quality to serve as a voice of reason, particularly in regulated industries, is highly advantageous, helping the engineers to adhere to strict compliance protocols.
With no HR function in place, certain situations can lead to awkward problems. Getting a medical leave, dealing with a sensitive private issue, or having a coworker that is hard to get along with – who can employees talk to?	Teaching people to resolve their issues at the lowest possible levels, before they escalate further, is helpful but can achieve only so much. This is an issue that remains unresolved at this point in the company's growth process.

Despite working out a number of solutions for the problems they are facing with the flat organizational model, this company has realized that the larger they grow, the harder it is to get things done effectively and efficiently. They know they are getting to the point when the flat model will no longer be sustainable.

Another company, a video-hosting start-up called Wistia, had a similar experience with the flat model and decided, in the end, to move away from it. Created in 2006 by only two people, it really enjoyed its flat organizational model, which seemed exciting and fun as opposed to the 'boring', traditional structure of a larger corporation. Early on, everyone chipped in with their ideas when it came to decision making on any project. The team looked for opportunities together to make improvements, but this lasted only until Wistia grew to just under 30 employees. In his October 15, 2015 essay, "Ditching Flat: How Structure Helped Us Move Faster," Wistia's CEO, Chris Savage, shared that as the company matured and grew in size, "the strengths of the flat organization turned into their team's biggest weaknesses." Relationships between functions grew more complex, and boundaries of responsibility and authority became unclear. It got harder to take risks, and it got harder to learn and to grow. As the flat management model got more and more in the way of the organization's success, Wistia decided to create a structure that clearly defined ownership of all processes – both teams and managers – and clear lines of responsibility through delegated authority (Shelly, 2016).

Holacracy, as an organizational model, also does not seem to provide lasting solutions in workplaces.

Medium, a blogging service that started out using the Holocracy model of decentralized management, had to move away from it as well; their website describes why it did not work for them. Despite its 'admirable' philosophy of putting responsibility into the hands of individuals at all levels, and allowing people with many talents to use them in multiple roles within organizations, Medium found it difficult to use for larger-scale initiatives, in need of coordination and alignment across functions. This, in addition to the requirement for a deep commitment to record-keeping and governance, proved to be time-consuming and hindered a proactive attitude. For this company, Holacracy basically defeated its own original purpose and got in the way of the work (Doyle, 2016).

Zappos, the online retailer tried the Holacracy management system and found that it did not work for them. According to a New York Times article by David Gelles, 'The Zappos Exodus Continues After a Radical Management Experiment', employees were initially excited, hoping the new approach would allow them to contribute to new areas of the company (Gelles, 2016). Unfortunately, as the new approach unfolded, the employees got confused about reporting channels, compensation plans, and job expectations. Within weeks of introducing the new system, 14% of the employees left the company. Even the most loyal ones admitted the experience was painful.

According to Gallup findings, published in *"The No-Managers Organizational Approach Doesn't Work"* article by Brandon Rigoni and Bailey Nelson, Google is another company that tried a decentralized management approach. The experiment of relieving managers of their duties did not lead to the expected positive results: it demonstrated that the people issues in the organization could not be addressed successfully without involving managers. Having a self-established job description was not enough; the workers felt a lack of clarity about job expectations and work progress, since a vacuum appeared quickly, one that required ongoing support from management, trusting relationships, and help making informed, unbiased decisions. "The many needs that great managers meet – for example, providing consistent communication and ensuring accountability – are among the most important drivers of long-term organizational success" (Rigoni & Nelson, 2016).

This gap in clarity and employees' unmet needs led to larger problems in the workplace, bringing down the quality of the work, affecting productivity and the ability to comply with customer requirements. After only six weeks from the launch of the experiment, managers were reinstated in their original roles. Google's experiment demonstrated the vital place of management within the organization. Besides, their research showed that workers with the best managers performed better, and the departments run by good managers had lower turnover.

Completely removing boundaries and giving all decision-making power to the front lines has not proven to be entirely progressive and even created setbacks for workplaces that have taken that route. When removing managers entirely, you cannot expect that workers will automatically assume full responsibility and take care of all decision making on their own. Besides, as organizations become larger and more complex, we cannot pretend that there are no issues between people in workplaces, the kind that need to be resolved by management.

We cannot expect people to manage themselves all the time, work out all of their interpersonal conflicts, and then still lead the organization to success. Interpersonal issues between the staff can be challenging. If those difficult conversations are not facilitated carefully, and if disciplinary action is put off, the workplace might become a very difficult place to function in. Issues should be handled as soon as they come up instead of postponing them. This approach prevents larger issues down the road. It is understood that the flat organizational structure can work for smaller size organizations, but the larger the company grows, the harder it is to control the decision making and conflict resolution without management and structure.

ADHOCRACY

Another alternative to a traditional rigid management structure is **Adhocracy**. *Adhocracy* allows for flexibility and spontaneity, negates all bureaucracy by making use of cross-functional specialized teams that are formed as needed, and focuses on projects of a temporary nature. These teams are only there to solve a specific set of problems or take advantage of certain opportunities. After successfully completing its purpose, the team is dissolved. These teams tend to work best if they get to operate in an atmosphere respectful of each other's expertise, with the team united by a common purpose while it lasts.

Ronna Lichtenberg, in her book ***"It's Not Business, It's Personal"***, describes the culture of Southwest Airlines, a company that views its employees as customers and treats them with the same respect and attention that customers get.

Southwest Airlines recognizes significant events in their employees' lives, thus getting to know them better. Even though the corporate structure does involve position titles, they don't think of themselves in terms of those titles, and, most definitely, do not divide people in terms of management and non-management. Lichtenberg compares the corporate behavior of Southwest to the individual behavior of successful people: they treat their subordinates as if they were their superiors. They provide emotional support and sustenance to employees and clients in a way that builds a strong relationship foundation, creating loyalty and affection. This organization does not place hierarchy before people, but fosters an environment for people to get the results they need to get for the company's success. The Southwest Airlines approach is an excellent example of a culture that successfully promotes the QIQO approach and contributes to a Caring Work Environment that encourages people to do their best (Lichtenberg, 2001).

During my interviews, high-level executives from a number of companies shared that one of the many challenges of being a CEO of a corporation with a strict hierarchical structure is that you have limited connection to frontline employees. Knowing how much power you have within the company, and actually fearing the potential consequences, people are more likely to nod their heads in agreement to any of the CEO's initiatives, just to be on the safe side.

However, even though people are less likely to speak up in a strictly hierarchical structure, everybody, regardless of their rank, can make a valuable contribution to the Continual Improvement of the business. Even more credit should be given to those corporations who create opportunities for executives to open themselves up to the mission of meeting people at all levels in the organization, learning more about how their people do their jobs, and bringing in diverse perspectives.

The industry itself may also dictate how much hierarchy is needed in the organization. For example, in aviation, by law, you must have a hierarchy for responsibility and clarity of accountability. In cases like that, when the flat model will not work, creating an agile team environment could be the solution. A CEO of a Canadian international airport shared about the team of 30 experts involved in the design of the $300 million building expansion at the airport. The team worked based on the free flow of ideas that go back and forth pretty quickly; the best meetings are those where you have a hard time telling who is a manager and who is reporting. That's why selecting the right people in management roles, those who are open to any new ideas from subject matter experts of all ranks, is so vitally needed.

In QIQO organizations, business titles don't matter that much – whatever you call yourself today, things might be changing in the near future. What is important is the knowledge you have gained in that field, and the value you bring to the table.

C. HOW TO DEVELOP & PROMOTE THE RIGHT PERSON TO MANAGEMENT

Gallup CEO Jim Clifton said, "The single biggest decision you make in your job – bigger than all of the rest – is who you name manager. When you name the wrong person manager, nothing fixes that bad decision. Not compensation, not benefits – nothing." I couldn't agree more with this statement, as management plays an essential role in the organization's success. Let's look at middle management.

Middle management has many different functions within organizations. One of the most important roles is ensuring that productivity goals are met. The best way middle-level managers can help the company to optimize productivity levels is by checking their own egos at the door and focusing on the team. To develop effective teams and operate those teams successfully, managers must possess great interpersonal skills, including the ability to rally people behind the shared vision articulated by the company leaders, inspire them to do their best by personal example, coach team members for success, and fairly and diplomatically resolve conflicts. Workplace conflicts are inevitable, arising both from personality clashes and from the pressure of meeting tight deadlines or navigating rapidly changing business priorities. Above all, leadership and coaching skills are the most needed qualities for managers.

Because of their unique position within the company, middle management often faces pressure from both sides – top management and workers in a variety of positions. Subordinates may view middle management as uncaring about the workers, while superiors may perceive middle-level managers as not doing enough for the company's bottom line. The position of middle management is risky, not only because of how much they have on their plate, managing multi-faceted and often conflicting expectations, but also because of how much they have to lose. Many middle managers are still working on building their own careers and struggle with moving up the ladder.

Of particular note, many of them are younger members of Generation X (born between 1975 and 1980), laboring hard in a workplace where rules were developed from the context and circumstances experienced by a previous generation, and most key roles are currently occupied by older Generation Xers (born between the mid-1960s and the mid-1970s), or even by Baby Boomers, who in their turn might feel no rush to leave their positions. Advancement opportunities for middle managers in traditional workplaces are few and far between. Limited room for vertical growth may add to existing challenges all middle managers face. Gen Xers, and those born later, work hard but continue to experience low job satisfaction, as they are unable to see their roles as important in large corporations.

How do these people get the middle level positions they are in? Many are promoted to managerial roles for mostly the wrong reasons: sometimes solely for their technical skills, or for performing well in the jobs they previously held within their departments. I never cease to be amazed by the number of people who make it to higher positions with no assurance that they have what it takes to do the prospective job well. The salesman selling the highest number of gadgets among their peers; a welder producing welds that resulted in fewest failures;

a machinist known for their precision machining skills; so often these high performers become department managers without any attention paid to whether or not they are good at managing or leading.

A common assumption, one I find puzzling, is that management skills will come naturally as long as a candidate has technical expertise in the appropriate subject matter. This type of candidate may be bossy enough to make sure people get things done, but they may not genuinely care about people, nor are they well-liked. These management experiments usually do not work out in the long run. Sometimes, the skills necessary for the new position are not difficult to acquire, but they are different from those the candidate possesses. It is a poor excuse for having in organizations so many of those mediocre managers we all know of, those who frequently serve as the focus of satire in popular culture.

This phenomenon was identified and explained as the Peter Principle, named after the Canadian educator Laurence J. Peter. First described in 1969, the Peter Principle tells us that in most organizations, managers rise to the level of their incompetency. Typically selected for promotion based on their current performance in the role they currently hold, management candidate selection is not based on their ability to perform well in their intended role. In observation, Peter found that employees keep getting promoted until they reach a point where they can no longer perform their duties effectively (Consultant's Mind, 2019).

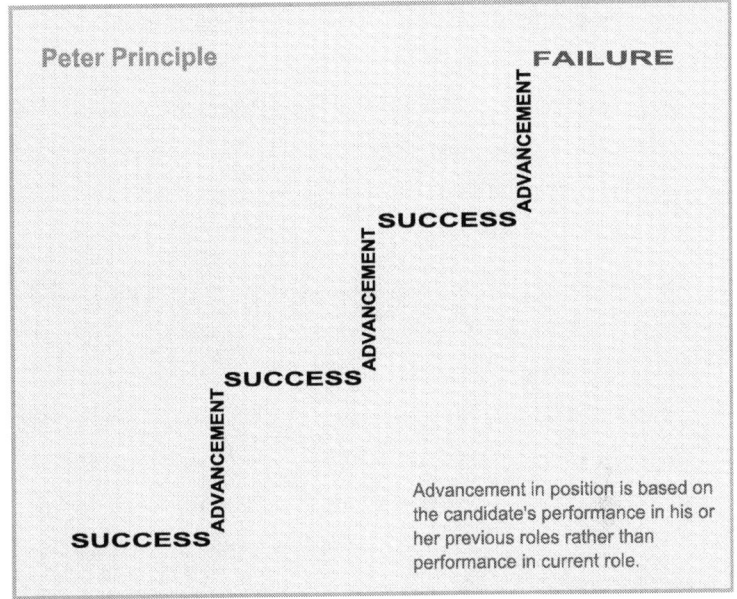

Picture 2. Illustration visualizing the Peter Principle (Harford, 2018).

Companies that choose managers based on the Peter Principle fail to realize that, to become an effective manager, even for the department they come from, the candidate needs a range of qualities and skills: planning, budgeting, and most importantly, the multifaceted ability to communicate and work effectively with different kinds of people.

The alarming situation that Peter warned us about is what happens if everyone in a workplace keeps getting promoted until they reach their level of incompetency? Eventually, all of the positions will be occupied by people who lack the competence to fulfill them properly. Employees promoted to their highest level of incompetency may remain in those jobs until the situation becomes apparent – but by then, much damage is likely to have been done. While they are 'at the top,' not only do they make their direct reports miserable, they themselves might feel trapped and barely able to keep their head above water.

- *I knew a talented industrial painter who got promoted to Coating manager at a manufacturing facility; he went from being a tradesperson respected for the quality of his paint jobs to a clueless department head who put his integrity at risk on numerous occasions. He could not keep up with his managerial responsibilities; he was overwhelmed, and he refused to ask for help when needed. This untenable situation ended with him leaving the company.*

- *Another example in my experience was an extremely abrasive 'know-it-all' designer who was promoted to Design and Development manager; she quickly showed her peers and subordinates that her lack of people skills and leadership qualities made her the wrong choice for the job. Her superiors seemed to be under the impression that things were fine; they kept promoting her until half of the design department's staff left the organization, and the remaining half mentally checked out and went into survival mode.*

- *At another company, a brilliant salesperson was promoted to sales manager. In his first six weeks of working, all twelve salespeople on his team became seriously upset with him. He had no idea how to manage twelve egos. Someone on his team was late to work five days in a row, and instead of asking his employee what kind of help he might need, the manager chose to yell at him. To make matters worse, he retained his sales territory as a part of his job, and that put him in a position when he was competing with his own reports for the highest sales numbers. After six months, the company fired him, instead of taking responsibility for what happened during his transition.*

The Peter Principle was clearly at work in all of these cases. Interestingly, as distinct as the effect of the Peter Principle is, it does not apply equally to all promotions across the board. For example, it is less frequent that women and minorities are promoted to the level of their incompetency, as discussed in the HBR article "*A Postscript to the Peter Principle*" (Ovans, 2014).

If someone is promoted to their incompetency level, they are most likely to remain in that position without further promotions. The opposite is not necessarily true; if someone stopped getting promoted, it doesn't always mean that they reached their incompetency level. It could be that they do possess the right skills or perhaps have raised their skills to the right level through training, but realized they do not like management roles or dealing with 'people problems' that managers have to get involved in. To find whether The Peter Principle occurs in your organization, look for people who have stopped growing, do not share knowledge, do not enjoy working with others, are eager to blame others and take credit for the accomplishments of others. What can you do if that is the case in your workplace? The proactive approach, aimed at preventing this phenomenon from taking root, is certainly the best option in identifying those situations.

With the QIQO approach, organizations make the connection between a poor promoting process and the detrimental results. That's why they ask the right questions before endorsing a candidate's move up the corporate ladder; they follow up by providing the proper training, and they do their best to ensure success by facilitating mentoring from a senior person for the advancing manager to learn leadership from. Caring Organizations that want to reward people who do well in their current roles do not necessarily give them managerial roles. They use a viable alternative stream for job promotion by creating a career path to turn those brilliant employees into senior specialists, or by offering sideways or diagonal transitions, as practiced in Lululemon culture. This allows the organization to foster happier and more well-rounded employees.

There are ways to deal with the results of poor promoting practices after the fact as well.

As much as it pains you to admit your promoting mistake, and as much as it pains the *'Peter'* to get demoted, this is sometimes the only viable solution. After overcoming the initial shock and the potential embarrassment of the act of demotion, the employee may feel relief in returning to the role they know how to do well. In a 2019 article, "*The Peter Principle and How to Beat It,*" F. John Reh suggests a win-win technique called *inverse promotion*. Instead of viewing someone who was demoted as a failure, as many tend to do, this approach recommends considering the person being demoted as a valuable asset for the company, who ended up in the wrong role. With *inverse promotion*, the person does not necessarily have to return to their original position; they can be transferred to an entirely new role, sometimes to a lower-ranking position but without an obviously lower job title (Reh, 2019).

It allows the now former *'Peter'* to save face while moving into a more suitable and fulfilling job; meanwhile, the organization can hang onto their expensive 'human resource' while refocusing their work to maximize their talents. By taking the proper steps, once you acknowledge the problem, you can address the consequences of the Peter Principle and focus on promoting the right person into the management role. As a last resort, if someone is clearly incapable of performing their job, it is best for them to be relieved of their duties. This method should only be used after you have diligently tried to locate a role that fits their abilities and strengths. When letting managers go, Drucker advises the responsible manager to make sure the one being let go understands that it's not due to incompetency and reassure them that they still may have a bright career ahead of them. It's so important to avoid shattering their confidence to the extent that it precludes them from successfully pursuing future endeavors (Cohen, 2013).

CHOOSING THE RIGHT CANDIDATE FOR MANAGEMENT ROLE

Having reviewed some of the many ways to prevent success, how do you begin to choose the right candidate for the management role? As always, there are different methodologies. Let's review some options, in the hope that you might find a methodology that works for your organization. Some companies hire managers based on their well-rounded skills and the ability to make fewer mistakes when it comes to critical decision making. Others look for candidates based on their ability to complement the existing management team, intended to fill in the gaps of what is considered the strength of the organization.

The most important criterion to look at is whether the person can align with, fully support, and become a champion of the company's vision, the direction it's headed in. Yes, this is already slipping into the field of leadership (which is definitely not the same thing as management), but the best managers are those who have leadership skills and can rally their people behind the right cause. If hiring decisions are already the most important to the company's success, then making the best hiring decisions related to management roles is even more critical.

When promoting the right person to the management role, the candidate's competence and character are essential. Identify a few strong candidates for the position, all of whom do meet the job's threshold requirements. Review their candidacies, ask for input from a few other key stakeholders, and consider the entire team while making your ultimate hiring decision.

I recommend against looking for the candidate who would be equally strong in all areas of the job. If you choose to bring on board someone with expertise in all areas listed, there is a chance that this candidate will not be able to offer strong representation for any of the key areas of the role. Instead, use the 80/20 rule, focusing on the candidate's ability to perform in the most vital areas of the job.

Once the top candidate is selected for a managerial role, their employers often expect a lot from them immediately. It's quite common to leave the newly appointed manager to figure out things on their own and to expect them to hit the ground running. Yes, top candidates can figure things out on their own. In my experience, for best results, the 'crawl, walk, run' rule should apply. The new manager will need thorough training to transition into their new role most effectively, to shorten their learning curve, and to eliminate unnecessary misunderstandings, bad habits, and other struggles. Appropriate and detailed training is best for everyone involved and makes the hiring executives look good for making the right choice for the promotion.

D. TRAIN YOUR MANAGERS TO BE INSPIRING LEADERS

There is a great deal of literature written on leadership; there are many programs that teach leadership. The paradox is that where there should be no shortage of leaders, true leadership is rare. There is still a lot of confusion as to what leadership is and what it is not. I know parents who instill in their children the value of doing well at school so that they can grow up and get leadership positions; the main motivation seems to be: "So you can give others the tasks you don't want to do yourself." This teaches our children that department heads are bosses who use their power to control people and demand obedience. It teaches nothing about inspiring people, taking the initiative to roll up their sleeves, and getting their hands dirty when necessary. What's even worse is when this kind of misconception comes from recognized leadership role models.

I have taken note of a quote that travels on the worldwide web, shared, reposted, and 'liked' by numerous professionals and industry leaders. Attributed to Facebook COO Sheryl Sandberg, the quote reads, "I want every little girl who is told she is bossy, to be told instead that she has leadership skills." Using 'bossy' and 'leadership' in the same sentence hurts our future. In fact, in today's workplaces there are already too many grown-up versions of those bossy girls and boys – micromanaging and un-inspiring individuals who were probably told too many times that bossiness means leadership.

Leadership is often misunderstood and, therefore, leadership positions are frequently sought after for the wrong reasons; from my perspective, mainly for the power that comes with it. The power over others is viewed as the extension of one's personal identity and an opportunity to boost one's ego. The allure of the higher titles on the organizational charts is associated with seeing leadership strictly as a position in management. While management roles are assigned and often have little to do with the candidate's leadership qualities, leadership as a concept is quite different, and has little to do with any positions and job titles.

'Telling people what to do' couldn't be further from the truth as to what real, effective leadership is about. It does not mean that the leader should be hogging all of the projects, stretching themselves too thin, and jeopardizing the quality of work and deadlines just because they believe that they are the only person who can get the job done right. Leaders must be able to delegate work and projects to people based on their current strengths, as well as their potential for developing those strengths for the future. Sometimes, it's about stepping aside, leaving behind their own ego, and admitting that someone else on the team is a stronger expert in a particular subject. Sometimes, good leadership is about followership as well.

HOW TO SPOT THE LEADERS

Contrary to the concept of being a 'boss,' leadership is about other people. Think of the people taking leading roles in your organizations: are they quick to give credit to their team members whenever possible, and are they ready to take the blame for the inevitable failures? This is a sign of leadership. While a manager has subordinates, a leader is defined by having willing followers. The manager focuses on *how and when*; leaders care about *what and why*. Both roles are essential and serve the organization in different ways, but to create a genuinely Caring Organization, managers need to become leaders.

Sheila M was a VP of Marketing at a clothing company; she aspired to become a Chief Marketing Officer. She approached accomplishing her goal by understanding that her job was to inspire someone else to the point of doing the VP of Marketing job very well, in order for her to be ready to move forward into her desired position. She created a safe space for people who reported to her – to learn, grow, and make mistakes. She protected her team with a firm belief that the team succeeds together and fails together. She ended up becoming a Chief Marketing Officer because of that mentality: inspiring people to greatness! This approach allowed Sheila to be seen as such, as well.

Inspiring people by your example encourages them to become better versions of themselves, by growing personally and professionally. These qualities of leadership don't depend on your position in the organization. Why not instill leadership qualities in those we promote into management positions? We need to teach managers how to inspire others to take action and ownership, instead of using managerial power to direct people to follow steps.

Managers who lead initiatives, instead of pushing those initiatives from top-down, can become the champions of many great beginnings that provide tangible benefits. Some examples include improving the safety culture of the organization, achieving *zero-defect production*, and fostering proactive communication. Most importantly, leader-managers must set a good example of a strong work ethic and adherence to agreed-upon values. If wearing **Personal Protective Equipment (PPE)** in the plant environment is an agreed-upon policy, managers must be the first ones to follow this rule, instead of breaking it. People do not tend to follow or support managers who stick to the destructive 'do as I say, not as I do' principle.

Suppose an organization decides to adopt the *smart meetings* format. It commits to running meetings effectively by bringing together only the right team of the experts needed, by adhering to the agreed-upon meeting agenda and parking all other arising issues, by closely watching the time, and by making sure that everyone around the table has a chance to speak up and to be heard before decisions are made. If that is the plan, then managers who call those meetings should be the first ones to uphold the new standard with all of its well-proven strategies to achieve the common goal of those meetings and come up with a plan for inspired action. If they do not respect the agreed-upon rules, then they cannot expect from others a different attitude.

Leadership certainly comes easier to some people; those fortunate individuals who seem to be born with extra charisma and are naturally inclined to care more about people and causes. However, even leaders who appear sure of themselves and confident in their results, face periods of struggle and confusion behind their seemingly effortless style. Leadership is not about always being perfect at what you do – it's also about stepping back and asking tough questions, re-evaluating your competence, constantly improving, and falling back on the core values that make up your character.

One program I highly recommend for those stepping onto the path of learning leadership skills is Toastmasters International. Their motto is "Where leaders are made." Toastmasters' well-honed curriculum simply and methodically teaches leadership skills in a safe, nonjudgmental environment. By completing different projects, by collaborating with others and discovering your leadership style, you learn to get projects done efficiently and cooperatively. This program is conducive to learning leadership skills because:

- You receive plenty of positive feedback on what you do right, which makes you aware of your natural strengths and the impact you make on others. Hearing specific feedback on how my actions impact others encourages me to do more, to develop my strengths, and to serve those around me further.
- You are gently pushed out of your comfort zone and nudged in the right direction. This is helpful, because our natural inclination is to stick with the familiar and avoid taking big steps until we feel we have gained enough knowledge and expertise on the subject at hand. Waiting for perfection keeps us from taking action. Immersion in the act itself is a great way to gain the necessary experience. Others with more experience are always around to coach, guide, and support you.
- You learn about your areas for improvement or, in Toastmasters language, 'points to grow.' The primary condition is that this criticism is delivered in a respectful manner with the future leaders' best interests in mind.

Caring Leaders don't waste their valuable time looking for ways to criticize; they are generous with positive feedback and like to catch people doing things right. In my coaching sessions for workplace leaders, I use a simple exercise that encourages executives to see the strengths in their management team and help them develop those strengths further. This exercise can be used any time someone comes to you with complaints. I sit down with the person and allow them to voice all of the grievances they have about their coworker or team member. We write down all of the concerns. Then, I encourage them to think about anything good in that person and their management style.

In one situation, I was dealing with a particularly negative executive of a food manufacturing company, Randolph S, who did not have an eye for anything good in people and was not used to giving praise.

As a typical *Type X* manager he was questioning the competence and character of Ashley M. another department manager on his team. The company that hired me let me know that this was not the first time Randolph had created a difficult situation with his team members, and asked me to interfere and facilitate better communication, so these two individuals could continue working together; the company really liked working with Ashley, but they were not ready to part ways with Randolph either.

During our session, I asked Randolph what, in particular, was not working with his team member. He said that nothing was working out; basically, everything was wrong with this manager, and he suggested perhaps, "She just was not the right fit for the job." Allowed to air all his grievances openly, Randolph produced a long list of Ashley's shortcomings – from 'lack of attention to technical details' and 'weak problem-solving skills' to 'dressed for work too nicely to actually care about the job.'

I diligently took notes, including this last piece of feedback for Ashley, and I reviewed them later with the full intention of turning the feedback into opportunities for improvement. Once Randolph was done, we took a pause. Then I asked him if there was anything positive at all about his colleague. The executive shook his head and said that there probably was not. I let him know that the meeting would not be over until he found something positive in Ashley's performance, anything at all.

It took Randolph a long time to come up with the first positive item; he needed a lot of help. I am recreating our conversation from the notes I took during our meeting.

"I guess she is good with people," he hesitantly offered.

"How so?"

"People seem to come to her with their problems."

"Why do you think they choose to come to her?"

"She knows how to listen to them and to empathize, I guess."

So, good listener, empathizes with people – I wrote. "And why do you think they keep returning to her with more problems?"

"She seems to help solve their problems."

"Ok, we will take a note on her problem-solving skills. Do you know how, in particular, she helps solve problems?"

"She is really good at researching complex topics, finding a lot of useful information, and if necessary, matching us up with the right type of experts from outside of the company."

"So, she has good research skills?"

"She actually sorts through her findings and distills the information down to what is most relevant to us."

"So, there is critical thinking, too then?"

"I guess there is then…"

This was not the end of our exercise, but you get the point here. By asking these questions methodically and getting some solid answers, we were able to discover many more excellent qualities that the manager in question possessed. The best part is that they came from someone who otherwise never thought anything good of people. A historically negative executive who seemed to see only people's shortcomings, now was encouraged to think actively about his team members' strengths and contributions as well. One of the most helpful outcomes of this exercise was that he would have to feel more compassion toward that person in the future, instead of vilifying them.

One of the crucial learning moments from this exercise is that, when all seems 'doom and gloom,' people think 'nothing I do is ever good enough' and lose hope and motivation for making any improvement. On the other hand, hearing about their strengths and acknowledging their contribution makes them more open to criticism so they can make improvements from a place of strength, confidence, and even a willingness to learn new skills.

UNDERSTANDING PEOPLES' STRENGTHS

Any opportunities for improvement that we may identify in ourselves or others are related to one of two broad categories: competence or character. I find it helpful to conduct personality tests in a workplace to find out what strengths each team member possesses and what weaknesses they have that stand between them and their path to success. There are many different personality tests out there. Myers-Briggs Type Indicator describes sixteen distinct personality types based on preferences from the four dichotomies specified in C.G. Jung's theory. There is a free online assessment you can take on www.16personalities.com. I highly recommend it, and I find it to be a reliable workplace assessment tool.

If all team members take a reliable personality test, you can develop a better understanding of yourself and your colleagues, become more compassionate toward people's shortcomings, and discover more effective ways to communicate and collaborate. Most importantly, it will help you to improve productivity by running more cooperative teams, by capitalizing on the cumulative strengths and offsetting the weaknesses, and thereby improve relationships between the people on your team.

Building trust among your managers will make it easier for them to take this further and build trust with their team members. Catching your managers doing the right thing and making excellent choices will, in turn, teach them the same approach toward the teams that are reporting to them. People stop trusting those who only notice mistakes and only give negative feedback. They need positive reinforcement too.

I once witnessed a heated scene on a plant floor in a manufacturing facility. The Plant manager and a Department manager were on a plant walkthrough, giving their feedback to the operators. One of the operators raised his voice at both managers; he was yelling that they only come to the plant to pick on workers or catch them do something wrong, which was why people on the floor did not want to see them there. "You never ever seem to notice anything good that we do!"

The Plant manager later admitted to me that being yelled at by a plant worker was a wake-up call for him. "Hearing those exact words made [me] realize how much truth was in them. I knew I had to do something about it." *This became the reason they revisited their communication methods between management and the plant employees. This company was able to eventually build trust between different layers in the organization.*

Focusing our attention on catching people doing the right thing is the most effective way to bring out the best in people and to inspire leadership qualities. The positive effect of this approach has the power to multiply exponentially. Even small gestures, like timely words of encouragement from the supervising manager, can go a long way. This not only enhances respect for managers in the eyes of their team members, but it can also generate powerful momentum to encourage people to feel better about themselves and contribute even more positively and enthusiastically to the company's success.

As Ken Melrose, the author of **"Making the Grass Greener on Your Side,"** said: "If you are not too big for small things, you won't then be too small for the big things that might happen as a result." Melrose describes how the corporate culture they built at The Toro Company takes advantage of the 'multiplier' effect, by recognizing employees for their small successes as well as their big ones. This is mostly done informally, on the spot, as part of everyone's daily work life, but it's done formally on occasion. One way to celebrate the company's success is 'Owner's Day,' an annual event to recognize and honor the people whose daily personal investments make Toro what it is. "We want employees to know that small things are important and add up to a healthy company" (Melrose, 1995).

Leadership behavior is critical, as the entire team looks up to their leadership. An old piece of wisdom, attributed to many cultures and languages, observes: 'The fish rots from the head.' In a business context, if the organization fails, leadership problems should be considered the root cause. On a positive note, all great things also start with leadership. Positive attitudes and productive behavior are contagious, too. Wise and caring leaders tend to pay close attention to what kind of habits they pass down to their direct reports, the middle level managers, and the rest of the organization.

Excellent research regarding this area of concern was done by Jack Zenger and Joseph Folkman, the CEO and the President of the leadership development consultancy Zenger/Folkman. Their research results are published in *"What Inspiring Leaders Do,"* an HBR article on 51 different behaviors transferred from leaders to managers to employees ((Zenger, Folkman, 2013).

Zenger and Folkman found that such positive behaviors as integrity, honesty, decisiveness, and performance, as well as negative behaviors like dishonesty and poor communication skills, can be passed from manager to employee. Does this mean that good leaders inspire other good leaders? And what are some of the most 'catching' behaviors? After matching 265 pairs of high-level managers and their middle level manager direct reports, and studying their *360-degree assessments* (assessment that includes feedback from an employee's subordinates, colleagues and supervisors, as well as a self-evaluation by the employee), the authors found highly significant correlations on a variety of behaviors. They distilled those behaviours to a total of 51. Among the behaviors that appeared most contagious, they listed those clustering around the following themes, in the order of most to least contagious:

- ☐ Developing self and others
- ☐ Technical skills
- ☐ Strategy skills
- ☐ Consideration and cooperation
- ☐ Integrity and honesty
- ☐ Global perspective
- ☐ Decisiveness
- ☐ Results focus

Studying overall performance, Zenger and Folkman found that direct reports of the worst-performing leaders performed below average themselves. On the other hand, highly effective leaders had direct reports who were also rated far above average. They reviewed the supposition that selection could have played a role in these results; a business bromide asserts "A Level Players hire other A Level Players, but B Level Players hire C Level Players." It turned out that the managers they studied had personally hired fewer than a quarter of the people who reported to them. It ultimately supported the hypothesis that leadership behavior is contagious: good leaders inspire better leadership behaviors among their middle level reports, while bad leaders cause the opposite results.

In the article, Zenger and Folkman cite research by IBM in which a question was asked of 1,700 CEOs in 64 countries: 'What do top executives want from their leaders?' It turned out that the three most desired leadership traits were the ability to:

- ☐ Focus intensely on customer needs,
- ☐ Collaborate with colleagues, and
- ☐ Inspire others.

They found that the leaders who scored highest on the competency measure of 'inspiring and motivating to high performance' did specific things such as setting stretch goals with their team. They expended significant time developing their subordinates, engaging in highly collaborative behavior, and encouraging others to be innovative. At the same time, they built emotional connections with their subordinates, established a clear vision, and emphasized effective communication. They championed change in the workplace and were seen as effective role models. Research shows that to be compassionate and inspiring, a leader does not necessarily have to be an extrovert either. The objective of inspiring leaders can be achieved by more than one method – by creating a vivid vision with a crystal-clear image of the future, and helping people develop their abilities in order to move together toward set goals.

E. THE IMPORTANCE OF PEOPLE SKILLS AND CHARACTER IN A MANAGER'S OVERALL SKILL SET

To inspire people, leader-managers need a robust set of people skills, often referred to as soft skills. Among those skills are promoting the company's product and values, having a creative and innovative approach to solving problems, fact-based decision making, and an excellent capacity to navigate interpersonal differences. Not only managers, but all knowledge workers need people skills in addition to their technical expertise. People whose value to the job is limited to their technical skills are the most likely candidates to be replaced with technology in the near future, while those with highly-developed people skills add more value by bringing out the best in people.

However, in most workplaces, teams operate under the impression that highly technical departments or staff members are more revered, seen as untouchable, and receive preferential treatment. I have personally witnessed many companies who have a so-called superstar, someone who rose to the top of their peers strictly through their technical expertise – whether perceived or real. Usually, these superstars are focused on their advancement in the company and don't mind doing so at the expense of others. In many cases, they skillfully disguise their inconsiderate approach, and often ensure that they are seen as caring more than anyone else about the company's best interests.

An engineer at an auto manufacturing plant climbed to the top of the heap by throwing her peers under the bus, taking credit for their work, placing blame elsewhere for her own mistakes and shortcomings, and engaging in many underhanded activities. This was done under the pretense of caring about company performance and customer satisfaction like no one else. Even though she was methodical about her work and had the requisite technical knowledge, many found it challenging to work with her. The staff experienced lost learning opportunities, because anyone who asked a question in the workplace was either ridiculed or yelled at for not knowing the answer in advance.

This person often caused workplace conflicts by mistreating her coworkers, especially those in supporting roles, whom she viewed as inferior. Some of those conflicts came to the attention of the General Manager. Unfortunately, instead of launching a proper investigation to get to the bottom of the issue, and setting clear behavior boundaries, to the entire team's astonishment and dismay, the GM rewarded the superstar engineer with a paid-for vacation with her family. The feeling of injustice made it a toxic work environment. Over the course of just a few years, many of the company's excellent and skilled professionals left the job. Turnover was extraordinarily high.

With the company culture focused on the bottom line and sweeping everything else under the rug, departing employees could not even bring themselves to speak the truth in their exit interviews. It took the company about ten years to finally understand what — who — was the common denominator in all of those cases. Finally, they took action to avoid further deterioration of their work culture, which included low employee morale, and an alarming declining status on GlassDoor.

It is time for companies to move away from allowing superstar behaviors, as they are dangerous in more than one way. Not only do they destroy employee morale, but they can also severely damage customer experience.

A Quality director of a manufacturing company in British Columbia shared an example of how detrimental superstars can be to the workplace. There was a salesperson at a gas company who gained his superstar status in the eyes of management for bringing in more money due to his apparent ability to sell more expensive gases. Because of his superstar status, most of his administrative work was pushed onto the inside sales staff, without providing them with any extra resources to handle their own demanding workload. He often pushed them to process his orders and fill out his paperwork ahead of their own work. If someone refused to give his tasks their immediate attention due to other priorities, the superstar salesman would make them feel guilty, or even have a diva moment by threatening that his customers would go elsewhere.

For years, he escalated things to senior management and got away with it, as his shining contributions to the bottom line blinded management to the cost of this behavior. He once made one of his coworkers cry under pressure when, torn between conflicting priorities, she realized she could not get her own work done. After years of ignored complaints, a workplace investigation was launched. The investigation showed that the superstar had regularly exaggerated urgency, apparently to force others into submission. It turned out, his customers simply wanted their orders processed in a timely manner. There was not nearly the level of priority, and absolutely no threat from customers to change their gas provider, as portrayed by the superstar. He simply wanted to push his unwanted work on the 'less valuable' peers.

Shortly after this incident, more information surfaced that had been carefully protected by the superstar salesman. The Quality Manager received a phone call from a customer concerned about the possibility of the liquified gas containers exploding. They did not know that the relief valve was there to let the pressure out. The Quality Manager drove to the customer site and demonstrated how the relief valve works. When asked who had provided the customer's training the last time they had come to the site — which is part of the sales representative's job description — it turned out that the superstar salesperson had never done the necessary customer training. This was a major eye opener for management: they finally discovered that the person they considered their best salesperson had been concealing poor customer service behind his 'diva' facade.

Many behaviors and actions that bring serious damage to an organization can remain hidden, particularly when an employer makes the mistake of granting someone privileged superstar status, and letting them bask in it while their shortcomings go unnoticed. Blinded by the performers' ability 'to put the puck in the net,' companies often seriously overlook the superstars' flaws in important areas such as interpersonal skills. Shielded by their untouchable status, the superstars can harm employee morale and the organization's overall performance, sacrificing company-wide efficiency and enthusiasm for the false glitter of burnishing their outwardly shining achievements.

Anointing superstars or unquestioned 'experts' in the workplace can actually lead to stifling an organization's growth. Victor Ottati, professor at the Department of Psychology at Loyola University in Chicago, warns about this in his article "*Beware of Earned Dogmatism.*"

> **"When you anoint someone as an expert, it makes them more confident. It also makes them more dogmatic in their opinions.**
> **They become less willing to embrace other points of view and more rigid in their thinking."**

Loyola University conducted an experiment that involved participants who believed that they were experts in the subject being discussed. They were asked a series of simple questions related to the subject of their expertise. Afterward, reviewing the objectivity and the open-mindedness of the responses, researchers concluded that the more a person perceives themselves to be an expert, the less open they are to new ideas and alternative viewpoints (Ottati, et al., 2015).

Managing top talent, keeping them challenged enough to maintain their interest while ensuring you can retain them is a demanding undertaking. With the right culture and incentive systems to support it, top performers can play an essential role in helping your organization meet its goals. One issue that top performers may have is distrust of their coworkers' abilities to also do a top-notch job; their natural inclination might be: "If you want it done right, do it yourself." While their strong work ethic may be commendable, the downside of this approach is that they tend to be unable to relinquish control, which thus suppresses teamwork. Even if they agree to share work with the team, they might start micromanaging others to make sure everyone is doing things 'their way,' the way they believe is the correct way. As the resident expert, they should know, right?

DEALING WITH DIVAS

What might be your best approach if you recognize the presence of one of those divas in your workplace?

When a newly hired or promoted manager steps into an environment with an already established superstar, it can cause ripples and disturbances if the issue is not approached in a diplomatic and effective way. If you inherited a superstar instead of hiring them, it may be wise to refuse to accept that status as is. First, familiarize yourself with the evaluation system the company uses to assess employee skills and accomplishments, so you can make an accurate, company-approved judgment on employee performance levels.

Some things to consider when you evaluate the employee performance program:

- Is the assessment tool well rounded?
- Does it only focus on employees' technical skills or emphasize their ability to do favors for management?
- Does it pay attention to a combination of capabilities? These might include:
    - Interpersonal skills
    - Communication skills
    - Leadership skills
    - Emotional intelligence
    - Teamwork values
    - Team camaraderie with minimal conflict

Take your time to learn how the superstar got to this point. For example, what methods did they use to climb to the top. The higher they rise using those methods, the more they feel encouraged to continue relying on those tactics and strategies. It's important to scrutinize those very methods that worked for the diva so far.

- Did they get ahead by hogging the most coveted projects, while pushing the less desirable work away?
- Do they protect valuable company knowledge from others in order to remain indispensable?
- Did they somehow convince the previous management team that they care about the bottom line like no one else?
- Does the company knowingly or unknowingly support the behavior of climbing the corporate ladder at the expense of other employees?

Even if those top performers got their reputation through significant contributions to the company's bottom line, accepting the existing status as gospel is a major mistake. The mentality of 'the end justifies the means' is ultimately damaging to your organization, and it would be wise to bring an end to that kind of thinking immediately. Start questioning the company's incentives program and challenge the very definition of 'success' as it has been viewed until now. If the rewarded behavior was anywhere along the lines of the cases brought up above, it may be time to challenge the value system the organization claims to be built on and the guiding principles it outlines.

People are always more inclined to display the types of behavior they are rewarded for. Change the reward system to move away from praising personal accomplishments in favor of developing a long-term team mentality, working towards excellence through sharing expertise, growing talent, developing team members by helping them learn new skills, and offering new opportunities. Lead by example, and the 'superstars' will have no choice but to rein in their undesirable behavior and follow the new mainstream culture. In the long run, this approach will be good for everyone, including the top performers.

UNSUNG HEROES

In the false thinking that the top performers deserve the most attention, managers often overlook another important category of employees. These are the quiet types, who typically produce exceptional results but prefer to keep a low profile. I call these people the *unsung heroes* of the workplace, who carry on their shoulders the brunt of the daily hard work. They find solutions to problems, conduct valuable research, proactively identify external or internal risks and opportunities, help the organization maintain compliance with requirements and regulations, protect the company from unnecessary and expensive lawsuits, keep employees and visitors safe, and do the least glamorous jobs for customers. These people prefer to produce their excellent results quietly, without attracting too much attention to themselves or their achievements. They easily get overlooked or taken for granted. Sometimes the company realizes their actual worth only after they leave.

I knew a manager who was a true unsung hero in his workplace. Robin S oversaw two different departments for years, stayed late and came in early, readily helped coworkers, identified training needs throughout the organization, and provided the necessary training – mandatory or otherwise – often putting the content together from scratch. He also had an extraordinary ability to get along well with all kinds of personalities. However, he was never seen as special in his workplace; not once during his seven years of service, and sadly, not even at the time of his resignation. After his departure, the senior management started ripping their hair out when they realized that the replacement hired at a higher entry rate than Robin's exit rate after many years of experience – constantly fell behind with their duties. They brought back Robin as a part-time consultant to help bring the new hire on board. Eventually, the company needed and hired not two, but three employees to do the work that one unsung hero had quietly done, year after year.

In their book **"Get Your People to Work Like They Mean It,"** Jean Blacklock and Evelyn Jacks warn us of the dangers of overlooking these hardworking, smart, loyal, positive thinkers who they refer to as twinkling stars. The authors explain that their friendly and low-key approach is often the reason why so few people recognize the stellar work and excellent skills of these individuals. Twinkling stars are a tremendous asset for any organization, contributing in many ways with their consistently high-quality work. They also value their managers' time and adapt well to making themselves a great resource when needed and in whichever capacity is required. They are self-motivated to provide the best value to their employer. Since these people are incredibly resourceful and versatile, their commitment to the company's success and their exceptional skills can be a smart manager's secret weapon (Blacklock and Jacks, 2006).

The *unsung heroes* may not need much input to feel engaged at work because of their nondemanding approach and easygoing personality, combined with their focus on productivity and results. Usually, a sense of accomplishment from a meaningful job well done is their primary motivator; they work outside of the spotlight and are not desperate for management's attention. This brilliant constellation of attributes and attitudes does not mean it's ok to allow them to be ignored either; they still like to know that their efforts are acknowledged and their contributions recognized. It's an excellent idea for managers to ask for their opinions and input when making important decisions. It should not be too hard for managers to see what is missing in the *unsung heroes'* job satisfaction, to fill those gaps with the types of rewards these individuals find satisfying. One thing is for sure. Becoming the next 'superstar' is not on their agenda. They are more interested in knowing that they have avenues for communicating their input to decision-makers and knowing that the job they are doing is important for the organization.

Blacklock and Jacks suggest creating a *participative management system* for building meaningful relationships with these solid performers, who often do the lion's share of the work. Participative management is focused on employee involvement in decision making, problem solving, strategy development, implementation of plans, and providing avenues for making suggestions and forming self-managed professional teams; all topics discussed in this book.

CHAPTER 4 – 'WE HAVE ALWAYS DONE THINGS THIS WAY': WHY RESISTING CHANGE ENSURES THAT COMPANIES STAY LESS-THAN-GREAT

> *"A man who is used to acting in one way never changes; he must come to ruin when the times, in changing, no longer are in harmony with his ways."*
> — Niccolò Machiavelli, The Prince

A. WHAT RESISTANCE TO CHANGE CAN DO TO YOUR COMPANY

In my role as an Organizational Excellence expert, I have helped companies ensure that the quality of their outsourced processes met all applicable requirements and adhered to the standards specified by high-profile clients. As a part of the supplier qualification process, I audited suppliers before bringing them on board. I visited their facilities to establish a personal rapport with senior management, reviewed their existing processes and management system, identified any procedural or regulatory gaps, and helped them improve their ability to provide all necessary documentation for project support.

As I was planning one of those audits, I made an appointment with the owner for a site visit. It was a machine shop with the ability to perform a niche process, so I took a machining expert with me to check out the equipment capabilities. From the moment we walked through the door something didn't seem right with this place. This company had no reception area, and there was no one to greet us. Instead, we found ourselves in a cluttered office space with a large fax machine in the middle. I was able to spot someone at a distance and called out to him, "Sir, we are here to see..." He turned around, he saw me, and he laughed, and laughed, and laughed. After coming back to his senses, this person agreed to take us to the owner, and as he led us through dimly lit scruffy corridors, he announced to at least two other workers how funny it was that I called him sir.

When we met the shop owner, I thanked him for making the time for us and restated the purpose of our visit. With a blank look on his face, this formidable-looking aging man pronounced somewhere above my head that he did not understand a thing. Well, I thought, it must be my accent. I slowed down and paraphrased what I said. There was a long pause with him staring me up and down, with his eyes stopping anywhere but eye level. He finally turned to my colleague and said he would give us a tour. I was the one with the questionnaire, but every time I asked a question, the shop owner rolled his eyes and deliberately replied by addressing my colleague, as if I was not even there. To get through this audit, I had to channel every question through my colleague, and he would translate it – from English to English – to encourage this owner to respond.

The lousy attitude we met permeated all other areas in this workplace. To get to the items we needed to see, we had to step over machine parts and bunched up cables, squeeze through tight spaces, and, at times, even limbo our way through the jungle of this workplace. As I was contemplating how this shop even survived with their disregard for safety, none of their staff seemed the least perturbed with the poor lighting, the exposed pinch points, tripping hazards, and the lack of personal protective equipment. Many things in this workplace suggested there was no 'woman's touch' to it, but I cannot say I did not see any women there. Unfortunately, I did. Stark naked women. Staring down from most of the walls. I would look away from one, only for my eyes to meet another, plastered on the next wall. If I felt invisible before, by this point, I felt exposed.

Nowhere on my checklist was a box for rating a supplier on sexism or bigotry, but for this shop to fail our audit, it didn't have to. They were so far from meeting our requirements on many grounds. Unable to provide adequate quality records or show traceability, they expressed zero interest in accepting help ramping up their documentation. Everything we saw, in terms of equipment and processes, was shockingly outdated. We also learned that no one in this workplace was computer literate. In fact, the company owned only one PC, which was referred to cautiously as 'the computer.' The only way they corresponded with the outside world seemed to be via the giant fax machine we had stumbled upon at the entrance.

On our drive back from this place, my colleague kept apologizing to me, even though we both knew it was not his fault. He informed me that what we saw that day was exactly how things were back in the 1970s and 1980s in regards to quality, safety, and the way people were treated in workplaces. He even admitted that those sexist posters and calendars existed in many shops back then.

To be fair, I haven't been around long enough to see for myself the *Workplace Culture* of those decades, so I have to rely on secondhand reports. Since that day, which took place only 3-4 years before this book was written, my perspective is cast in a whole new light when people venerate 'the good old days' in front of me. After experiencing this glimpse into the past, I now appreciate even more the progress made by organizations and individual leaders; it left me more grateful than ever before for the change that is the catalyst of our progress.

This example shows how employees get used to the way things are run in their workplace. The 'We Have Always Done It This Way' mentality gets so entrenched in people's brains that it translates into all of their daily activities. Once accepted as the company culture, it becomes quite a task to introduce change, keep up with modern best practices, and become leaders rather than complacent, accepting, and resigned. Limiting themselves to their immediate environment, without a reality check on how business practices have progressed and evolved elsewhere, employees tend to go with the flow. They fall behind the times when ignore red flags of their workplace and do not raise concerns. Here are some of those red flags that indicate a company with a backward mentality:

- Holding on to outdated manual machinery and tools, while your competitors have multiplied their throughput and productivity by moving on to newer equipment and more efficient production methods;
- Refusing to challenge your procedures to identify waste in current processes and eliminate it at its root;
- Keeping an old-timer on staff, the kind who repeatedly disregards company policies and defeats its values, just because they have been with the company for so long;
- Persisting in following archaic management methods, stifling the creative learning process, and fostering disengaged employees;
- Ignoring customer feedback and other important signs; 'shooting the messenger' instead of turning complaints into opportunities for improvement;
- Resisting new ideas without giving them proper evaluation, just because they come from someone else, especially people with lower seniority in the company. This is the infamous *Not Invented Here* approach, usually taken by defensive bosses whose only goal is to protect their power base and status. This tends to cause stagnation in employee engagement, while stunting the company's growth (May, 2016).

Management behavior that insists on clinging to the past prevents companies from realizing their potential, growing their market share, and making the progress they are otherwise perfectly capable of making. Employees who work for them may, for a while, go along with the low-engagement approach, becoming entrenched in this backward thinking, and attached to their routine. However, in my experience, the employees who remain for too long are those who do not believe they can find a job elsewhere, and may not have much to offer to evolving workplaces, because they do not like to challenge their comfort zone, which of course cuts off their capacity to learn, grow, and develop. Others eventually get exposed to new ideas coming from the outside world and, as a result, develop a more critical eye for their immediate surroundings. They begin to see the difference between their company's outdated ways and how things really should be. Frustrated by management's inaction on making overdue workplace changes, they tend to leave.

Turnover is only one of the problems faced by employers with such a backward mentality; losing orders, losing customers, and being forced out of business by their more forward-thinking competition is only a matter of time.

STICKING WITH THE STATUS QUO IS NOT FEASIBLE NOW

Why do companies get stuck with their outdated and unprofitable status quo? When a company first starts out, things seem magical and exciting for the founders. They are in growth mode; they make a significant breakthrough to enter the marketplace, establishing themselves, and gaining a customer base. Then they grow more comfortable with who they are, they relax about their place under the sun, and become complacent. Routine takes over, numerous meetings begin to suffocate the desire to continue making progress, and, especially culpable, the mentality of 'If you want something done right – do it yourself', begins to surface.

The business owners stop growing and pushing boundaries; consequently, the business also stops expanding its boundaries. You know you did something right in the first place – but if not vigilant, you risk allowing that old success feeling to lock you in to the status quo. 'We have always done it this way,' usually for quite a long time, represents an established best practice that brought in business and earned stuck-in-the-past employers the status of a trusted provider of a product or service. Sticking with what they are good at works for a while – hence the mentality of 'don't fix if it ain't broke.' This can only work for so long; even a well-established process, without the lubricant of Continual Improvement and innovation, runs the risk of becoming outdated. The danger to companies in today's rapidly evolving and challenging environment is quite high; when you stop changing, business requirements do not remain static, so things start to deteriorate.

This is precisely what happened to certain industry leaders that once were household names: famous examples include once-highly respected and profitable companies such as Kodak and Blockbuster. Business history is rife with widely celebrated behemoths who lost their place under the sun and had to file for bankruptcy after many years of enjoying tremendous success. The reason for their demise could be blamed on rapidly evolving technology, but responsibility for failure can most often be pinned down on company leadership, where an inability to change can be highly damaging when times demand an evolving approach.

Blaming failure on external circumstances represents a victim mentality as if company leadership is patently incapable of flexibility, awareness, and implementing innovative solutions to meet the requirements new circumstances, technology, or whatever the situation calls for. Well, why do some companies adjust to changing circumstances, while some don't? The QIQO approach encourages us to look within, taking responsibility for both our actions and our inactions, choices that may have contributed to failure to act, and to implement new processes and yes, even values.

From that perspective, resting on your laurels hinders further progress and eventually leads to the demise of a company. Exploring opportunities outside of their comfort zone might not always come easy. Still, it may actually prove useful to the organization's survival, ability to remain competitive, and lasting success in this ever-changing world.

B. COMMON CHARACTERISTICS OF QIQO COMPANIES

"Happy families are all alike; every unhappy family is unhappy in its own way," said Leo Tolstoy in his novel Anna Karenina. According to this principle, a variety of attributes can lead to an unhappy family, while all happy families share the same set of attributes that lead to their happiness. Can the great Russian author's words also be applied to successful organizations that follow the QIQO principle? Are there common characteristics that can be considered must-have ingredients behind every brand that successfully manages change?

In my search for answers and solutions, I found this to be a reliable indicator: while unique products, excellent value, and superior customer experience are essential for business success, a strong organizational culture that unites great people around a shared vision seems to be the number one condition for lasting success. Working toward that great future state becomes the purpose of the organization's existence; it is supported by core values and is driven by guiding principles. Everyone at the organization is encouraged to practice the core values and stay focused on the guiding principles in their daily work.

According to the research in **"Good to Great,"** author Jim Collins found that *specific values* do not matter as much as *having those values* in the first place. As specific values vary from one organization to another, adhering to those values and reinforcing them through daily decisions and actions, becomes quite important to nourishing, fertilizing, and sustaining a strong, stable corporate culture.

At some point, a dilemma arises for organizations who want to stride along to keep up with a dynamic business environment whether to preserve core values behind their brand or to embrace change. Despite the pride they take in the historical company legacy, and the respect they have toward the brand founders and other visionaries of the past, companies cannot get too attached to traditional business methods if they wish to remain successful. Therefore, to encourage a forward-thinking business mentality, at least one of the values the organization upholds must reflect innovation, experimentation, and Continual Improvement (Collins, 2001).

They know they must stay in tune with ever-changing customer needs, welcome innovation at all levels, and, most importantly, allow their employees to make mistakes while exploring and experimenting with new methods. They are willing to take risks, change their ways when it becomes necessary, and even reinvent their business. To explain the seeming contradiction between upholding these two opposing concepts: to remain faithful to timeless principles and yet keep up with a changing world, Collins brings up a great analogy: while the laws of physics remain 'relatively fixed,' engineering practices continuously improve.

A good example of a global company revisiting its core values to embrace change is Siemens: they changed their mission from 'maximizing shareholder value' to 'serving society.' As part of this transformation strategy, called *Vision 2020*, they included embracing Artificial Intelligence and The Internet of Things. It required a larger scale of cultural change to shift decision making from the central management sphere over to business units. It eventually switched focus from its core oil and gas industries to digital technologies and smart infrastructure.

Siemens USA CEO Barbara Humpton, quoted in a recent HBR article, *"The Top 20 Business Transformations of the Last Decade,"* declared that "the biggest obstacle to any transformation is 'the way we have always done things'" (Anthony, et al., 2019).

Not everyone can afford a major transformation; money can be an issue, especially for startups. Mistakes can be costly, embarrassing, viewed as a waste of resources, and of course, they are never anyone's end goal. They can, however, be used as an excellent learning tool. That is what successful companies do. One approach to dealing with the waste factor is to 'try frugally and fail fast,' as does the Indian multinational conglomerate holding company, Tata Group.

Ratan Tata, the head of Tata, promotes the concept of frugal innovation, by embracing the power of failure as a part of his business strategy. He introduced an annual award for the best failed idea to support the spirit of innovation even if the idea tried did not meet with success (NextBigWhat, 2011). Hill Holliday, a Boston-based marketing and communications agency, learned to welcome failure into their organizational culture to drive their team's creativity and cultivate the guts for risk-taking. That's why they introduced their annual *Epic Fail Award* (Proulx, 2019).

Given our culture's focus on being successful and not admitting when we are wrong, developing a tolerance to failure may be one of the hardest things to do when it comes to changing the organizational culture. Some failure is a necessary part of growing, learning, and embracing the change that is frequently an effective catalyst for our progress. Not everything can be planned for or fully anticipated. Not every situation can be forestalled, even if anticipated. Accidents do happen. Mistakes are made. Albert Einstein, Henry Ford, and Alexander Graham Bell have provided role models for people who learned from their mistakes and allowed room for innovation in their efforts. Successful organizations welcome failure, encourage their people to challenge each other, challenge the status quo, make mistakes, learn from them, and embrace change together.

Within the last two or three decades, we have seen more tremendous change in the way our society operates and how businesses are run than anything that has happened in the previous decades of the 20th century, which is saying a lot, given world wars, widespread medical challenges like influenza and AIDS, and radical economic shifts. Businesses of the past also faced major changes due to technological and social shifts in perspective. The discovery of the steam engine led to mechanization of factory processes through water and steam power. The invention of electricity allowed for mass production and assembly lines, which led to the advancement of telecommunications. The Internet and the rise of digital technology entirely revolutionized the way the world operates: the faster the change, the less time to prepare for it. As Ken Auletta noted in his book *"Googled: The End of the World as We Know It"*, "It took telephones 71 years to penetrate 50% of American homes, electricity 52 years, and TV three decades. The Internet has reached more than 50% of Americans in a mere decade." With the invention of the Internet, the changes we have encountered are arriving faster than ever. The globalization of business became easier to understand and the impact is ever more apparent Auletta, 2009).

While some organizations blame technology for their inability to cope with change, many successful organizations have reinvented themselves to meet the demands of a rapidly changing global environment. Productivity, quality, and personal satisfaction have increased in those organizations that have begun to focus on the management practices that invest in building high-performance teams, united by a shared vision, and ready to take on any challenges on the way to their destination.

Despite the significant role of technology in altering our lives on so many levels, the *Good to Great* companies examined in Jim Collins' book didn't often mention technology as one of the main factors driving change for them (Collins, 2001). In fact, 80% of the interviewed executives did not list technology among any of the five top factors that had the most impact on their transition. Only two out of 84 interviewed mentioned technology-driven change as number one. Here are some of the technology-related lessons we all can learn from the *Good to Great leaders*:

- Avoid technology fads and bandwagons, and apply only carefully selected technologies that fit with your core ideology;
- Use technology as an accelerator of momentum, not the creator of it;
- 'Crawl, Walk, Run' can be a helpfully cautious approach, even during rapid technological change.

In some cases, it takes an outsider with a fresh perspective to notice when things are getting stagnant, and that the system has begun to weaken. It is hard to maintain a sharp pair of eyes when you are too engrossed in daily operations to fully grasp technological advancements pertinent to your industry. A strategic decision can be made to walk away from the old methods and habits, and start planning for the transformation to new and higher levels. At a moment in time like this, leaders should consider:

- Keeping an open mind to hear out fresh ideas.
- Taking some time to pause, for a deeper, more reflective look at the overall business – both its achievements and shortfalls.
- Conducting a thorough evaluation of external and internal opportunities.
- Renewing their focus on customers.

In his book **"Cold Hard Truth"**, Kevin O'Leary said that when his company introduces a new computer program or phone system/

inventory tracking device, he makes sure he is the first one to sign up for training on how to master it (O'Leary, 2011).

C. THE ERA OF DISRUPTIVE CHANGE

In all previous industrial revolutions, changes were life-altering for our predecessors. Today, we are living through the Fourth Industrial Revolution — *Industry 4.0* — where change is moving faster and more drastically than ever before. Driven by internal forces or dictated by external conditions known as *PEST factors*, change happens whether we want it to or not.

> **PEST**
> **PEST analysis** (Political, Economic, Socio-cultural, and Technological) describes a framework of macro-environmental factors used in the environmental scanning component of strategic management. It is part of an external analysis when conducting a strategic analysis or doing market research. It gives an overview of the different macro-environmental factors to be taken into consideration. It is a strategic tool for understanding market growth or decline, business position, potential, and direction for operations.
> Variants that build on the PEST framework include **PESTEL** or **PESTLE**, adding essential legal and environmental factors for consideration. ("PEST analysis" Wikipedia, 2019).

As the founder of *Total Quality Management (TQM)*, Dr. Deming wisely said: "Change is inevitable; survival is optional." Advances in technology create changing possibilities, affecting public opinion, resulting in changes in customer expectations, wants, and needs. It's up to us: whether we gear ourselves up to get ahead of life-changing challenges, whether we choose to keep up with changes, or whether we allow ourselves to lag or fall behind.

HOW TO ADAPT EARLY

Successful companies do everything in their power to adapt early. In recent decades, the *original golden rule* for businesses was to identify your customer needs to meet and exceed customer expectations. These days, that rule is no longer enough; this is not how companies like Apple get ahead. The *new golden rule in business* seems to be: Give customers the ability to do what they cannot currently do but would want to do if they only knew it was possible.

Do you ever have clients that do not really know what they want? They do not know what they can ask for. By giving them a range of possibilities, it opens up a dialogue. You understand their needs and desires, and they aren't afraid to ask important questions. The technology-driven transformation will not wait for any of us. If new technology created a possibility for something new to be done, it would soon be done. If you don't do it, then someone else, for sure, will. When things in our company are moving slowly, we lose our competitive edge and fall out of alignment with our marketplace. That's why it's important to master the *Art of Change Management,* something that provides the company with a way to ensure the success of the inevitable transition and provides sustainability in the midst of the change.

How do we prepare ourselves for the unknown challenges the era of disruption brings with it? Here are some thoughts on planning for the unknown:

Start thinking about what you can offer to your customers to address future needs. New technologies do not always mean that the old technologies will be discarded. Investigate creative ways to integrate new and existing technologies to provide the best value. *Industry 4.0* may sound overwhelming when we think of it as the era of disruptive change, **Big Data,** and the digitization of manufacturing that these innovations bring with it, but it offers tremendous opportunity and flexibility as well.

Yes, transformational levels of innovation are required to stay successful. That does not mean that the goal of Fourth Industrial Revolution is to disrupt; and the goal of *Big Data* is to collect the most significant data possible. The digitization of the economy does not necessarily mean further improving the efficiency of existing processes. If the product itself is outdated or the service we provide no longer meets our customers' needs, there is no point in automating or digitizing the processes behind it.

To be prepared for *Industry 4.0* means to be able to challenge our own status quo, how we do things, and the way we think of our customers and our abilities to provide their needs. If the organizations' past goal was to meet or to strive to exceed customer expectations in the new era, that is no longer enough. We must proactively think of our customers' future needs and expectations, sometimes to conceive of needs that the customer themselves may not realize they have yet.

Innovative organizations value any idea based on its ability to resolve the *root cause* of the customer's pain. They understand that the solution to that pain lies somewhere outside of our company's current capabilities, just like, on an individual level, we know that magic lies outside of our comfort zone. Forward-thinking companies do not allow themselves to be limited by their existing capabilities and technology. They step out of their comfort zones and start working with new tools and systems that come with *Industry 4.0*. QIQO organizations view those tools as a means to an intended end, but not the end itself. They understand that today's technology provides options for solving a wide array of problems and they refer to technology for help when needed.

Big Data is there to support the organizations' needs. Do current data limitations impede your organization's progress? What are the data you need? How do you collect it? How do you analyze it? What problem will it help solve? A precept often attributed to Albert Einstein observes: "Not everything that counts can be counted and not everything that can be counted counts." Don't just collect Big Data to use as your next tech fad; instead, focus on what goal you are striving to achieve with the help of this tool.

What processes are you planning to automate? Have you considered other methods of Continual Improvement of your business processes before looking into automation? What is the goal of your automation? Do you really understand the current process and know where the inefficiencies lie, in addition to the causes behind those inefficiencies? What is your strategy for integrating people with technological changes? Are you going to lay off your people or find a way for them to utilize their talents elsewhere? It's always best to find ways for people to move on to better and bigger things due to the automation of the previously manual processes, so that they can still be a part of the team and add value to the customer and the bottom line in new ways. For people to contribute in new and meaningful ways, leaders need to help them change their mindset, gain new knowledge, and develop new goals.

Most importantly, to overcome the paralyzing fear of instability and job insecurity, helpful strategies might include involving people in the change, perhaps via a survey, or find other ways for them to contribute their opinion on the following vital questions that every organization faces during the times of change:

- What should we stop doing?
- What should we do more of?
- What should we start doing?

Things to stop doing: actions that hold the business back should be identified and acknowledged as no longer serving the business.

Things to do more of: actions that might constitute the current strengths of the business; we should capitalize on those. Which areas can we place a deeper focus on, to master those skills and become a leading authority in those subjects?

Things to start doing: actions that might include the digital technologies we need to learn about, pinpointing new knowledge to gain.

Knowledge has an expiry date, especially technical knowledge, that continues changing at high speed. The complexity of the issues contemporary workplaces deal with makes it very hard to expect one expert to have all the necessary knowledge. That is why, in today's business environment, it's all about preparing high-performance teams that are empowered to learn continually and grow; the intention here is for everyone on the team to become a problem solver who can be trusted to make good decisions when needed. The team must stay on top of upcoming changes in the industry, if you want your organization to stay ahead of new technology trends, and not to be caught off guard by disruptive change.

Maintaining a risk-averse stance when it comes to new and emerging technologies is certainly understandable, but if the future is now, what can we do to enhance our strengths and explore the many options being presented to us at what sometimes seems like the speed of light? Perhaps begin asking the kind of questions provided below, using the answers to see where the search leads you:

- How do we identify what data is useful obtain?
- What are the risks of cybersecurity when storing Big Data?
- How do we finance replacement of the technology?
- Will the ROI pay off?
- How will the new technology integrate with existing systems?
- Will we have access to the right skilled people to test and utilize those digital and operational technologies, so our company is able to capitalize on the advantages they offer?

While there is definitely risk with trying anything new, excessive caution is something to guard against: you could pay a bigger price in the long term, with the risk of arriving too late to the party, when all of the competitors have gone ahead. The best approach would be to understand the purpose of the available new technology, especially focusing on what goals you are trying to reach. Focus on incremental changes and collaborate with other companies that may have similar experiences and challenges. This is not necessarily about sharing confidential information, but more in the vein of problem solving to handle a shared challenge, as most of what you are facing is probably familiar to others, and may include common issues faced by many employers.

D. WHAT LEADERS NEED TO KNOW TO MANAGE CHANGE

Any changes in societal systems, including most introductions of new technology, have historically faced resistance. During earlier industrial revolutions, there emerged a community of **Luddites**, who originated resistance to using new technology as a movement. They disliked the technologies emerging at the time and opposed the process for mechanizing manufacturing, seeing the low-skilled machine operators as a direct threat to the individual craftsmanship of the skilled artisans of the time. From smashing textile machines to barging into mills and burning factories, these rebels of the time thought they could deter employers from installing machinery, and thus could stunt technological progress. The group of resisters was squashed into oblivion by the government; however, the concept re-emerged many years later as a word for regular, everyday *technophobes*. One of the main reasons behind resistance to change was the fear that change will only benefit a handful of the elite, and cause problems for the masses. Additionally, the benefits of accepting the change seemed only possible or accessible in the faraway future, while the disadvantages seemed near.

While change around us today seems much more all-encompassing, resistance to it is not any less than before, and the inherent challenges of **Change Management** are still present. According to HBR, nearly 70% of **Change Initiatives** fail (Nohria and Beer, 2000). Many reasons for failure may show up in specific organizations, according to various surveys, but the top three reasons that surface most commonly include:

- Employee resistance and turnover during the transition;
- Communication breakdown and lack of clarity around the change;
- Costs exceeding budget, not only financially, but overuse of resources in general.

Understandably, most companies do not like to talk about failed projects. In the absence of a healthy organizational culture of Continual Improvement, instead of investigating the reasons for the failure, facts get hidden when people and companies are too concerned with not looking bad in the public eye.

A Quality Management professional and ISO 9000 Auditor, with over 40 years in the field, discussed his experiences with Change Management with me. He has worked for three major employers in his career: the United States Navy, a large IT company, and a well-known car manufacturer, where he led change projects, but he observes he has yet to see significant lasting changes. Among the failed change initiatives were such projects as the implementation of **Six Sigma, Lean manufacturing systems**, and other quality improvements. What he witnessed most of the time is that the change initiatives started well, with lots of excitement in the beginning, soon going sideways, and eventually, the effort makes a U-turn and dies down.

In one company he worked for, when a project failed, no further discussions about what happened ensued. The company had decided to implement Six Sigma, a set of tools and techniques used by companies to improve production processes, eliminate defects, and guarantee quality. In the beginning, there was a lot of support from the top management;

an experienced consultant was hired to help with the implementation; the whole team was pumped up with excitement and anticipation.

Within the first six months, 27 employees had been trained as Six Sigma Green Belts, and twelve as Black Belts. Everyone was looking forward to their turn to get the training. Somehow, though, after the initial six months, the euphoria died down, and soon the entire project was abandoned. Even the staff that received the coveted training were no longer excited about what they could do for the company with the knowledge it provided them with. More than anything else, they seemed to care about adding their brand-new designations to their resumes. From the senior management perspective, once the training stage was over, no further activities were organized, and no action was taken to sustain the change. The progress stopped there, while the most crucial part of the change, building sustainability, was supposed to start once the trainings were completed. As soon as the mentality "It was good enough," settled in, the opportunity to make it excellent was killed. Good is the enemy of Great, as Jim Collins has noted.

ADKAR

ADKAR is the *Change Management* model outlined by Prosci Solutions, an advisory services company that specializes in Change Management. The steps of *ADKAR* must be taken in sequential order to achieve the cumulative effect for sustainable change.

Awareness of business reasons for the change. *Awareness* is the goal/outcome of early communications related to an organizational change.

Desire to engage and participate in the change. *Desire* is the goal/outcome of sponsorship and resistance management.

Knowledge about how to change. *Knowledge* is the goal/outcome of training and coaching.

Ability to realize or implement the change at the required performance level. *Ability* is the goal/outcome of additional coaching, practice, and time.

Reinforcement to ensure the newly implemented change sticks. *Reinforcement* is the goal/outcome of adoption measurement, *Corrective Action*, and recognition of successful change.

One company I knew of did well with the first step in the Change Management process per the ADKAR model, which is raising the Awareness of the need for change. The Desire to engage and participate in change also seemed to be there. The company believed in the vision of a better future so deeply that the CEO agreed to spend a hefty $11K for a three-day Change Management course. Out of that, the company got tons of useful tools and checklists to be used in the workplace – so the step of gaining Knowledge was also achieved. Where they got stuck was implementing the new knowledge in the workplace, making it company-wide. For the initiative to take root and keep going, there had to be a push from the top; this did not happen. The CEO left the company, and the necessary support ended. The commitment that once was there swiftly died out. People moved on; the focus shifted. Three years later, they were back to square one, all of the original problems still an issue and no progress to show for the investment of money, time, and effort.

Sustainability is important to any change initiative. Without sustainability, the best efforts will be a complete waste, and the intended business results will not be achieved. It is the responsibility of leadership to recognize what obstacles exist for effecting lasting change, and how to deal with each of them. Here are some of the common leadership mistakes when it comes to sustainable change:

- Allowing complacency in themselves and others;
- Failing to lead by setting a personal example;
- Not articulating a powerful vision;

- Allowing obstacles to block the vision;
- Failing to create a step-by-step plan with some early wins built in.

To lead the change with their own powerful example, leaders themselves must first fully believe in the change, without any doubts or negativity toward it. As a leader implementing a new change program, you must fully understand the change initiative to the extent of becoming a champion of it for the rest of your team. Do you know the rationale behind the change and how it will impact everyone else? Do you believe this change is worthwhile, timely, and expedient?

What if the change in your company is happening for reasons entirely out of your control, such as a merger or acquisition, and you, as a leader, do not 100% agree with it? Perhaps there is a misalignment in the process due to trust issues existing between the various groups within the organization. In that case, I would recommend that you and the rest of your leadership team go through the process of building alignment among yourselves. Everyone on the leadership team could voice concerns, and provide their perspective on the pros and cons of the upcoming change. Once you've had a chance to be heard and to hear your team members, if you are outnumbered in your position, you would choose to align with the company's decision and agree to give it your best try, wholeheartedly. Only after all of your own questions and concerns are addressed can you contribute to the project with a wholehearted approach that allows you to lead and coach others through the change.

E. 7 STEPS OF CHANGE MANAGEMENT

(Inspired by John P Kotter's "Leading Change")

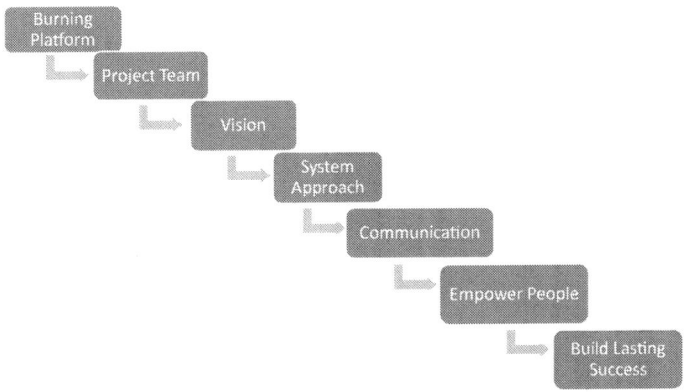

Picture 3. 7 Steps of Change Management Inspired by Kotter (Kotter, 2008).

STEP 1: FINDING YOUR BURNING PLATFORM

Human nature being what it is, people tend to get attached to the familiar, their status quo; only a few people look forward to making changes in their life and routine. If there is no **burning platform**, for instance, the customers are happy, and the company is making enough money – then why change? Without a *burning platform*, it's hard to kick off even a minor change, and only a small percentage of those initiatives achieve the intended business results. A primary role of a Leader is to thoroughly address the *Why* behind every change. If you want to move away from your status quo because your competition has moved ahead of you, then merely implementing a slogan like 'Competition never sleeps' will not help. Instead, bring in hard data on what the competition has accomplished. As W. Edward Deming said, "In God we trust, all others bring data."

Let your team know what to expect. Paint alternative futures for them.

Option 1: We continue this way, and what happens is we stay this way. Accept that competitors are moving ahead of us.

Option 2: Make the change, with the potential to double our revenue, profit, or reach another, more desirable outcome.

If you or your business aren't headed toward your desired future, the only way you can get there is to realize that and to alter your direction today. To initiate the necessary change, it's important to first foster an atmosphere that will help your team to begin to feel the need for it. Money is good for enticing people to make changes, but money is not everything – so not everyone is motivated by it. People need more from work – a positive atmosphere, flexible hours, good managers. Look at the size of your company and the average age of your workforce – a company with the average age being 42 years old will require different motivations than that required by a company with an average age of 28. Paint a picture of the desired future state that pertains to and suits the specific kinds of people working for you, taking into the account their personal needs.

Many people lack, in their personal or business lives, the perspective that allows them to acknowledge the very need for change and to feel a *sense of urgency* to make it happen. For example, an American businessman and Quality Guru, Philip Crosby, was a long-time smoker, according to his biography. His friends advised him, over time, to stop smoking; he never listened, until he was told by a doctor that he only had one month to live, if he didn't quit smoking. Imminent death made him take immediate action. The doctor painted a picture of a grim future, and he was able to act appropriately and timely.

Some workplaces face a burning platform every day due to the nature of their business. This was the case in my first place of employment, a daily newspaper, where every day we had to fill, from scratch, the pages of the new issue and get it published. In companies where the work is project-based, I have seen a sense of urgency go up and down following a project's life cycle. Yet, some other workplaces only experience the burning platform when a crisis hits. Then everyone runs around in a frenzy, stressed out, pointing fingers when things don't get done on time. In my experience and observation, this is not a real sense of urgency. When the calendar is filled to the brim, everything becomes urgent. I once had a customer who kept putting in the subject line of every email he sent out – URGENT! URGENT! It desensitized us to the word 'urgent,' and we stopped taking it seriously. Your organization needs sensible planning to prioritize tasks in the order of their importance and purge the least important ones entirely.

If the burning platform is not consistently visible in your workplace, then, as a leader, you have to create it, so that it's shared and felt by everyone throughout the organization. Your people and the organization need to be fully aware of all the issues surrounding them and be ready to take action to address risks and take advantage of any opportunities on your way to a clearly defined, desired future. As a natural outcome of incorporating this step, people should be encouraging each other to rally behind the change.

STEP 2: BUILDING YOUR PROJECT TEAM

Draw the right people to the team. For the change initiative to work best, you need to assemble a diagonally cross-functional team made up of individuals at all levels and with different areas of expertise. Aside from their expertise, identifying the team members' personality profile is also essential. You are looking for people who can check their ego at the door and work together for a higher purpose. For best results, choose to incorporate a variety of personalities: from creative types for brainstorming ideas to analytical types to keep the team level-headed. Also, be aware of how those personalities may clash at certain points as the team goes through its stages of development, such as ***forming, storming, norming,* and *performing,*** adapted from Bruce Tuckman's *Team Development Model of 1965*. Assign a good facilitator to unobtrusively navigate the team to work together toward the desired future state.

As a leader, it is essential for you to model the trust and team spirit that you want others to display. If you need to adjust the way you work, do that first. Change yourself first, if you expect your team to make changes in the way they work; it's the strongest approach to be successful at promoting a major change to all interested parties: to the rest of the company, to other external, associated parties, such as vendors, distributors, and to customers.

STEP 3: GET THE VISION RIGHT

A helpful definition of *change*: the transition from a current state to a desired future state to fulfill or implement a vision or a strategy.

Regardless of what prompts the need for change in your organization – the external PEST factors or internal policy, systems, or structure – you need a strong, clear *vision* to help you take steps in the right direction, as a team. The *vision* ideally paints a compelling picture of the desired future state we touched on in *Step 1, the Burning Platform*. The vision allows people to see what futures are possible for them, other than the default future that is inevitable and predictable if they change nothing about their status quo.

I can't put it better than John Kottler's description: For the vision to be effective, it must meet the following criteria:

- **Imaginable:** Conveys a picture of what the future will look like;
- **Desirable:** Appeals to the long-term interests of employees, customers, stakeholders;
- **Feasible:** Clear enough to provide guidance in decision making;

- **Flexible:** General enough to allow initiative and alternative responses;
- **Communicable:** Can be fully explained within five minutes, or written on one page;
- **Moving:** Incorporates an emotional component, such as a commitment to serve people.

Once you have identified your *vision*, develop a *strategy* to support it. Since the future hasn't happened yet, there is always an element of uncertainty about it. Describing the future in terms of abstract aspirations such as 'maximizing shareholder value' or 'promoting superior customer service' does not help people imagine. What exactly does it mean to 'improve customer satisfaction' or 'increase sales by 30% in the next quarter?' People respond more favorably when they hear about the future described in terms of what it will look, feel, and sound like.

Studies have shown that a *vision* communicated via image-based words triggers a stronger performance than a vision with similar content but without the visual component. In one study, two teams were tasked with developing a toy prototype. The first team was given the following vision: 'Our toys will make wide-eyed kids laugh and proud parents smile.' The second team's vision was: 'Our toys will be enjoyed by all of our customers.' The results of the experiment showed that the first team had better performance and developed a much better toy. It worked like that because the people on the first team were able to imagine the future of the vision given to them. After all, everyone can relate to being a proud parent, and everyone wants to hear those wide-eyed kids laugh. In this case, the image-based words inspired people to work together toward the crystal-clear snapshot of the future state they were sharing.

STEP 4: COMMUNICATE FOR BUY-IN

One of the common reasons a change initiative fails is a lack of buy-in into the new process. Everybody has their familiar ways of doing things, and they are attached to those methods, habits, and systems. It's a leader's job to get the team to buy in to new processes. A successful communication strategy is to get to know your audience well and hone your message to tailor it to the audience's specific needs. To avoid useless, generic memos, ask yourself the following questions:

- Who is the audience, and what do they know already?
- What do we need to communicate?
- Who relays which message?
- In what order do we communicate the messages?
- What are the best channels of communication?
- The intention of your message must be very clear to you:
- Is it meant to drive behavior change?
- Are you aiming at educating and engaging people?
- Is your objective to raise awareness or to mobilize commitment?
- Do you have a way to measure whether this communication has achieved its objectives?

Be mindful of people's feelings toward the change, and plan to address them accordingly. Remember the beautiful picture of the future state you painted for people? Paint it again.

At every opportunity, bring up the vision of what it would look like for everyone to unite in a common, higher purpose. It's human nature to wonder 'What's in it for me?' so begin your communication with how it affects one individual and then expand the communication to include the whole.

Any change, any deviation from normal routine is hard to effect in normal circumstances. People especially resist change when they sense that the new process is only being implemented for the sake of change. Explain the reasons behind the change. Aim for the heart, not just the mind. Dr. Martin Luther King, Jr. built one of the best image-based visions in his famous speech *I Have a Dream,* delivered during the March on Washington on August 28, 1963:

> **"I have a dream that one day on the red hills of Georgia, the sons of former slaves and the sons of former slave owners will be able to sit down together at the table of brotherhood."**

You, too, can look for the element in every story that will inspire employees into action. To support your employees, help them to buy in to the need for urgency, and help them feel empowered, not stressed. Middle level managers can become your most powerful allies when it comes to creating and enhancing employee buy-in, because people tend to listen to their own direct superiors. That's why, as a Caring Leader, it's essential to bring middle management employees fully onboard; help them see the path by fully explaining the company's reasons behind the change. Once they are clear on the need for change, they can help you convince their people.

Simple, heartfelt communications always succeed over general statements. Vagueness does not help anyone solve problems. Realistic optimism is most effective for motivating people. You have an integral role to play: being an example, and embodying the willingness to change. If you want your project to work, long term, it's necessary for you to 'walk the talk,' lead by example, be authentic, and most importantly, tell the truth. Don't hide things.

I once had to deliver some bad news to a work team, news that would affect the entire workplace. As you might imagine, human behavior revealed itself in the first questions people asked, which focused on their own situations: How the change will affect me personally? Will I get to keep what I currently have? Good answers, well prepared plans, and reassurances work best at the beginning of the process of leading your employees through unpleasant change. Even when changes are intended to bring a positive outcome, not knowing how to get there can bring some slow downs, unless everyone is well informed and, hopefully, on the same page. How you communicate the vision, the path, and the eventual outcomes can make an enormous difference. Your clarity will help reassure your staff.

It is essential to be prepared for all kinds of questions, doubts, concerns. It is also important to be ready for resistance; typically, the mid-managers are both your best potential allies, but also the hardest to convince. They could even become a bottleneck if their concerns and issues are not addressed properly. That brings us to the next step.

STEP 5: EXERCISE SYSTEM APPROACH

To improve the chances of success for your change initiative, consider implementing your process using a *system approach*. A *system* is a set of interconnected parts forming a complex whole. It's also a set of detailed methods, procedures, and routines devised to carry out a specific activity or resolve a specific issue. An organization is a system relating to other systems contained within the larger systems of industry and society. Any proposed change is usually oriented to changing a business process to assure and increase value, for the business itself and for its customers. Being a system in itself, in any business a change in any one process has complex consequences and affects various parts of the overall system. In most Change Management scenarios, a *process* is changed not just once, but repeatedly in a series of progressive refinements. Each stage of implementing and refining a process has its own implications that inevitably affect the rest of the system, introducing a ripple effect that may have unintended consequences. Change must be managed with insight, curiosity, and care.

To exercise *a system approach* is to thoroughly analyze what, who, and how the change will impact each element of the system. In Caring Organizations, leadership takes into account the repercussions of any modification on other processes – direct, indirect, and those spreading beyond the organization's boundaries. It may create conflict with other priorities. The easiest way to begin undertaking this approach is by reviewing change from the perspective of resource allocation. A good question to start your inquiry: are there any parallel projects that will be affected by and/or have an impact on the change I am managing? Will we have to pull resources from those projects to accommodate the change?

As an example, let's consider the role of middle level managers. It is essential to have them on your side, as their input is crucial to assist in promoting the change to the rest of the team. In your planning process, it is important to understand how much responsibility middle level managers already have on their plates. All stakeholders of affected processes must be able to demonstrate, particularly to the satisfaction of frontline workers and middle level managers, that the proposed change is beneficial, and at a bare minimum, not harmful to the business.

Middle level managers are in charge of ensuring the smooth execution of daily operations. They must remain focused so that the people responsible for daily operations are capable of delivering timely progress of all existing projects and thus, an uninterrupted flow of work throughout the company. Any change initiative will impose an immediate time-crunch, with extra workload for the middle level managers. If you are able, try to estimate how much extra workload they will face.

Is it a tolerable increase, or will it put an unreasonable strain on them? If your mid-level managers cannot openly resist change, they may express their doubts by stalling progress on implementing the changes you have initiated. If this happens, it might take some time to discover where the delays are coming from. For a while, there will be a false impression of things going well – and senior executives will believe it, because initially, people rarely talk about their often valid doubts, concerns, and resistance to added responsibility.

The workers in the midst of the process will know what is going on. If they see their managers exhibiting only half-hearted effort and limp commitment to the change, they will have a hard time taking the new project seriously. Management engagement and enthusiasm must come first, as it's directly responsible for implementing the change. As effects of the change may spread both inside and outside of the organization, any new initiative should be reviewed from the perspective of any constraints it may impose on parts of the organization, especially constraints it might experience due to existing agreements such as union contracts, vendor contracts, and any commitment to existing policies.

Initial changes usually bring the most tangible results, but, as time goes on, more resources must be expended to obtain lasting, sustainable results. Once the most apparent problems have been addressed and resolved, further changes will become incremental, resulting in less visible benefits, even though the resource output may remain consistent. Since most of the effects on ancillary processes may be somewhat invisible, it's human nature to start paying less attention to possible implications of changes on other areas of the overall system. At this stage, it is important to follow through with the *system approach* until the end, to ensure the success of the change being implemented. Here is where **Empowered Action** becomes an important tool for reaching a successful conclusion.

STEP 6: EMPOWER ACTION

You can have a beautiful vision painted on the wall to inspire change; you can have a great cross-functional team assigned to it; you may have communicated the change effectively to get buy-in; and you have probably thoroughly reviewed the implications of the change on the other parts of the system. This still doesn't mean your intended change will be successful. As a leader, you are responsible for taking steps to *empower broad-based action*. Anticipating pitfalls that lead to losing momentum, which can lead to overall failure, giving up, or dropping the effort that began with such strength and determination, is very much a part of the planning process.

Just announcing to your people that the change is happening is not enough; promoting optimism and building confidence around the change effort is key to maintaining momentum. Easy to say, but how do you build trust and enthusiasm for the long-haul? In every organization, there is always a group of individuals who are more enthusiastic about change than most of the staff. Focus on one relationship at a time. Provide the enthusiastic participants with opportunities to harvest 'low hanging fruit,' meaning results or rewards intended to build a foundation for tangible success and strengthen confidence. Focus on one to two goals at a time, instead of too many projects at once. Remind the enthusiastic early adopters of the importance of those priorities, to keep their awareness levels high. Support them in every way you can, perhaps by removing obstacles for them, or by highlighting and recognizing their efforts.

Doing this builds your team, slowly. Then you can rely on them to bolster others, with their examples of 'if we won you can too' scenarios. This attitude is likely to become quite contagious, in the best possible way. Most employees enjoy the benefits of being members of powerful teams, and to be able to act in the context of successful efforts. Seeing examples of early victories and being a part of celebrating small wins helps bring awareness, and once people see the benefit of the change, it makes it easier to rally them up behind the change.

STEP 7: BUILD LASTING SUCCESS

For many companies, achieving a sustained, comprehensive change is an ongoing challenge. Some may have mastered partial solutions. Some companies that have incorporated a structured Change Management system—such as *TQM* or *Six Sigma*—still experience trouble with sustaining change because they have lost crucial leadership and focus on the vision. To keep the image of the vision alive, tell vivid stories about the new direction and why it succeeds. Remind your people about what the default future would otherwise be; what would happen if we change nothing, and things unfold as our past predicts? Make sure your planning incorporates the continuity of behavior and results that help a new culture grow. Adjust company recognition and award systems to include stewardship and openness towards the change you are seeking.

It is highly advisable to avoid rushing to do everything at once; look carefully at all aspects of the change, to grasp and understand the big picture. If team members feel misled, or unable to understand the whole story, they will most likely grow more and more skeptical and cynical. Depending on the scope of the changes you are considering, develop a long-term road map that you will be working on gradually. Small, consistent steps are better than one big leap. Think of it like a rubber band: if you stretch the rubber band too far, it's going to break, snap back, and hurt you. You cannot force change upon people; you certainly cannot rely on scaring them with a loss of employment or of any other benefits, either. It won't be sustainable, and you will find yourself back to square one. The status quo will have won if you cannot implement real change in a way that takes into account implications and effects on the entire system, a system that matters to everyone in very different ways.

F. COACHING THROUGH RESISTANCE

For the intended change to become a permanent part of the corporate culture, Caring Workplaces take all resistance into account. In order to control or manage resistance, we need to understand its nature and origin. Sometimes, resistance to change means your people are clinging to established methods without questioning the status quo. At times, attachment to the past can take on fanatical and even comical forms.

A college teacher of mine, Benjamin R, told me a story that took place in his family. He came from a Jewish family that was big on following its traditions. One of the family traditions was to make a special meatloaf to be shared by the entire family when they gathered for their annual Purim dinner. The meatloaf was made using the family heirloom meat grinder, which was passed down from generation to generation. When one of the older family members passed away, my teacher inherited the meat grinder. That year it was his turn to cook the meatloaf based on the family recipe, and to host his relatives for the holiday gathering.

Well, the first thing he did was to take apart the meat grinder and thoroughly wash it out to get rid of the old residue, including some leftover old meat that was stuck in it. He set the dinner table using his best heirloom dinner set. When the extended family gathered around the table, Benjamin proudly brought in his meatloaf on a beautiful serving plate. Having meticulously followed the family recipe and having watched his mother and aunts make it year after year, he was confident about the quality of his creation. He was looking forward to his relatives' response to this masterpiece he had so lovingly recreated. To his surprise, as the relatives started trying the meatloaf, they winced and commented that something was seriously wrong with the meatloaf: it tasted nothing like it should. When they learned that Benjamin had thoroughly washed the meat grinder and freed it from all the leftover meat, the Aunties got really upset with him. They said the flavor the old meat remnants added to the dish was the best part of it! Without it, the meatloaf did not taste the same.

In this situation, the change was clearly intended for better results; nevertheless, it faced rejection. Most likely, nothing was wrong with the 'new' flavor of the much-loved old recipe. That one person, altering the usual course of events, did a simple thing that was taken as a threat to a long-standing family tradition.

In workplaces, we often face this reaction in a similar fashion. If change is introduced, as we have noted, employees can be quick to resist without giving it a chance or without fully understanding the benefits of it. People tend to focus on what they currently have and what they potentially would lose because of change: maybe they fear for their job security, or are used to associating change with increased workloads and fewer opportunities. This often originates from a lack of clear communication around the subject. People also bring a lot of baggage from their past unresolved resentments to their new workplace. It requires a lot of work and dedication from the leaders to undo the previous damage.

In one of my past workplaces, one employee saw change as an immediate threat to his job. With any change to the company processes, procedures, or equipment, he anticipated personnel cuts, and believed that he would be the first one out of the door. He kept bringing up examples of what "just happened to him in his previous workplace." Through closer discussions, it became clear that the damaging experience he kept referring to had taken place at least fifteen years prior to our conversations, but to him, those memories were as vivid as if they were from the day before. He relived his past hurt anytime a change in the workplace happened. It took a lot of coaching to help this individual recover from his fears and anxieties about change; he was a valuable team member, and it was certainly worth the time invested, once the problem came to light.

When people resist change, leaders need to understand what is behind their reaction. Get to know what feelings people might be experiencing that may contribute to blocking the change: possible reactions could be coming from feelings of fear, anger, insecurity, anxiety, or an array of other emotions. People love their comfort zone and grow complacent. If you are facing employee resistance toward change, leverage your team's relationship to understand and address concerns on a personal level.

Invest in your people. Engage, coach, mentor, and enrich people's roles in ways that will keep them interested.

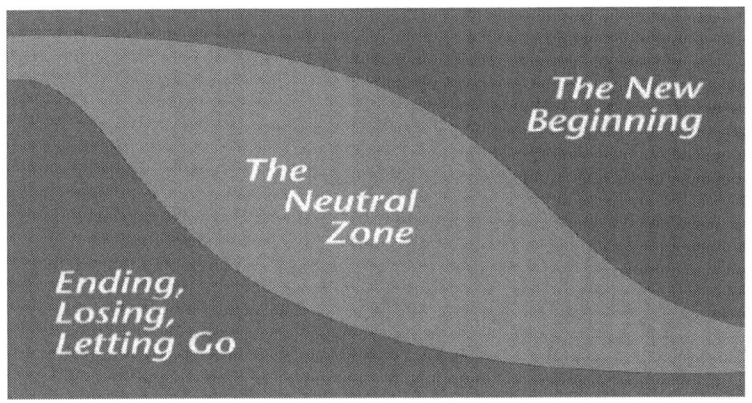

Picture 4. Bridges' Three Phases of Transitions (Baker, 2015).

If the reason for the change initiative's failure is determined to be a communication breakdown, develop a strategy for communicating key information as discussed earlier in this chapter. Don't take for granted that all the right people will somehow find out everything they need to know in regards to the change process. If you don't manage the communication channels properly, people will begin relying on the company gossip grapevine for their information, which frequently leads to confusion and other unhealthy outcomes.

One useful model to describe the emotional impact of change on people is called William Bridge's *Transition Model*. Its creator, a change consultant, published this in his 1991 book *"Managing Transitions"*. This model describes how people's attitudes change as they transition from one stage to the next (Bridges, 1991).

Typically, people undergoing change start off with a pessimistic view, having a hard time letting go of the old and familiar ways, and they carry a feeling like they are trapped in complete darkness. Then they gradually migrate towards the neutral zone, where feelings balance out. Eventually, adjustment occurs as people move to a more optimistic zone where the picture of the new beginning is clearer. As we can see from the graph, the transitions are far from linear and people's feelings about the same change can often change back and forth. It is a leader's job to support and encourage the staff through each phase.

Caring Workplaces come up with lasting solutions to sustain the new, changed reality. The main component of lasting change is to establish a supportive and sufficiently strong organizational culture, in which people are not afraid to make mistakes. This culture promotes openness and truthfulness. Building a *Freedom to Fail Environment* where people are not afraid or embarrassed to admit they made mistakes is key; in this kind of environment, leaders admit their mistakes as well and follow through with a solution. As a result, new and winning behavior continues to emerge, despite the pull of tradition, turnover of Change Leaders, and other factors typical of any culture shift.

CHAPTER 5 – ZERO FOLLOW THROUGH: THE FLAVOR OF THE MONTH THAT LEAVES A BAD TASTE

A. WHAT IS FLAVOR-OF-THE-MONTH SYNDROME & WHY IT NEVER CATCHES ON

Jack Welch, former CEO of General Electric, once said, "If the company has been through enough change programs, employees consider you like gas pains. You'll go away if they just wait long enough." (Welch, Jack & Welch, Suzy, 2005).

In my experience, I have found that the more unsustainable change initiatives introduced, the more skeptical people grow about motives for change in your organization. Yet, change without proper follow-through, a guarantee of disappointment for employees, is still a common phenomenon in workplaces.

I once knew a CEO who was always full of bright ideas. He would loudly announce those ideas at the town halls, expected a lot of enthusiasm from his staff, assigned action items, and selected responsible personnel to implement those changes. He gave his team due dates for different milestones, but he didn't collaborate with them much about how they should reach each milestone. People would act upon his ideas – research, gather materials, and set up all the groundwork necessary to implement his vision.

On the due date, when staff presented results and interim work to the CEO, they would realize that he was not particularly interested in hearing about the progress they'd made. To their astonishment, he'd lost all of his enthusiasm toward that change. His mind had moved onto another idea, something 'bigger and better,' and suddenly he'd expect the staff to dive in to the newest, latest, greatest idea, and abandon the last idea entirely.

Similarly, in another corporation, the bright minds would come up with a new great initiative every year during their Strategic Planning gatherings. Inspired while the executives got together at an enjoyable, relaxing company retreat, working with a well-recommended new consultant-facilitator, they would come up with great new ways to improve their business.

Every year, the executives brainstormed ways to improve company-wide communication so that they could more effectively reach the company's performance goals. The year I observed them, the theme was 'The Right People on the Bus' inspired by Jim Collins' work; I joined them for this project. When the new strategy was being deployed by the management, the engagement levels from the workforce were low. The team shared with me that they were certain "This too shall pass," just like the annual initiatives before it.

"Last year it was CCC [the company-wide Clear Concise Communication initiative], the year before that it was the Hedgehog [this was the concept of sticking with one defining idea, based on philosopher Isaiah Berlin's essay "The Hedgehog and The Fox"] and now this!"

The old-timers assured me that the Right People on the Bus concept would last, at most, for a month or two, then it would die down as, predictably, management would fail to stand behind it. Every concept that came out of the prior years' strategic planning sessions sounded exciting and promising, until it wasn't any more.

The company caught onto the fact that year after year, company-wide communication come up as a problem again. What were they doing wrong? They changed their consultants, restructured the 'executive' teams, altered the combinations of people engaged in the strategy sessions. They did everything they could think of to finally find a communication style they could adopt for their business successfully; after all that effort, the results were still not there.

In fact, after they invested in a new program every time, the results were further and further from the expectations. The leadership team saw less and less enthusiasm and support from the team back in the office with whom they shared the details of the program. It turned out that the problem of poor communication was with the leadership who would each year go after a new shiny object instead of properly implementing the already started program.

How often have you seen a brilliant concept generate excitement and buzz among the team, only to die down later? Leadership fails in workplaces, not because they don't initiate great plans, but because their plans lack follow through. Next time, even if you are presenting them with the greatest idea, you will be faced with skepticism. The more often you indulge in new flavor of the month, the higher the chance that in the end you will be stuck with a bunch of cynics on your team.

ACTION PLAN SPECIFICS

As with any project, a great idea needs to be managed. To stand behind their initiative, leadership has to break it down into tasks, assign responsibility, specify time-frames, and allocate resources accordingly. The tangible action plan has to have a way of measuring its progress on an ongoing basis, leading up to the date of completion, so that feedback is shared, for clearing hurdles, overcoming challenges, and making positive progress.

How will you measure progress, to assure the timeliness of the tasks, proper use of resources, and meeting performance expectations? To do this, controls need to be in place. In the book **"Practical Drucker,"** by William A. Cohen there is an explanation of Drucker's three major characteristics (Cohen, 2013):

- Controls can be neither objective nor neutral;
- Controls need to focus on results;
- Controls must consider both measurable events and unmeasurable events.

CONTROLS CAN BE NEITHER OBJECTIVE NOR NEUTRAL

Whatever measurement we apply to any event we want to track – even in a scientific approach — there is always room for bias and error in judgment. The fact that we have to choose what process or strategy to measure based on our necessity also makes it subjective. The most obvious example of this phenomenon is the **Hawthorne effect**.

In the 1920s, researchers in the Western Electric Plant Hawthorne Works, near Chicago, studied the effects of improved work conditions, in particular, when adding enhanced lighting in the productivity area. As the lighting was improved in the areas where workers did their jobs, productivity improved as well. This repeated through several increases in the wattage of the light bulbs. As the experiment continued, the researchers decreased the illumination but, surprisingly, witnessed further improvement in productivity. This phenomenon, named later as *Hawthorne Effect*, showed that people work more productively because of the attention paid to their work, not necessarily when their work conditions are improved. Bringing us back to Drucker's point, leaders in workplaces must be aware of the bias and subjectivity that comes with measurements, and should choose wisely how to measure the strategy's effect in the workplace. This is an excellent approach to getting a strong grasp on the results of the improvement they are implementing.

CONTROLS MUST FOCUS ON RESULTS

The controls leaders put in place should always be chosen with the end in mind. It's easy to be distracted by day-to-day operations, with a strong pull to focus on efficiencies and doing things right. This is the essential difference between leaders and managers, as Drucker explained it. While managers must ensure the effectiveness of the processes by doing things right, leaders need to stay focused on the bigger picture, to guide the organization in the strategically chosen direction. Focusing on the right things to do ensures the effectiveness of the strategy in achieving the intended business results.

CONTROLS MUST CONSIDER BOTH MEASURABLE AND NON-MEASURABLE EVENTS

Measurable goals are more attractive, because they yield the desired outcome of the strategy in quantifiable terms. Suppose your goal is to enter a new market, aiming to conquer a region you had never done business in before. In that case, you can quantify it by setting the target number of customers you want to obtain the new region. Given that you know your baseline – which, in this case, would be zero – you can easily count the number of new customers you gained by the end of the review period.

How can you measure controls over workplace events that are not quite so easy to put a number to? Sometimes the non-measurable effects of strategic planning are not only worthwhile but perhaps even more important than the obviously measurable ones. Drucker reminds us that leaders have to look at non-measurable effects and find ways to make them measurable. For example, a goal such as "to increase visibility of our product in the market" cannot be measured as it is stated.

The company can invest in campaigns to increase product awareness in the market. However, leadership has to find a way to quantify that increased visibility; perhaps by the number of referrals or stores that carry their product. Whenever possible, non-measurable — or, more accurately, not easily measurable — goals must be turned into measurable quantities to assess the level of success for the strategy deployment. As previously noted, an important point to keep in mind: ***not everything that can be counted, does actually count.*** Make sure the controls you put in place actually help you control the right processes, which might more reliably ensure the right outcomes that help implement the strategy chosen for your organization.

Suppose your team sees that you are keeping track of what matters to the organization, and you serve as a great example of self-discipline and accountability with your behavior. In that case, it will usually translate to all other levels and very likely defeat any flavor-of-the-month mentality that may exist as a remnant of past leadership attempts. For the controls to work and support your company's strategy, they should be pertinent to the purpose they serve, without being too costly to implement or overly complicated to sustain. The controls should yield the outcome we need, so we know how well our strategy is working, how our goals and objectives are being met, and where we as leaders need to make the appropriate adjustments to keep our business on the intended course.

Once you have the right control in place, proceed by conducting periodic reviews, and by all means, make the results visible. Share any information that can be shared. This brings visibility to the course of action taken. People want to be informed of what is going on. This keeps interest levels alive.

Often, Continual Improvement teams are formed within organizations to champion the improvement initiatives for certain processes. Whether with the help of an external consultant or relying on their own efforts, management should aim for assembling diagonally cross-functional teams with the best internal experts. Leaders usually are familiar with the normal stages of the team's life cycle, such as *forming, storming, norming,* and finally *performing.*

The stage of *performing* is not achieved by all teams – only by high-performance teams. This is the most coveted and challenging stage of the Change Management life cycle. Ideally, the team members are able to put aside their differences, learn about each others' strengths and perspectives, and appreciate diversity as they start producing desirable results.

COMPLETING THE PROJECT

Once the team's project is over, however, the last and, nevertheless, most important stage – **adjourning** – is rarely discussed. The team itself, and the rest of the organization, do not really know when the formal end of their project has come, unless *adjourning* takes place.

Before adjourning the project team, a comprehensive project report should be issued to outline actions taken from start to completion, to review the results achieved within the scope, and restate goals once determined for this project. The team certainly deserves recognition for their efforts before the project is officially completed, and the organization as a whole needs closure.

From time to time, companies change direction, and even a great initiative may discontinue due to the new strategic course. Even if the focus shifts away entirely, as a leader, you still owe it to your team to provide feedback on the work they put in, and to explain the reasons for the course adjustment with a sufficient amount of detail. An important part of this step is to ensure that the team is recognized and celebrated for their contributions, and best practices and/or lessons learned are captured for the future use by this or another team.

Whether due to project completion or a shift in strategic focus – if the team is done with its mission, there is another option instead of adjourning it. If something new is on the horizon, leadership can reassign the now-seasoned team to undertake a different task. No matter what the outcome, the team needs to see honesty and transparency in management methods.

B. CREATING A CULTURE OF FOLLOW UP (AND FOLLOW THROUGH)

To know whether or not a specific initiative was effective in yielding the intended results, a thorough review process is necessary. If the strategy or project you've invested in fails, saying "In the future, I will do things differently," is insufficient and not helpful to your team. It's equally important to understand both the reasons behind the failure and why things worked. To capture all *lessons learned*, establish a program for *continual review* for every product, strategy, and policy.

Each case's individual circumstances may reveal some unique components, but the good news is that you don't have to reinvent the wheel to learn helpful lessons. Great systems already exist and are ready to be used by your team. One of them is the tried and tested **Plan Do Check Act (PDCA) cycle.**

Business professionals who attend my Business Process Improvement training courses often ask me when to use *PDCA*. They wonder if it's too heavily based on a scientific method, when all they actually need is a daily operational tool that can be easily applied to any situation regardless of its scope. My response is that PDCA is a healthy mix between a scientific approach and everyday operations. This cycle is a highly versatile tool that can help you handle any improvement initiative in a workplace setting. Another aspect of the PDCA tool that seems to throw people off is the abbreviation itself: *Do* and *Act* are separate steps, but in the English language, both of those words have similar definitions and pertain to the same action. We can overcome this confusion if we remember that *Act* in the PDCA cycle stands for *Acting* upon the newly gained knowledge, which is the first task before implementing the improvement. Better yet, this fourth step could be called **Adjust,** if that's easier for everyone involved.

Using PDCA can be helpful in a broad range of circumstances, for example:

- Starting a new project or implementing any change.
- Evaluating the results of a strategy deployment.
- Developing a new or improved design of a process, product, or service.
- Defining a repetitive work process.
- Planning data collection and analysis to verify and prioritize risks or opportunities.
- Analyzing the *root cause* of a customer complaint or a quality problem.
- Investigating a workplace incident or a near-miss with a potential for injury.
- Evaluating and developing supplier relationships and resources.
- Undertaking daily problem-solving tasks.

HOW TO APPLY PDCA?

Here are step-by-step instructions on how you can make this tool work for you:

- **Plan:** Before launching a new initiative, evaluate its impact on the rest of the organization to make sure it does not duplicate or negate any existing efforts, and does not absorb too much in the way of needed resources from a project that has started elsewhere.

Once it's clear to all key stakeholders that the initiative does need to take place, the *Planning* stage begins. Set a clear goal that your organization intends to achieve, define specific ways to measure the goal, and outline what resources are needed. A written plan can be as short or long as necessary, depending on the situation you're applying the PDCA tool to. For a project or strategy, spell out the scope, the time-frame, responsibilities, milestones, resources, expertise needed, etc.

If you're using PDCA to investigate a workplace incident, to determine the reason behind a product defect, or resolve another workplace issue, start off the planning process by formulating the problem. This may seem like an easy thing to do, but oftentimes, this might be one of the most resource-consuming phases of the PDCA process. When done right, it will set your team up for success. Brainstorming is essential to stating the right problem to solve. At this stage, ask yourselves what other information is needed to understand the problem and its root cause thoroughly. What resources would be required to solve it? Are those resources available? What are possible solutions for this problem; consider as many options as seem viable. Think about the implication of the effect this process you are trying out may have on other parts of the organization.

- **Do:** At this stage, the plan is tested in manageable size steps, typically under controlled conditions. This allows the team to explore options, by testing multiple solutions and hopefully eliminating the less effective ones. The aim is to do proof-of-concept before rolling the most feasible options out on a larger scale. You can test the solution to your problem or a new, improved process on a smaller demographic; this way, you avoid accumulating the unnecessary cost of rolling out a program that won't work for your organization. You can select your test group based on who the solution pertains to the most, who the process owners are, and, who would give you the most timely and honest feedback. The feedback you receive will help you move into the next step of PDCA.

- **Check:** At this point in the process, the project team studies and analyzes the results of implementing the plan, taking into account the feedback and experiences resulting from the trials. In a different version of this cycle, ***Plan Do Study Act (PDSA)***, this third step is called **Study**. Did the plan work? If not, what were the complications? Are there any bugs in the process that need to be worked out? What improvements are necessary for the future? This step allows you to evaluate the solution you have implemented so far and revise it as needed before rolling the new process out on a larger scale.

- **Act:** Outcomes from the *Check* stage determine your choices to complete the PDCA cycle. The evaluation results will dictate whether the initiative has been going well and can now be rolled out on a large scale. It will also highlight challenges that require tweaking. The PDCA cycle may also reveal if something was not a good idea, and why the company should not proceed with it. If all goes well, the improved process can be standardized and implemented on a larger scale. If there is more to do here, you'll have to go back to the *Do* step, testing the improvements again to ensure the process will be effective.

An organization that applies this approach to strategic initiatives can obtain great benefits; however, the magic happens when the rest of the team learns how to use these tools in their own decision making. Providing thorough, hands-on training on how to implement this process, typically with an experienced facilitator, is an excellent step in the right direction. Once training is complete, encourage your team to keep using this tool and make it part of running your business. This turns PDCA into a valuable asset for maintaining ongoing clarity and developing leadership skills in many departments.

As a Caring Organization, you can make it easy for your team to use PDCA by making the tool visible and handy. Have a reference guide to PDCA posted on a wall in the highest traffic meeting room, or perhaps set up a huddle board where people gather to discuss daily business, review metrics, and learn from their successes and failures. Do what you can to take the mystery and the seeming complexity out of PDCA, by simplifying the tool and starting by spontaneously capturing on the PDCA board the thought process that someone from your team is already sharing verbally. Even in passing, people can share great insights. Capture it. Then pass the pen to one of the team members. You can start with supervisors, to encourage the rest of the team to get more comfortable with the PDCA cycle.

Eventually, you can begin assigning random employees to champion a PDCA on a particular problem their area is facing. Once people grasp how this tool works, invaluable skills for brainstorming and capturing ideas, running through various scenarios of why things went wrong (or right), prioritizing contributing factors, identifying the root cause, and solidifying the appropriate action will become a habit. Learning how to make fact-based decisions is something that inevitably leads in the right direction.

Leadership following through on important initiatives will raise employee engagement on many levels. With the team's confidence in leadership growing, if an occasional initiative falls through the cracks (which inevitably will happen sooner or later), this rare event won't raise much scepticism among the team members. Since the team has seen enough evidence that leadership is reliably following up on the projects they launched, they will understand if something fell off the company's radar, especially if it's dropped in favor of greater opportunities to pursue or higher risks to manage.

Mastering PDCA can help create a company-wide follow up culture based on collaboration and open sharing through feedback loops. In this kind of culture, Continual Improvement is no longer an abstract concept – it's a standardized process that is written up, can be easily followed, and refined along the way, as more information becomes available. The whole team is responsible for the results; no one is singled out as a culprit. If your team discovers a certain initiative does not work as intended, you should feel comfortable pronouncing it obsolete. With the data to back up your decision, you are no longer feeding the flavor-of-the-month mentality; you are feeling confident about taking the right action.

The Continuous Improvement cycle, using tools such as PDCA, does not have a final destination. It's a journey that continues. Make sure you understand the problems of your workplace, bring the right people on board, identify the right tools, and do not give up.

C. HOW TO GET THE MOST OUT OF EMPLOYEE SUGGESTION PROGRAMS

Employee Suggestion Programs are popular and have been around for a long time. The initiative is believed to have originated in early 18th century Japan, when the Eighth Shogun (a military ruler nominated by the Emperor), Yoshimune Tokugawa, posted this statement outside of the castle: "Make your idea known. Rewards are given for ideas that are accepted" (Schroeder and Robinson, 1991). The concept was adopted in other cultures and evolved in many forms. Even though suggestion programs can only yield what can be considered small data, the idea is prolific even in today's era of Big Data. With the mindset that good ideas can come from any source, pretty much every reputable organization finds it helpful and worthwhile to implement some version of it.

However, even programs built with the best of intentions can easily devolve into a flavor-of-the-month disappointment, if you let them. The employee who came up with the idea may be frustrated if they never hear what came of it. We already know the consequences of having disengaged staff that grow skeptical and cynical. That's why it's really important to think through every detail up front and develop a system for administering the program that will last to bring many benefits in your workplace. Fresh viewpoints, a diversity of ideas, and additional brainpower, yielded by well-executed suggestion programs, have a lot to offer, compared to brewing ideas only behind closed doors in company boardrooms. These programs can help reduce incident rates, improve product quality, devise new product offerings, increase process efficiency, reduce costs, enhance customer service, and lead to innovation in other areas.

In her article "*An Effective Employee Suggestion Program has a Multiplier Effect,*" Freda Turner estimates that approximately 37% of submitted suggestions have merit, mostly by saving an organization money, time, and/or identifying strategies for increased effectiveness. General Motors Corporation attributes increased efficiency in their manufacturing processes to an initiative called the **Global Manufacturing System (GMS)**. GMS is designed to improve peoples' performance, safety, quality, responsiveness, and cost. Employee suggestions are vital to the successful implementation of GMS. GM workers at one plant suggested 44,000 ideas in just one quarter, which contributed to a savings of $900K! Employee suggestions have been effective in reducing the time it takes to assemble a vehicle by 15%. Extraordinary results can surface when people are empowered to voice their ideas and have proper channels to submit them (Turner, 2003).

One company, a packaged potato chip manufacturer, was facing an issue with inconsistent weight of their final product – a bag with potato chips. The management team struggled to find a solution that fit both the purpose and the budget, when an ingenious idea came from the shop floor workers: to set up a fan on the conveyor line to blow away the potato chip bags that were too light. This simple concept ended up solving the problem; no further expense or action was required!

Does your company have a suggestion program? How does it work? Who is in charge of administering it? Most importantly, what is the process of follow through on the ideas submitted? Pay attention to whether the box is empty most of the time, or if new ideas keep coming. A weak flow of suggestions could signify that the program is not administered effectively or that the company culture does not encourage free thinking. The entire team should feel free to share their thoughts and ideas without a concern for being judged.

Some companies set up their suggestion systems in an anonymous manner. I do not believe in anonymous suggestion programs. To me, they should be used only as a stepping stone in an effort to improve the worst-case scenario toxic culture where no new opinions are encouraged. What is the point of having a suggestion program, if you cannot go back to the idea originator to ask additional questions, collaborate, and make them a part of the solution? In fact, one of the main reasons why employee suggestion programs fade away is when the idea originator is too distanced from its implementation.

I have seen a company that did not heed this advice and implemented a program where the suggestions were sorted by a program administrator and placed on the desks of department heads based on the perceived pertinence. The idea originators could choose to remain anonymous or put their name down to qualify for $100 if their suggestion ended up implemented. Most importantly, the originators had no obligation to research their idea for feasibility or conduct a simple cost-benefit analysis. The program's success was measured by the number of suggestions implemented. The department heads were judged by the length of time they took to implement the idea that had arbitrarily landed on their desk.

People felt free to submit any suggestion that popped into their head and seemed, to them at least, a good idea at the time. Certainly, the ideas flowed in. One person suggested that the company should invest in an air hockey table, and was overheard later bragging to his colleagues that "it was the easiest hundred bucks he ever made in his life." Another suggested to invest in skiing lessons for every employee and then sponsor a company-wide ski tournament in a mountain resort a few hours away from the town. Implementing this became not only a significant expense *for the mid-size firm, but also a logistical nightmare for the already busy Department Manager assigned with the task of organizing the event; they were expected to do so single-handedly. The idea originator walked away ($100 richer) from the responsibility of helping with project implementation. He stated that coming up with such a 'fantastic' suggestion was more than enough, and he did not have any more time to spare. No one explained to him, that as much as new ideas are appreciated, generating one does not require nearly as much work as executing it.*

Another company collected employee suggestions once a week and passed them around the office to assign ownership for the implementation. People rarely got ownership of their own suggestions. With lack of interest from the new owners, many suggestions never got implemented. This caused the employees a lot of frustration, disillusionment, and distrust, not only in this particular program but in management as a whole. Eventually, this approach choked off the flow of new ideas. To cover up for their own deficiencies, management said, "Oh well, we tried. Those ideas weren't much good anyway."

In both of these cases, suggestion programs were eventually revitalized by rewriting the rules. The new rules included channels for the idea originators to take responsibility for their suggestions, including the research of pros and cons, some version of cost-benefit analysis, and most importantly, joining the team implementing the suggestions. As a result, bonuses were given out for legitimate efforts such as effective implementation of or an honest attempt at innovation, and not merely for writing down the first thought that popped into an employee's head, for the sake of qualifying for a monetary reward. This ensured that the ideas were well thought out, and that the resulting actions were beneficial for the organization. Employee morale was vastly improved by bringing up engagement and empowerment.

When building and managing suggestion programs with Continual Improvement in mind, Caring Organizations treat every employee as a potential source of a million-dollar idea. Unique life experiences and a proactive mind can make anyone a good candidate for authoring the next winning idea. While innovation is often (mistakenly) linked to technologically advanced or mechanically inclined minds, the winning combination is actually a healthy mix of technical vs. non-technical suggestions.

At one point in my career, I had a chance to work with a Russian inventor, a brilliant engineer who was in charge of building multiple plants in mining and heavy manufacturing industries in the harsh conditions of Siberia. He shared his approach to generating high-quality ideas. He made a point to specifically include non-technical personnel on his high-performance teams. In his distinctly no-nonsense manner, this inventor admitted: "If, roughly speaking, ten ideas from those non-technical team members are good for nothing, the 11th is always this genius idea that could never occur to any of my engineering staff! They simply don't have a mind that is open enough to think that freely."

Thinking 'that' freely is the power of so-called good ignorance! Peter Drucker was known to attribute his supreme success in business management consulting not only to the knowledge of the industries he worked with, but also to his ignorance of those industries. His ability to ask questions, the right questions, that only a person with a fresh pair of eyes could ask, contributed to his capacity to make such a difference.

The value of ignorance was proven during the World War II, when the U.S. built Liberty Ships at the British government's request; the British were too busy and too under-resourced to keep up with the growing need to replace their lost ships. The Liberty Ships ended up manufactured per simplified British Designs by Americans who knew nothing about building ships, used non-expert manpower, and unapproved fabricating techniques, the only techniques available to them. Nevertheless, the efficiency of their assembly lines reduced the expected shipbuilding time significantly, and decreased the cost. Time and Cost were two of the most valuable resources, desperately needed to gain an advantage during wartime (American Management Association, 2019).

D. PROS AND CONS OF HIRING CONSULTANTS

Continual Improvement works best when everyone in the organization is involved. As we often see, companies get comfortable once they put in place a Quality manager, a Continual Improvement manager, or, speaking in more conversational terms – that Lean guy or that ISO lady (the ISO 9000 Management Representative), the one who will step in with the right tools and fix the challenges the company faces. This becomes a problem if the organization gets used to relying solely on the existence of such a person single-handedly spearheading the CI program. Improvements must take place where the actual work is done, with the involvement of the same people who work in those processes throughout the organization. As the saying goes: "The wisdom of the many is always better than the knowledge of one."

When we are too close to the processes, we lose that much-valued outsider's perspective – the good ignorance of the Liberty Shipbuilders during the World War II. We find it hard to detach ourselves from what we already know; our pre-existing knowledge affects our view of the current problem as our prior experiences can bog us down with what worked and what did not work in the past.

That's when we can really use an impartial outside resource, equipped with a fresh pair of eyes and a combination of problem-solving tools in their arsenal from years of experience gained from many different companies. An outside consultant is not enmeshed in any political connections or special friendships within your organization where they feel overly cautious, trying to avoid offending someone during the course of their work. They are not attached to any ideas from the past, and their minds are not clouded with prior failures.

External consultants come with a clean slate and can be excellent facilitators. In the last interview he gave, in 1993, Dr. Deming said: "To get out of the pit we require an outside view. No chance from the inside. A system cannot understand itself. Understanding comes from outside. An outside view provides a lens for examination of our present actions, policies. Knowledge from outside is necessary. Knowledge from outside gives us a view of what we're doing, what we might do, a road to improvement, Continual Improvement." Deming was convinced that the internal committee could not produce profound new knowledge even if the committee was expanded. He believed the outside view was more trustworthy in encouraging foundational long-term improvement (Stevens, 1994). Consultants are usually hired during the change-over in a system, since they are excellent at implementing management change processes, especially if they're qualified with soft skills handling people through the transition. They can be of great help when you introduce brand-new concepts to your team or need an impartial facilitator. Their lack of familiarity with the 'way we do things around here' their lack of attachment to old successes and failures, makes them excellent paradigm-shifters.

I have had consulting jobs with companies that didn't have time or manpower to solve their own problems and needed to bring in someone with outside knowledge to help find solutions. For best results and to build sustainability for the improvement, I teamed up with the internal process owners and developed them into future champions of Continual Improvement. This approach saves money for the hiring organization: the employees gain knowledge and expertise from the consultant, and learn how to pass on know-how that will remain in-house once the consultant is gone. Good consultants do not stretch their billable hours beyond necessity. Before they move on, they groom someone with skin in the game into the role of the **Internal Consultant,** someone who can continue building buy-in from the team. This way, six months of efforts don't go to waste, and the initiative does not die off as soon as the consultant leaves. Once the project is over, you still have an in-house expert, a go-to person who can answer questions for others and represent the newly adopted initiative.

It is important to consider who you bring on board. The consultant must be qualified, but not everyone with industry knowledge is necessarily the right person for the job. Excellent skills communicating with your employees at all levels, both individually and with groups of various sizes, is essential. If you are new to hiring an outside consultant, it is best to stick with a plan – specify the scope of the project, the time commitment, the milestones, progress tracking methods, and an accurate and meaningful measure of success. To keep a good handle on the progress of the consultant's job, maintain open communication with the consultant throughout the life-cycle of the project. The results of the project should not come as a surprise to you at the end.

So long as expectations are set out clearly and proper communication is maintained, numerous benefits accrue to expanding your company's horizons to include outside expertise. This is true, no matter how many highly intelligent people your organization already employs. Looking for ideas outside of your company is a concept that came into use sometime in the late 19th century. Some of the earlier consulting firms specialized in technical research. Later, in the mid-20th century, they were known for helping organizations build structure, more specifically, the multi-departmental structure; for example, within the DuPont Company. More advanced consultant roles have now morphed into strategy developing roles (Poznan, 2018). Other forms of consulting have become popular in today's world, such as *co-creation*, *crowd-sourcing*, or *wikinomics*. Companies use suppliers and customers to run ideas back and forth as they are looking for innovative solutions to commonly shared problems, seeking ways to improve processes that would benefit all parties. Asda, a UK-based subsidiary of Walmart, for example, is known for obtaining help from shoppers testing out its products (Wooldridge, 2011).

Whatever the approach is, from hiring external consultants and seeking out ideas from clients, to collaborating with the masses, the same thinking underlies all of these efforts: The surest way to secure a bright idea is to attract lots and lots of ideas. When there is an abundance of fresh perspective, there is always room for innovation and expanding the boundaries of the organization's knowledge.

CHAPTER 6 – KNOWLEDGE IS POWER: SPREAD THE KNOWLEDGE, SHARE THE POWER

A. WHY PEOPLE HOG INFORMATION & OTHER PRECIOUS RESOURCES

In the early 2000s, during an ISO 9001 Audit of the Quality Management System at a mid-size manufacturing company in California, I came across two assembly employees, who stood side by side and worked off notes handwritten on paper. Each worker kept her notes in her apron pocket and both were cautious not to let others see their notes. Neither these two nor anyone else on their assembly line even glanced at the company-approved work instructions posted on the wall at their workstation.

By doing this work day in and day out, each worker had mastered the skill of assembling the product, and also developed their own unique method of getting the job done more efficiently. Closer review of this situation revealed that their employer used the number of gadgets produced per minute to measure the assembly department's success. Individual workers' performance was assessed by how many gadgets they made in an eight-hour shift, along with the rate of gadgets passing the independently conducted final inspections. That's why each worker was trying to get ahead by using individual trade tricks they learned through trial and error. Showing their methods to their coworkers or supervisor was the last thing on their mind.

Back in those days, the ISO 9000 family of standards had as its motto "Do what you say and say what you do." "Working from unapproved work instructions" was not only a write-up in the audit report, but was also a big no-no as a business practice. In response to this discovery, management decided to review the potential process improvements the workers had thought of with the possibility of incorporating them into standardized, controlled work instructions. However, taking this action solved only one part of the problem. The root cause was still in effect; why did the employees feel the need to hide their best practices in the first place?

REINVENTING THE WHEEL

A lot of time and effort is wasted searching for knowledge that already exists on paper or in people's minds. It's pretty common for people to tightly hold onto the information they have accumulated. They often do so in response to circumstances that can be readily addressed. Why do people conceal the knowledge they have? What makes them go out of their way to hide it from the rest of the department and organization? For most employees, especially during economically unstable times, it's primarily a feeling of insecurity; fear of being outshone by colleagues, fear of being overlooked for promotion, or fear of losing their job all together.

In their prior career, many have witnessed difficult times, perhaps even an economic slowdown when many lost their jobs. Previous experience has taught them: "You must make yourself indispensable to your employer" to survive layoffs and other undesirable practices. Those who survived this ruthless economic elimination came to believe that the only way they could increase their value is by holding tightly onto crucial information, which includes best practices, on-the-job-learned know-how, or even valuable industry contacts. When facing a real or perceived threat, people decide they must become the top-notch expert, with enough power over the others in the organization to hold steady in their position. The saying 'Knowledge is power' gets seriously misinterpreted when people start using hoarded knowledge to maintain power over each other. In contrast, through sharing knowledge, the entire organization could gain power in the marketplace, yielding growth opportunities that could benefit everyone.

Are employee insecurities around sharing knowledge well-founded? As leaders, we must take a closer look at the organizational culture we've created or maintained. Sometimes, hoarding information becomes a part of the culture as a direct result of management rewarding people strictly on their technical knowledge, or demonstrating lack of interest, through inaction, when people openly refuse to share their knowledge even when it could help others. If that is the case in your workplace, either management must make a change, or the management team should be changed.

Leaders should closely examine their own behavior patterns first. Are they good at sharing their knowledge with the team, or do they hang onto their specialized knowledge too? I have witnessed management members feeling so threatened by a bright employee that they denied the employee credit for their hard work, and diminished their contributions, while blowing any of their mistakes out of proportion.

This type of manager cannot be called a true leader; they operate by ego and a false sense of pride, with a need for more control, to hoard power over people. I believe leaders should start earning people's trust by following what Ken Blanchard recommends: to practice shining a light on others, and to recognize that life is about giving and not as much about taking (Witt, 2018). Only when a leader is able to surrender a need for power and control can they begin to create a space where it is safe for everyone to share and to be themselves. The benefit for the whole company is that no one needs to waste their time reinventing the wheel or hiding great insights that can benefit everyone. To build trust with your team, practice open, sincere, and effective communication. After all, knowledge is only power when it's used. Everyone wins when we can use the shared knowledge.

With respect to the organization's confidentiality policies, share all relevant and pertinent information whether it's the financial performance, the projects coming down the pipeline, industry trends that may affect your business. Employee surveys often reveal that the number one item employees wish they had more of was more information about the business, while management often parcels out information in small portions as the need-to-know arises. Best company practices include sharing pertinent information with employees on a periodic, roughly, quarterly basis. Quarterly or at least semi-annual town halls are great for that purpose, but maintaining open communication channels throughout the year allows people to stay in the loop on all important developments. When you understand that the benefits of knowledge multiply when shared by everyone, you are all rowing the same boat as a team.

HANDLING TOUGH TIMES

No one likes to be caught off guard by bad news or watch their colleagues being laid off one by one – that spreads panic and anxiety. Leadership is called upon the most at a time when layoffs are inevitable. It's so important to look out for the interests of the team even during the hardest and most unpredictable times. Try to repurpose people's talents in ways that may be beneficial to the company, if the choice to do so is an option.

If layoffs are inevitable, we don't want to spread panic by making announcements too early, but letting people rely on rumors is even worse. When confronted with specific questions from your team on whether or not there is a prospect of losing their job, learn subtle ways to let people know to listen to their gut feeling, get their resume ready, and keep an eye on the job market. At least that way, there will be trust between you and the rest of your team. By keeping communication channels open and building trust, you put yourself in a better position where you can rely on your team whenever they have information you might have wished they shared sooner.

B. PROMOTE & REWARD SHARING AS A COMPANY BEST PRACTICE

How often have you come across a manager who has a hard time accepting ideas of other people, or felt the need to prove them wrong no matter what? In my decades spent in the corporate world, I have seen many examples of those types.

One manager would flat out reject any idea proposed by a subordinate. Occasionally, if it was too hard to resist the appeal of a winning idea, he would sit on it for a decent period of time, only to present it eventually as his own. Another manager was the My-Way-or-the-Highway type, whose desk was referred to (in inner circles of his direct reports) as the Bermuda Triangle because of its ability to make any suggestion or a proposal that landed on it disappear. (See Chapter 3 for more information.) When confronted about it, he was often heard blaming the idea originators for wasting valuable company time with 'pointless conversations' on ideas that were "good for nothing anyway."

Where does this attitude come from, and how do you explain it? It turns out, this is one of the seven fatal ways of thinking, as perfectly described by Matthew E. May in his book **"Winning the Brain Game"** (May, 2016). Called **Not Invented Here (NIH),** it's the rejection of any good ideas only because they are not your own. The biological explanation of NIH syndrome has to do with the fact that we do not receive the same chemical reward from using other people's ideas as we would if we came up with our own solution to the problem.

From a psychological viewpoint, as the author maintains, when we develop deep but narrow bands of knowledge, also known as **Subject Matter Expertise (SME),** most folks tend to associate our knowledge with our self image. When another person's idea takes off and ends up solving a problem, we feel that their knowledge is taking away from the power we have accumulated through great effort. Affected by the diminished view of our abilities, we allow the 'I should have thought of that' attitude take over, and we then pledge to restore and preserve our expertise at any cost.

As a leader, what kind of behavior do you project out to others, and what kind of behavior do you support and encourage in others through your organization's incentive programs, performance evaluations, and employee recognition channels? As we mentioned in Chapter 2, performance evaluations often focus on individual achievements and end up promoting the *SME* or Superstar mentality, at the expense of teamwork values. The same goes for knowledge sharing. When was the last time the Employee of the Month award given to a person who spent their afternoon teaching a new hire how to use the company ERP System or someone who shortened a colleague's learning curve by sharing the know-how they obtained through their own years of schooling or hands-on work expertise?

Do your employees understand the many benefits of knowledge sharing, or do they fear repercussions? A wise leader seeks to understands the underlying reasons for peoples' concerns and strives to remove any anxiety or reservations around sharing knowledge.

HOW THE SHARING CULTURE APPROACH HELPS EVERYONE

To incorporate the **Sharing Culture** into the fabric of your organization, explain the benefits it offers. Make them clear and visible. Here are some questions and areas of inquiry to get you started:

- How will everyone benefit from this type of culture? Define all stakeholders. What information do they need, what do they need it for, and when do they need it?
- Will employees have a better experience when quickly and easily accessing the company's latest and greatest best practices?
- Will the customer benefit from receiving better customer service from better-informed personnel?
- Will the organization as a whole start to raise its collective knowledge levels, thus honing its competitive edge?

People need to know the reasons *Why* and they need to know what's in it for them. It's important to communicate what your employees themselves get out of all this. To instill a culture of learning and continually improving, get to know the distinct language that every group in the organization speaks. Just as it is common knowledge that management speaks the language of finance, the rest of the employees have their own language as well. The most commonly used language is: "What's in it for me?" Before adopting any new approach, people want to understand the personal benefits to them. If they are going to change their ways and put an extra effort to achieve higher results, they need to know how things will change for the better. It is management's role to find what motivates people, and then make it clear that their role in sharing and expanding knowledge supports overall company performance. It's also essential to show how improved results will positively affect their lives.

Whether it translates to shared profits and improved work conditions, if your peoples' lives are made easier in a specific, tangible way, or if there's an opportunity to become a part of a coveted project, the impact must be clear. To solidify this new approach, redefine your culture to encourage teams to succeed together as opposed to perpetuating the old and ineffective model where individual workers compete for resources or managerial approval.

> **If your team members still care about making themselves indispensable, rewrite the definition of 'indispensable' to describe someone who readily shares their knowledge, trains coworkers on what they know, and helps others succeed.**

Measure an employee's progress milestones based on how much time they invest in training others, including the quality of the training. One company, for example, had a policy: no manager will get promotions, and no team members will be offered management positions unless they contribute a minimum of two articles to the company's **Knowledge Management System (KMS)**.

Once the *Why* behind this thinking is understood by all involved, and employee buy-in is secured, clarify how employees should be sharing their knowledge. How do they get the assurance that their knowledge is worthwhile for the company? What is the process for reviewing and accepting their knowledge? What channels should they go through? Will they be getting value — short or long term — out of this endeavor? Will anyone recognize their contribution? Is there any risk that their contribution might be misattributed?

C. CREATE A KNOWLEDGE MANAGEMENT SYSTEM ACCESSIBLE TO ANYONE NEEDING INFORMATION

Knowledge only becomes power when we can use it and act upon it. How can most employees access the right knowledge on organization's products, processes, customers, and equipment if a large amount of it only resides with certain SMEs within the organization as tribal knowledge? The organization may either be aware or unaware of all the knowledge acquired and collected within its walls, but if it remains unconcerned with it, this mindset can damage the company culture and hold its progress back.

First of all, if tribal knowledge is allowed to remain tribal, it is almost guaranteed that some of the negative workplace phenomena we discussed earlier will continue to flourish: information hoarding, lack of cross-training, and excess reliance on the so-called superstars. When knowledge is not documented, it's hard to distribute it company-wide; when it's not captured electronically, it impedes the processes of adopting new technology.

What happens to the tribal knowledge when the corporate wisdom carriers are no longer there? Lack of succession planning is a real threat to modern workplaces, because of both planned and unplanned scenarios. We already know that Baby Boomers — born between 1946 and 1963, the largest generation before the Millennials — are well on their way to retirement. When these experienced and highly knowledgeable people, who have held high-profile positions in the company, leave, what happens to the knowledge gathered and stored in their heads? It simply walks out the door with them. An organization can also incur damage to its workforce in a rather unplanned but still must-be-anticipated scenario — a large-scale disaster of natural or human-made origins.

To avoid losing all that knowledge at once, some companies started taking action by practicing so-called 'phased retirement,' starting with a gradual reduction in hours for the valuable workplace experts, allowing them time to transition into their retirement years, while preparing other team members for success. For example, a U.S.-based health-care company, Abbott Laboratories, allows veteran workers to work four days a week or take 25 more vacation days a year (Wooldridge, 2011).

Implementing a KMS as an effective repository of all pertinent information, for future use by the entire organization, as needed, is now becoming commonplace. A KMS is any kind of IT system that stores and retrieves knowledge to improve understanding, collaboration, and process alignment. KMSs can exist within organizations or teams, but they can also be used to centralize your knowledge base for your users or customers Birkett, 2020).

Here are a few points to consider when building a successful KMS:

- **1. Where do you start building a KMS?** The process starts at the top, with high-level executives who possess valuable knowledge that they must be willing to share. If top leadership exempts itself from sharing what they know, the entire initiative will fail.

- **2. What kind of information should be shared?** An organization accumulates a lot of knowledge over the years, but not all of it is relevant. The process of choosing what is relevant requires structure. Your leadership team should start by defining what information is pertinent to the scope of your business, the context of your organization, and its core capabilities. You don't want to overdo it and flood the database with too much information. Sifting through the stored information to locate what's useful would become a nightmare for the users later. Carefully select the information and mark it with clear, meaningful identification.

- **3. Do workers participate in the knowledge sharing?** Workers have a lot of knowledge on how to get the job done, whether it's approved, or possibly, unapproved, methods they have discovered the hard way. This knowledge could present valuable tips and tricks of the trade known only to a small number of people. Discovering these hidden gems and adding them to your KMS can be more valuable than expected.

In a well-established culture of QIQO, success stories are not the only information to share and capture. Since Caring Leaders admit their own mistakes and view them as learning opportunities, they create a safe environment for everyone else to share their lessons learned: cautionary tales, failure stories, near misses. All of this can save the organization from reinventing the wheel, repeating history, and wasting resources down the road.

- **4. How to categorize the information?** There is no magic formula that works for all when it comes to categorizing foundational corporate knowledge and the best form to present it in. Think of what's meaningful to you based on the nature, scope, and size of your business. You could categorize it by product type, process, customer, or project. Whatever it is, have the end goal in mind. I recommend observing the natural, intuitive patterns your employees currently follow when looking for information. Consider running a poll among the future users of your KMS to learn what people think would work best. Hiring an outside consultant experienced in building these systems could be a major help if they work in conjunction with your process owner or a team of experts.

- **5. High Tech or Low Tech?** The form in which you present your KMS can be as high tech or as low tech as you want it to be. It could be as simple as a meaningfully constructed spreadsheet, with hyperlinks leading to the electronic sources of your information. It could be any in-house or purchased software; you could capture the know-how in videos, tutorials, webinars, work instructions with photos, PowerPoint presentations, a Frequently Asked Questions listing, an interactive forum, case studies, project documentation, and more.

- **6. Who can access the KMS?** Once the KMS format is agreed upon, decide how to control access – who needs this information and where to access it. Who gets revision rights and who gets viewing rights only? Consider how long the information is used for. Is there an expiration date for the knowledge?

Just like food and other consumer products, knowledge also has an expiration date.

In certain fields such as exact sciences, IT, medicine, knowledge expires much faster than in others. However, all accumulated knowledge collections must be reviewed from time to time for accuracy and adequacy. Make sure the review intervals and updating responsibilities are specified in your brand-new KMS.

- **7. The two parts to KMS.** KMS is so much more than the IT platform that enables it. There are two parts to it – the capabilities that technological advancements make available for us, and the genuine human effort behind sharing valued content and mapping it out. Knowledge Management is not nearly as much about technology, as it is about the objectives of your business, and that does not start with technology. It starts with observing and analyzing business objectives and business processes, for the purpose of sharing the important, even essential information needed to run the business properly, efficiently, and effectively.

The purpose of a well-designed, accessible KMS is to make the right information available to the right people at the right time so they can make the most educated decisions in the timeliest manner.

You don't necessarily have to spend too much effort on its form, as long as it's user-friendly and provides the right content. Once you have captured all the pertinent internal knowledge, determine what type of knowledge from the outside world is relevant; anything that adds value to your organization's strategic goals, anything that can be well integrated.

D. CREATE A CULTURE OF CONTINUOUS LEARNING BY PROVIDING PAID TRAINING

Training is the most basic form of knowledge sharing that takes place in any company. This is just the start of learning individual and company-wide job requirements, but it's not nearly enough. Quick, job-related instructions shared with an employee on the go are often called 'training,' while actually, it's not. Nothing is wrong with providing on-the-job training; knowledge transfer and skills learning does not always have to take place in a classroom setting. It's important to understand that training is never a one-way instruction or task demonstration. The feedback received from the trainee is as valuable as the information given to them in the first place. What have they learned? Do they understand the *Why* behind a certain process? People have different learning styles, but I can tell you that no one is good at memorizing and retaining instructions if they are not sure of the logic behind those steps and their sequence.

ASSESSING YOUR TRAINING TEAM

Who are your trainers? Do you have designated trainers in your facility, or do you assign pretty much anyone to train others on what they have learned already? Even if it's the latter, you can implement a system where you pair up a more experienced employee with someone new to the task. Before getting started with this informal training style, agree on a standard way of doing the job. Ask your staff questions such as: what are the best practices, and what are the safest work methods?

People with many years of experience can grow complacent; they tend to cut corners just because they have done this job for so long "without ever getting injured." This is what I like to remind those types of on-the-job trainers in the organizations I work with: "Your complacency minus your years of experience could be a deadly combination for someone new on the job." We must be careful so that when we transfer knowledge, we do not transfer bad habits.

Create a cross-training matrix for your organization's key skills that you need adequately covered. Define those skills in three levels – the beginner, the expert, and the trainer levels. The trainer level implies a lot more than having mastered the technical skill itself. It also includes the soft element of human interaction, the ability to instruct, demonstrate, ask reinforcing (open-ended) questions, patience, diligence, and, above all, the sincere desire to see another person succeed in their job. That's when the *Sharing Culture* we previously discussed comes in handy. With incentive and recognition programs that value people for going beyond their personal achievements, well-thought-out training programs usher in a level of competence and confidence that encourages pride and engagement at your company.

If training is not just on-the-job instruction, what is it, then? It's staying on top of your field and learning the latest and greatest as agreed upon in the relevant industry. That's why I value organizations that allow their employees to grow, develop, work toward certifications, degrees, and anything else that helps them advance their skills further, so they can build competence and become more valuable.

General Electric is an example of a successful company that is sincerely invested in its team's training and education, with a focus on standing out in front of its competition through truly mastering Continual Improvement. Pretty much everyone who joins GE is required to take a Six Sigma course, and then use their newly acquired knowledge by applying those methodologies to a project at work. Those more advanced in Six Sigma, Master Black Belt professionals, are required to train other employees to become Black Belts as well. Through this and many other initiatives, the company maintains its excellence and established leadership in the marketplace.

If you don't have the time to arrange for the right training program, then I highly recommend outsourcing the logistics and the IT support for your planned KMS, and focus only on the content. If your team members do not have the time to attend classrooms, there are many online programs suited for different schedules. Besides, you can always offer incentives for those willing to spend some of their personal time to expand their knowledge base. That way, you can also identify the most engaged team members, who, in turn, will be a valuable resource and will contribute their skills and education to the company's KMS.

To create a well-populated knowledge repository and establish succession planning, organizations benefit greatly by relying on their semi-retired resources to mentor their younger, less experienced full-time coworkers, to build them into strong experts in their fields. The experienced ex-managers can serve as consultants on call, summoned when their help is needed for specific projects. According to Forbes magazine, about 70% of Fortune 500 companies have a program like this, while only about 25% of smaller companies do. There are many benefits to having great mentors at work on a part-time or full-time basis. The one benefit that stands out to me the most is the potential for grooming newer hires to foster growth in the fields of management and leadership.

As much as it can be learned from attending educational programs, there is nothing like a well-developed relationship with a hands-on, caring, and wise mentor, who is there to help your people navigate through the intricacies of problem solving and decision making like a leader, with a focus on real-life scenarios from your own workplace. It seems to work best when the two people are chosen and paired up in this mentor-mentee relationship. Otherwise, a mentor could be putting a tremendous amount of energy and time into a prospective mentee, but if there is no 'chemistry,' no clicking between them, then this effort could be a burden more than anything.

In a devoted work culture that emphasizes Continual Improvement, the learning never ends, and the mentor could also have a mentor of their own or be a part of a mastermind group. If you have found a great mentor, one who is invested in peoples' growth, and can serve as an excellent role model, consider yourself lucky, because those relationships can do miracles and be mutually rewarding in both short and long-term scenarios. I have had some excellent mentors in my life who have helped to bring out the best in me, supported or challenged me when I needed it, and facilitated my capacity for navigating through life and work situations while finding the right answers for me. My first experience witnessing mentorship programs at their best started long before I fully understood the meaning of the word mentor.

During my childhood, growing up with my grandparents near me, I saw people come to our house to see Grandpa all the time. Depending on the time of the year, he would take them to his study room upstairs or outside to the garden house, where they spent hours, with a pot of freshly brewed tea and other amazing homemade goodies generously served by my grandmother. I knew they were not family friends or relatives, who were also frequent visitors in the house. I asked Grandpa who these people were. He told me: "They are my mentees."

With a strong devotion to the legal profession, having served in multiple roles from prosecutor, lawyer, district attorney, and judge, by the end of his career, my grandfather opened his own legal consulting firm and helped many people, including supporting numerous cases on a pro bono basis. He took it upon himself to also tend to a younger generation of legal professionals on a completely volunteer basis. During his off-hours, in his own house, he would meet with them to go over the details of court cases, review the results of subpoenas, and prepare the mentees for upcoming court hearings, etc. I saw different generations of these mentees come and go; I also learned that Grandpa's mentees went on to succeed in their chosen field. Some became prosecutors and even judges one day. This is the power of having an excellent mentor.

However, it does not always have to be the top-down approach when it comes to sharing knowledge. A younger or more junior employee could become an in-house expert in certain areas and prepare presentations or training sessions on the subjects that they are knowledgeable about. This could be especially true when it comes to mastering the new technology faster and helping others in the workplace to become proficient with it.

Another initiative that can be 100% managed by in-house experts is something popularly referred to as Lunch and Learn sessions. These topics share presenter expertise that may interest the rest of the organization or even a certain group. When the employees get to suggest or vote for topics of interest, the engagement level is usually higher as well. When team members are given these leadership opportunities – a chance to reinforce their knowledge, to showcase their expertise – it can be invigorating for everyone. Not only does the speaker get the satisfaction of others recognizing their expertise; it can also energize the rest of the team to expand their confidence and step into mentorship and trainer roles themselves.

When investing in peoples' training, a company always exposes itself to a level of risk; their newly developed in-house experts can just turn around and leave to explore new horizons somewhere else. There are ways to provide some assurances through putting legalities in place. The main point is this: yes, there is always a risk that the person will still leave before the company can claim its ROI. Some managers worry if they can afford the risk of investing in people's training. Think of it this way: one of the best managers I had in my career would say: "But what if we do not invest, and they stay!" Point well taken!

CHAPTER 7 – QIQO: REAPING WHAT YOU SOW

A. COUNTERACTING GIGO WITH QIQO

When I was growing up, the concept of reaping what you sow was one of the biggest lessons instilled in our minds from all directions – family, school, popular culture, cartoons, or children's books. One of those childhood stories was the fable of *The Ant and the Dragonfly*.

The hardworking Ant spent the entire summer stocking up on food and fixing up his dwelling in preparation for a long cold winter ahead, while the airhead Dragonfly spent her time dancing and prancing day in and day out. She found the Ant extremely boring and ridiculed him for wasting away the beautiful sunny days on chores. The hard-nosed Ant stayed focused on his task with nearly religious zeal. He warned his neighbor that the harsh winter would be unforgiving to those unprepared, but the Dragonfly deliberately ignored his advice. Sure enough, winter came upon them with all its harshness. While the Ant faced the freezing temperatures in a warm home with his large family, well-fed and comfortable, the soaking wet and starving Dragonfly had no place to go. One day, shivering, she knocked on his door begging, for food and shelter. With his zero-tolerance toward irresponsible behavior of any sort, the Ant felt no mercy and shut the door in her face.

Even though the Ant's 'I told you so' attitude and lack of empathy didn't make him appealing to me, he brings the point home in a business context. The moral of this story is simple: planning ahead is wise and might save your life. This was one of my earliest introductions to the concept. As I further interacted with the outside world, I saw many other manifestations of this concept and heard different variations of the phrase itself used. Just like the hardworking Ant from the fable, sometimes the stories left a bit of a bad taste in my mouth. Although we discussed this earlier in the book, now I wish to draw a closer connection to one of the variations of this fable: the risky, time-wasting, disappointing **GIGO attitude**.

When allowed to persist unaddressed, GIGO keeps managers mediocre, workers disengaged, performance poor, and workplace improvement close to zero. There is one thing that flourishes in the GIGO environment – excuses. Have you noticed that excuses are rampant in a workplace that commonly repeats the phrase: "Oh, well, you know – Garbage In, Garbage Out?"

The mentality behind poor or mediocre performance provides an easy-to-blame culprit for workplace inefficiencies and non-conformities. A machine-shop employee who cuts a part to a wrong dimension has the perfect excuse: a draftsman specified wrong tolerances on the drawing. An assembly millwright puts a product together using the wrong components and blames it on the material handlers who staged the wrong parts. You arrive at a hotel front desk after a long day of travel to have the reception clerk tell you that they are all booked, because something must have gone wrong in their software, which did not hold your reservation. You are now on your own in a foreign city at a late hour trying to figure out where to spend the night. Due to a GIGO attitude, the hotel representative shrugs and continues pointing you to the computer screen, which does not display your name. He feels righteous in his own way: it was not his fault, the system is garbage, and he is powerless to do anything about it. At the end of the day, blaming the situation on GIGO doesn't help.

Doing a half-hearted job to push a task off your plate as fast as you can only creates *Garbage Out* flowing down the pipe. You can't expect someone to take your garbage and create something meaningful from it – **Garbage In, 'Gospel' Out** simply does not exist. A lose-lose situation is embedded in GIGO's definition; when you embrace your helplessness to change anything, just because of the cards you have been dealt. This becomes a vicious circle.

This is exactly why I propose replacing this victim mentality with the much more productive and powerful QIQO model. QIQO fosters an environment for taking personal accountability for the quality of your output. By continually remaining aware of the needs of those who rely on our input for producing their output, and by making a conscious effort to each and every time stand behind the quality of what comes out of our hands or our computers, we all share accountability for the outcome of the process.

In QIQO, everyone understands they are a part of a larger system where all components are interconnected and are interdependent. Everything we do ultimately affects the entire system – that's why we don't make the excuse of being served a poor-quality input. We take charge of what we're served and raise the right questions right then and there. By speaking up on time, and collaborating with the suppliers of our input, we find what is missing, clarify what is vague, correct what is wrong, and always try to sow good seeds, so that we too have something useful to reap at the other end of the process. Doing this together makes the rewards of the QIQO efforts that much more satisfying. It helps sustain a chain reaction of primarily win-win scenarios in the future, thus fostering an environment of developing empowered and accountable individuals.

B. HOW QIQO HELPS TO OVERCOME THE SILO MENTALITY

In a true QIQO culture, everyone is focused on producing quality results, whether or not what they produce is something tangible. Even if your hands are not touching the company's product (for example, you oversee only a portion of the process, or the documentation that goes with the product), your output will still become someone else's input.

A sample sequence of events and decisions is described below:

A ***Request For a Quote (RFQ)*** comes to my inbox from a customer. I thoroughly review the information given in the *RFQ* to evaluate for the presence of all vital details; the quantity, the delivery expectation, the materials to be used, and any other parameters and characteristics of the product. If I am missing any information important for the integrity of my quote, I need to ask questions, research the information given to me, collaborate with the customer, or provide options for others on my team to follow up on. In a QIQO environment, we remain keenly aware that everything we produce becomes an input for the next internal function or for the company's customer. Whatever steps we take or fail to take will affect those important people down the line.

In the QIQO approach, we treat ourselves and all other internal and external functions associated with us as parts of the same complex system. We recognize that any change we make on our end inevitably affects other parts of the system. For example, changing the material a bicycle is made of affects not only its weight but its speed and handling. Switching a project deadline to an earlier date might well add to its overall cost or take away from the scope of the project or reduce the quality of the product we offer. In a similar manner, we cannot shrink the budget hoping to keep all other aspects of our project the same. We must make sure our output meets the quality, timeliness, and cost requirements of the project. We cannot expect good quality to be produced from garbage. In a QIQO environment, we know that we cannot change anything in one part of the system without reviewing the implications on others. Since no change is ever isolated, why make the change *in* isolation?

Yet, many organizations, regardless of the industry and sector they are in, operate in **silos**. What are *silos*, and what are they needed for?

Silos

1: A trench, pit, or especially a tall cylinder (typically wood, steel, or concrete) usually sealed to exclude air; used for making and storing silage.

2a: A deep bin for storing material (such as coal).

2b: An underground structure for housing a guided missile. These are weapons that can hit military targets, such as missile *silos* and headquarters, swiftly and accurately.

3: An isolated grouping, department, etc., that functions apart from others, especially in a way seen as hindering communication and cooperation. Big, complex companies are typically structured, so that decision making is separated according to function, geography, and product. This system design naturally creates *silos*. (Merriam-Webster)

4: Information silos: In business management and IT, a silo describes any management system that is unable to operate with any other system, meaning it's closed off from other systems. Silos create an environment of individual and disparate systems within an organization (Beal).

Silos in farm settings serve an essential purpose: they prevent grain from spilling out, and protect it from the elements to increase its storage life. What if someone came along with a wrecking ball and demolished those silos? Would the farmer appreciate it? Most likely not. In the same way, departments in organizations are often like silos. They are necessary structures that are meant to cultivate and utilize expertise.

After all, different teams usually specialize in different areas – and that's a *good* thing. To stay on top of their field, most people tend to become narrow specialists. A Jack-of-all-trades is a master of none, right?

From this perspective, we should not attempt to dismantle workplace silos. At the same time, real-life silos need ventilation to keep the grain from going stale. In organizations, the knowledge cultivated inside *unventilated thought silos* can also go stale when departments or separate teams don't communicate effectively with each other.

One engineering director that I knew took the silo mentality to the extreme. Anytime someone came to his department for their technical expertise he would challenge the request with a question of his own: who is going to benefit from this information? He had built walls between his group and other work functions, and whether he chose to help with the issue at hand was completely dependent on your answer. If the benefit of the shared knowledge or a credit for the solved problem might go somewhere else, he flat out refused to help.

People like this not only deprive others of learning opportunities; they limit their own opportunities as well. When you operate strictly within your silo, isolated from what exists outside the department you hold hostage, your knowledge becomes limited. Disconnected from the context of the whole organization, this strategy inhibits your growth, and keeps your entire team from realizing its full potential. To keep your products and services fresh and innovative, each team or workgroup needs to integrate a process of sharing ideas and exchanging specialized knowledge with teams outside their immediate process area. (See Chapter 6 for more information.)

Since silos are built for a good reason and a specific purpose, our goal is not to completely demolish them. Instead, we need to teach the inhabitants of *thought silos* to communicate with each other effectively.

First, let's take a closer look at this phenomenon and what causes it. How can you tell if your workplace operates in silos? Do you hear at work: "I thought that was the IT department's job." or "You are the

Project Manager, shouldn't you be dealing with it?" Here is a more subtle indication: "If I had a dime for every time I helped someone to succeed in this organization, I would be filthy rich by now!" If your employees walk around making comments like that, chances are you work in a siloed environment.

Nowadays, employees are more technologically interconnected than ever before, which facilitates global teamwork, but it also leads to a lack of face-to-face contact. Opinions and assumptions get in the way. Instead of learning facts about each other's work, geographical distances, physical spaces, differing cultural norms, and unresolved managerial differences may prevent people from seeing each other's perspective and impedes their ability to listen. Sometimes security issues leading to restricted access to information are also reasons why silos develop within companies. An ever-increasing reliance on technology prevents us from using or, more critically, developing interpersonal skills.

Silos may exist both horizontally and vertically – between peers in various departments, in some cases between plant and office, and often, between workers and management. People segregate based on the work process, differing personal goals, and within the white/blue collar class divide. They see their own narrow agendas, squint through tunnel vision at their individual or departmental goals, and typically don't see themselves as part of a larger team united by a common purpose. Focusing exclusively on their own agendas, they don't realize that too much segmentation hurts everyone.

Issues modern workplaces face are too complex to be resolved by one expert, no matter how knowledgeable or hardworking they are. Those issues most often span disciplines and require different specialists to integrate their expertise. To avoid problems with silos down the road, the best approach is to start off on the right foot. When dealing with a work project, launch it with a kick-off meeting, during which you review and analyze all of the project requirements. This is the best time to decide what expertise is needed for the successful implementation of this project. Define each role and select the best methods of collaboration between the various experts. Before actually calling in experts for the project, check if there will be any conflicts with their normal workloads or their commitments to other projects that are taking place simultaneously. Ensure that any areas that might be left under-resourced are fully covered.

Regular Updates: To keep key stakeholders on the same page during the project life cycle, have periodic meetings in an open format with the entire project team, as opposed to privately discussing the affairs with one or two executives who can only speak from their viewpoint. Hold open team discussions on shared goals, tracking progress made toward reaching those goals, and definitely, help managers decide how to best share the work. Acknowledge all contributors, especially the unsung heroes, who don't normally get credit for contributing to 'somebody else's project.'

Reward Team Effort: Recognize individual team members' efforts by finding ways to measure their contributions to the team's success. Remind everyone regularly: no one is an island of their own, and every team is only as strong as its weakest link. Allow people to bring their issues and biases to the surface, and foster an environment where the team members are not afraid to challenge the views, opinions, or perspectives of someone with more seniority. It's not easy to change a prevailing mentality, especially if it has been festering in the company for a long time. The good news is: handled correctly and carefully, it can be done.

Shifting from *Silo Mentality* to *Sharing Culture* might involve:

- Team restructuring.
- Changing where key teams are physically located in the office.

- Technological changes that make it easier to communicate and perform duties.
- Generating discussions between key players and fostering teamwork.
- Introducing and instilling the concept of the Internal Customer.

The last point is the most important, in my experience.

C. INTERNAL CUSTOMERS ARE JUST AS IMPORTANT AS EXTERNAL CUSTOMERS

Have you ever worked for an organization that cared about their customers, clients, or patients (if you work in health care)? How do you know your organization cares about customers? Usually, you know this because your work puts great emphasis and importance on:

- Identifying customer needs and expectations;
- Making plans for and executing production of high-quality products;
- Providing the exact service the customer is looking for.

I have worked with many organizations that care about their customers and place great importance on their needs and expectations. Why do you think clients are important? We want to provide outstanding customer service, not only because our customers rely on us and pay for our services, it's to honor the promise our brand makes to customers. For the long-term survival of our company, it's rather obvious that we want to keep customers. Well, how about the people inside the organization who rely on our input to help make those products and services?

I knew a Customer Service Representative, Kelly R, who continually did an excellent job fulfilling customers' needs. She solved all of their problems, found timely answers to the trickiest questions, and she made herself available at odd hours for any product-related inquiries. In reviewing customer satisfaction surveys, this rep got the highest scores. When asked how we could improve our service further, customers often replied, "Clone Kelly!" At the same time, other customer service reps, sharing the room with this person, couldn't have been more miserable working with her. Known for her negativity and spiteful nature, she often threw her colleagues under the bus, always 'saving the day' in the customers' eyes. She sabotaged the work of other departments, was known for slamming doors, and walking out of any meeting at the first sign of things not going her way. Despite all this, she was allowed to stay on board because of her superior service level in the eyes of the customers. It was painful for everyone else, but that situation lasted until she eventually crossed all the lines of acceptable workplace conduct and was let go.

In her pursuit of excellence, when it came to meeting and exceeding customer expectations, her chase focused on undying customer loyalty. Admired by the company customers, Kelly, at the same time, never learned the basics of how to treat her coworkers right. After witnessing this seeming paradox, I realized that it simply never occurred to her to view the people she worked with as her customers! This experience made me choose, as one of my professional goals, to educate people on the concept of the Internal Customer.

EXTERNAL AND INTERNAL CUSTOMERS

External Customers are the people who pay for and rely on the products or services your company offers. When brainstorming problems and designing solutions, these customers are who you have in mind. An *Internal Customer* is someone who works within the company. It could be any function, department, or individual within your organization that receives assistance from you in the form of information, service, or product in order to get their job done. A basic definition of the *Internal Customer* is anyone who needs your input to generate their output. Your Internal Customers' output becomes the input for the next internal process or even for the External Customer (depending on the function).

SIPOC:

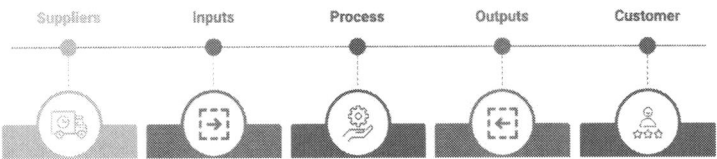

SIPOC is a process-based approach that can explain the relationships between *Internal Customers* and **Internal Suppliers**. We rely on our *Internal Suppliers* to provide us with **Input**. Through our value-added activity, (**Process**) we generate the **Output** needed for our Internal Customers. Sometimes, the supplier and the customer are the same person. If you, for example, are in charge of the Estimating function, your Internal Supplier could be your Sales Department that is passing on to you the *RFQ* they received from the outside customer. Based on the information provided, you compile an accurate estimate to the same Sales Representative, who now becomes your Internal Customer. In his turn, the Sales Rep turns your estimate into a quote readable by the External Customer, and sends it off to them. We are all interconnected: it works best if the organization makes a point of teaching all of its functions this simple but powerful concept – an Internal Customer relationship based on the **Process Approach**: Quality of Input equals Quality of Outputs.

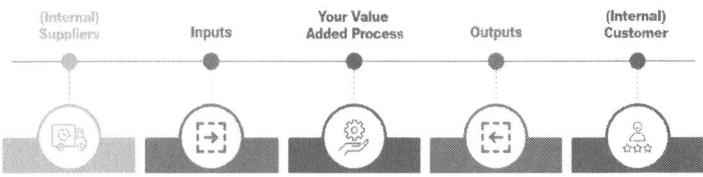

Since suppliers and customers can be both internal and external to the organization, inputs can also be generated internally or externally. It's important to consider that your process must always add **Value**. To determine what adds *Value*, ask: does my activity change the fit, form, or function of the product, and would a customer be willing to pay for this step? If yes, then go for it. If not, you should probably rethink the idea. If your activity is another inspection, an additional check-off point, moving parts from one bin to another, submitting paperwork for more signatures, etc., then reconsider your process from the Value perspective.

> **When we serve our Internal Customers well by adding Value, together we ultimately deliver better value to our External Customers.**

I suggest requesting that everyone in your organization reviews the simple tool I have put together (see below), to identify all their Internal Customers and Suppliers. By understanding how they all are interconnected, you can provide quality service to them. This tool is easy to use in any environment, industry, or sector, regardless of the scope or size of your business to help you learn and implement a very useful Internal Customer/Supplier philosophy.

INTERNAL CUSTOMER QUESTIONNAIRE

Each work function in your organization completes this questionnaire together with their entire team.

WHY: Internal cooperation and customer satisfaction are essential to External Customer satisfaction and overall company performance.
WHO: An Internal Customer is anyone within your organization who relies on your products or services to produce goods of their own.
WHERE: Any department, branch, or adjacent team member/coworker.

Your Internal Customers
1. List each department/function you believe is your Internal Customer/who you supply to:
2. Internal Customer #1: _____
3. List essential processes/products you supply to this Internal Customer on a regular basis, and rate yourself/your department:

Product/Service I Provide to Internal Customer #1	Rating of Service Provided: (Exceeding Expectations) (Meeting Expectations) (Needs Improvement)	Comments/Notes/ Observations
How would you rate interactions/ communication with this function?		

4. Please repeat steps two and three for each Internal Customer on your list. (Use additional tables to include all of your Internal Customers.)

Product/Service I Provide to Internal Customer #2	Rating of Service Provided: (Exceeding Expectations) (Meeting Expectations) (Needs Improvement)	Comments/Notes/ Observations
How would you rate interactions/ communication with this function?		

Your Internal Suppliers

5. List each department/function within that you believe is your Internal Supplier:
6. Internal Supplier #1: _____
7. List essential processes/products this Internal Supplier provides to you on a regular basis. Rate the quality of work you feel you are receiving:

Product/Service Internal Supplier #1 Provides Me	Rating of Service Provided: (Exceeding expectations) (Meeting expectations) (Needs Improvement)	Comments/Notes/ Observations
How would you rate interactions/ communication with this function?		

8. Repeat steps six and seven for each Internal Supplier on your list. (Use additional tables to include all of your Internal Suppliers.)
9. When completed, please return the forms to the Program Administrator.

Leadership can assign a well-trained internal staff member, or better yet, invite an impartial, external resource, to administer this program and facilitate the process with all of the work functions within the organization, until all stakeholders have participated in the exercise. These are some examples of the departments that should go through this exercise: quality, engineering, manufacturing, procurement, planning, health & safety, compliance, legal, HR, finance, accounting, sales, marketing, shipping-receiving, sanitation, etc.

Whatever your organizational chart looks like, do not leave any functions behind, even those who, at a glance, do not appear well connected with others. The information identified through this company-wide initiative will be used later to construct all the charts to reconcile all of the discovered gaps in the process.

Once all functions have participated in this exercise, Internal Customer/Supplier pairs should be matched up to review their initial self-questionnaires in order to establish the following:

FUNCTION A'S QUESTIONNAIRE:

- Who have they identified as their Internal Customers?
- What kind of product/service do they believe each of their Internal Customers relies on them for?
- How do they rate the services they provide to their Internal Customer?

Then, compare the questionnaire filled out by Function B, identified as the Internal Customer who described Function A as their Internal Suppliers.

FUNCTION B'S RESPONSES:

- Did they name Function A first as an Internal Supplier?
- What products/services do they rely on Function A for? In which order?
- How do they rate the services Function A provides them as their Internal Supplier?

Organizations that I have introduced this tool to have come across some interesting and surprising results. The biggest discovery happens when one department lists another as their Internal Supplier, but the latter never thought to place the former on the map as one of their Internal Customers. Different functions often lack awareness of who within the organization relies on their services and depends on the quality and the timeliness of those inputs.

In addition, various functions fail to recognize that their Internal Supplier might be their Internal Customer too. An engineering department in one manufacturing company identified their reliance on the quality department as an Internal Supplier to complete a timely contract review in order for the engineering team to be able to launch their projects. However, they failed to recognize themselves as the quality department's Internal Supplier too: in order for the quality department to complete the much-needed contract review on time, they relied on the engineering team to provide the original contract on time with all the change orders that customer added to it.

It's fascinating to review those questionnaires in pairs, comparing the results of your self-assessments against your counterparts' ratings for those specific services that the Internal Customer-Supplier relationships are based on. Quite often, Internal Suppliers give themselves a much higher ranking than their Internal Customers do for the same services. This exercise is an eye-opener and an excellent way to begin a dialogue on how to reconcile the two parties' feedback and agree on what actions are needed to close the existing gaps in the quality of those relationships and the deliverables.

Knowing who your Internal Customers and Suppliers are is a prerequisite for building the culture of QIQO. However, this knowledge alone is not enough. To align with the concept of QIQO, we must maintain the high-quality services we provide to our customers. How do you know if you provide quality input to your Internal Customer? We are not usually the best judges of the quality of our products and the value of our processes. The actual definition of what constitutes quality and what adds value is determined by the customer, the client, the user of our processes. Quality is not what you put into in your product. Quality is what the Customer gets out of it. To be a good Supplier, we must understand our Customers, and their needs and expectations really well.

This exercise teaches us the importance of being a good Customer too. Stephen Covey advises: "First seek to understand, then to be understood," in his landmark book, **"The 7 Habits of Highly Effective People"** (Covey, 2013). This simple approach is a great foundation to help people consider other functions in terms of the Internal Customer/Supplier relationships. It's easier to spot your direct Internal Customers and harder to remain aware of those indirectly affected by the quality of our work. The Internal Customer can also be a Situational Customer, depending on your service for a specific time for a specific reason. It can be someone you work for, as well as someone who works for you.

The results of the surveys conducted by teams throughout the organization can be used to develop a company-wide map of Internal Customer/Supplier relationships – using such tools as SIPOC or other similar charts. All of the responses can then be put into a matrix. Once you have your entire team thinking along the lines of Customer/Supplier relationships, it's time to turn this awareness into a permanent part of your company culture, using the methods we discussed earlier to build sustainability.

PERFORMANCE REVIEW AND REWARD

If you abandon the process half-way through or fail to put to good use the incredible information you have gathered from the various functions within your organization, what is going to happen? Everything will revert to the old routine. Why? Because organizations have outdated but familiar procedures, performance review and incentive programs that, by the force of entropy, maintain the status quo. In order for the QIQO culture to establish itself, update your performance review system to incorporate some of the great feedback received from Internal Customers.

Start measuring people on the improvements they make toward delivering excellent, reliable, consistent Customer Service. Review the system periodically. Maintain accountability on all levels. Whatever behaviors you want other people to present, you as a leader should focus on becoming the best example of those behaviors in your own daily actions.

D. HOW TO INSTILL A WINNING CULTURE — A DIFFERENT KIND OF WINNING

Growing up — perhaps as one of the last generations before electronics and technology took over children's minds and lives — my three siblings and I had a favorite game to play. Using any materials, we could get our hands on around the house, we would build entire cities with neighborhoods, schools, hospitals, transportation. Then we would populate these cities with families, made of toy characters of all sorts. We employed numerous sets of Lego-type blocks in our creations, and when we ran out, we used other toys, action figures, dolls, school supplies, and various household items.

The cities we built had elaborate infrastructure, and every household was complete with sets of parents, children, their chores and errands, family dynamics and friendships, visitors and outings, etc. Each of us four children were responsible for a family to take care of. It was up to us to have 'our family' establish relationships with the others. We deeply cared about the civilizations we built; weeks at a time passed, and we managed to keep them intact. Now that I think about it, kudos to the patience our elders showed, as we refused to pick up our toys for so long. Every day, we came back to our characters and resumed playing out their roles. At times, our characters faced complex dilemmas and interpersonal issues to solve. Somehow, every one of us knew the importance of getting along, in order to find, together, the solution to those complicated matters.

Given what's available to children today, the games we played might not seem like much, but they taught us a lot. They taught us to empathize with those in sorrow and to cheer for our neighbors' successes. They taught us resourcefulness, collaboration, and negotiation skills. If someone else had a piece of the puzzle that would perfectly fit in the house, we were building:

> **We learned that cooperation was the only way to get what we needed,
> if we wanted to ensure the sustainability of our made-up cities.**

Early on, my siblings and I learned that there were different kinds of winning. Of course, you could win by hogging the resources of your choice. All you needed to do for that was to arrive early at the scene, and appropriate the best available construction materials to make sure your 'family' got ahead. You could also trick your younger brothers into giving you the items they had in their possession. Sometimes, that actually was tempting, as sibling rivalry kicked in. However, the excitement of being number one and sporting the best houses and cars did not last long when we saw our playmates struggle to keep up, having to make do with less desirable, less plentiful, and more mismatched materials. Playing stopped being as much fun when we won at the expense of others.

We learned through our experiences that finding creative and innovative solutions together was more satisfying and rewarding than putting our energy into ensuring those personal but solo gains. By sharing our knowledge, skills, and the most coveted resources, we helped each other thrive. That way, our games lasted longer, everyone felt appreciated and cared for, and together we came up with more ideas on what other activities we could pursue. This fulfilled us on so many levels. Most importantly, it shaped our criteria for success and solidified our definition of winning.

Despite the external world's focus on only one kind of success (the King of the Hill kind), we seemed to instinctively realize that there are different kinds of winning situations. Short-term results accrue when you hog the best resources, which is very similar to what happens when this approach is applied to workplace benefits. You can climb to the top by taking credit for someone else's work, by throwing your colleagues under the bus, or by throwing a tantrum, perhaps cheating here and there, or appropriating someone else's idea. In all of these scenarios, winning means you must, by default, generate at least one loser.

Another approach is to win through your hard work by building meaningful connections, earning trust, investing in others, and gaining long-term happiness; this is especially possible when you surround yourself with productive and effective people. If we were able to achieve this type of experience as young children, why is it that, so often in our workplaces, we mostly encounter the former scenario, rife with winners and losers?

People who achieve great professional heights at the expense of others do not become winners in the long run; they typically fall from those great heights eventually. The story of Enron Corporation, one of the largest companies in the U.S. at the time, the high flying, well-respected, even envied corporation that disintegrated almost overnight in 2001, teaches us a great lesson on the cost of choosing short-term wins versus long-run success. This story came to represent the epitome of everything that goes wrong in the corporate world when the rise to the top is driven by greed more than anything else.

"Winning isn't the billion-dollar bank account or the private yacht. It isn't walking into a room and striking fear into employees' hearts. It's not about being profiled in Forbes or fawned over on the pages of Wall Street Journal. Winning is… about using the skills and talents you have, to make more of your life and do more for others than you ever thought was possible" (Luntz, 2011).

Where does the competitiveness and the ruthless one-upmanship of today's workplaces come from? Does it have its roots in the human need for hierarchy? Just as humankind's history has taught us, the need for hierarchical life was ingrained in our ancestors' minds as civilizations evolved for thousands of years. Everyone benefited from living in a society that was based on principles of hierarchy. This included even those at the bottom of the totem pole; they had protection from wild animals and hostile tribes, they got to eat and be sheltered. All they had to do in return was to live by the rules of their tribe and to respect authority. Outliers did not live long due to the many dangers of being alone. The more affable types survived and got to pass their genes to the generations to come.

The structure of the hierarchy was supposed to reduce the amount of squabbling between tribe members by introducing order and setting examples of acceptable behavior. Those examples usually came from the top, even though, unfortunately, not all leaders set good examples; this is similar to the case of Enron Corporation. Even in hierarchical organizations, climbing to the top works best when leaders have both *Competence* (the power that comes from acquiring and mastering so-called hard skills: such as subject-specific skills, business acumen, decision making, strategic thinking, and computer technology) and *Character* (the power that comes from possessing and using people skills: caring about others, empowering growth and development, instilling the values of excellence and teamwork). The skills of valuing the people around us and cooperating with them are extremely useful in today's workplaces. While this skill may sound intangible and even fluffy to some, it's solidly backed up by research showing that employees do thrive, and are motivated to contribute more to the goals of the organization when they feel their efforts are recognized.

There are two types of HR practices defined by research: **commitment-based** and **transaction-based**. The *commitment-based* HR approach focuses on the long-term relationship between the employer and the employee, supported by investing in training, developing, and mentoring the employee for their long-term success. Just as the name suggests, the *transaction-based* approach is primarily about compensating the employee for the work they do for the company. As a UK study showed, the commitment-based approach leads to better results: more engaged employees, offering a consistently higher quality of service, and overall improved financial performance (Doke, et al., 2010).

The leaders' primary role is to create a work environment conducive to personal and organizational growth. The best environments are those that allow people to thrive, do their best, and use their talents in the most effective manner. Instead of bogging them down with work they are not good at and do not enjoy, they capitalize on peoples' natural strengths, and provide opportunities for developing their strengths further, so that people can better contribute to the organizational goals. The best leaders are well-liked and supported by the people who choose to follow them. Without followers, there are no leaders.

Instilling a culture of 'a different kind of winning' is, in our current business climate, important for your organization's long-term success. The entire organization wins when the definition of winning does not imply, require, or allow that there must be losers in the game. For the entire organization to *win*, there cannot be any *losers* within it. Since we are examining the organization from a system perspective, the important thing to understand is: for the whole system to win, the consistent support of leadership helps to shore up weak links or develop staff skills, so that underperformers are no longer stuck in jobs that they are unsuited to. The system will always be as strong as its weakest link — as **The Theory of Constraints** teaches us. If one process becomes a bottleneck in the operation, then the whole system is affected and will not operate at optimal capacity.

CHAPTER 8 – CREATING ACCOUNTABILITY IN A NO-BLAME ENVIRONMENT

A. HOW TO CREATE AN ENVIRONMENT OF ACCOUNTABILITY RATHER THAN ASSIGNING BLAME

In my field, I offer a wide variety of employee skills training. *In one situation, while delivering a manufacturing team training session on Root Cause Analysis and Corrective Action, we focused on addressing underlying causes of an identified problem in a truly effective manner. I explained that the RCA must be conducted in a **No-Blame Environment,** where people are not afraid to speak up about any workplace issues, freely share facts, and come forward with their own mistakes, as opposed to sweeping trouble under the rug. During a break, the supervisor of the group took me aside and suggested in private that I "lay off the no-blame environment part" from my content. As he put it, he wouldn't want anything to take away from the credibility of my message, as he was finding the rest of my session highly useful for his team.*

Intrigued by his suggestion, I asked for more input. He agreed to elaborate. Turned out, their work environment was far from being no-blame. In fact, the opposite was true. All the workers, including the supervisor himself, were afraid of management's wrath when it came to any mistakes, incidents, late delivery, property damage, non-conforming outputs, or near misses. As a survival strategy, they tried their best to hide and deny any involvement they may have had with any of the above-listed occurrences. Sweeping problems or mistakes under the rug was a common phenomenon at this workplace. In order to begin to resolve this situation, the conversation had to be taken to different, managerial, levels.

The damage caused by this type of work environment is hard to quantify, but it is, in my research, observation, and opinion, quite serious. If people are hiding valuable information for fear of management using it against them, everyone loses. People miss out on growth opportunities, and the company does not learn any lessons from addressing recurring mistakes. What we don't know, we cannot learn from; thus, no Continual Improvement, no progress, no savings, no getting ahead of the curve.

Instead, the company suffers from stagnation; this stems from unaddressed underlying causes that tend to resurface anytime, any place, and it perpetuates constant reinvention of the wheel, with the consequent added cost of the rework and loss of competitive edge. Even worse, if mistakes are not known, acknowledged, and addressed, people can be hurt or even killed due to lack of awareness and attention. It's certainly not a safe nor sane approach to doing business in a complicated world of regulation, laws, safety measures, especially considering how carefully highly sophisticated machinery and materials must be handled.

Most importantly, there is no real way to hide mistakes. The truth will always surface. How it surfaces is a most urgent concern for a company, in terms of safety and legacy.

No matter what, the tension encountered by company staff, who are stuck balancing the need to tell the truth and the cost of admitting problems, can be quite intense. The conflict arises because management also faces the need to meet the requirements of a positive cash flow and a black ink bottom line. All of the company's processes should support its strategic goals. Individuals and teams working on those processes are responsible for delivering quality outputs and are accountable for things that go wrong. As research indicates, the challenge many workplaces face is determining how to establish a safe and stable work environment where everyone stays accountable for their action or inaction, while seeking to achieve desired results in a non-blaming manner. Is it possible to require lasting quality and hold people accountable, while maintaining a non-threatening environment? Is this a utopian dream, or a potentially profitable reality? Here are some inspiring examples of how this might be possible, to help devise a roadmap for Caring Leadership.

Let's review the two crucial aspects to this process: *Creating Accountability* and *Creating a No-Blame Environment*.

CREATING ACCOUNTABILITY

A Navy commander shared his experience: whatever he produced at work, his superior would check after him, make all the corrections deemed necessary, and leave him out of the loop. As a result, the commander did not feel fully responsible for the quality of his own work. At his next job, it was a big eye-opener for him to have a manager with a completely different attitude: "You have prepared this report; you know what you are doing. Now, where do I sign?" This changed everything. He not only felt a lot more responsible and accountable for his work; he felt respected for his expertise.

To learn accountability, people must feel responsible for their entire task. To set staff up for future success, management must ask questions and plan strategically: explain the intended outcome of the task but ask the employee how they think the goal should be accomplished. If something goes wrong, it is important to avoid asking questions that imply blame. Implying blame will not achieve the desired outcome. Human nature will take over. The employee will not be inclined to think about how to solve the problem at hand; they will be more focused on finding excuses to escape consequences. Instead, ask the kinds of questions that help the person contemplate how the problem occurred, what went wrong, and most importantly, what could be done to prevent a (costly) recurrence in the future. Good leaders include themselves when taking responsibility for what went wrong, while generously giving praise deserved for successful implementation of the task or the deliberate problem-solving effort.

It's helpful to maintain ongoing, two-way communication between leadership and team members. It's also important not to wait for things to go wrong before you talk to your team members. Know what people are working on, take the time to have a quick chat with them to learn what they are accomplishing and discovering. If all goes well, ask about their progress too. If they seem to be struggling, check to see if they need help. Take interest in how they are doing on a personal level too. One of my first managers showed me so much care and appreciation throughout our daily interactions that not only I was inspired to do my very best every day, I was more than happy to step up and put in extra effort any time he asked me to.

KNOW STAFF WORKLOAD AND PRIORITIES

Today's organizations are too complex and often come with multiple reporting channels, and dotted lines across various corporate levels and jurisdictions. For Caring Leaders, it's a must to know your team members' normal workloads and to be in tune with any additional responsibilities that may get thrown at them. You have to be able to step in when needed to bring clarity to ever-changing priorities, the kind that may cause time crunches and schedule conflicts. Knowing your team's workloads and priorities also helps to keep people accountable. In workplaces with multiple reporting channels, especially in larger corporations, it's easy to hide behind a smokescreen of unclarity. Meanwhile, you as the leader are tasked to remain positive about the work being done, and should focus on staying in the zone of constructive feedback about any shortcomings.

KNOW STAFF CAREER OBJECTIVES

With daily operational tasks, it's easy to get swept away into monotony, pushing and moving things day in and day out. In the midst of all the activity, busy managers may overlook the fact that each team member also has their own longer-term career objectives. Original job descriptions evolve, understandably. Challenges arise when the scope of work expands exponentially and resource provision remains static; in this pressure-cooker environment, employees eventually grow to feel used and start experiencing burn out. They may lose trust in their own worth and place in the corporate structure if leadership doesn't help them move toward their specific, unique career goals.

Career goals — just like personal aspirations — unfold differently from person to person, and what's important to one valued team member may not matter to another. However, in a Caring Organization, leadership understands that staff members, especially those who have dedicated so much time to meeting the goals of the company, also require support to move in the direction of their dreams and goals.

If your internal experts spend most of their time performing tasks that are neither inspiring nor challenging them in a meaningful way, while falling far behind with their strategic core actions and personal goals, at some point, the quality of their work will suffer. This will result in poor outcomes instead of providing the far more desirable QIQO type of performance. Leadership can mitigate this by stepping in with creative ways to provide more resources for adequate support.

CONSULT WITH YOUR EMPLOYEES

People like to feel recognized for their knowledge and expertise. Instead of depending upon one-way, top-down communication, ask for their expert opinion and their advice. Hands-on staff know their jobs to a deeper level of detail not always visible to an outsider. If asked, they are able to help establish and document best practices and/or address some of the toughest problems your customer is facing.

CREATING NO-BLAME SYSTEMS

After you have built trust and become more involved in supporting your staff with their career aspirations, you have laid a strong foundation for establishing a **No-Blame System.** In this open and honest environment, your devoted, hardworking people can get support and don't waste their talent and the company's precious time fighting disrupted system flows and inefficiencies. As a part of the accountability structure, assign each team member to take responsibility for the outcomes of a certain work area. This approach works well: certain employees' names and maybe even photos are posted on the wall as a sign of their accountability for a safe, orderly set up at the workstation, a production line, or covering a larger area, as a designated contact person for a 5S type of program.

People take pride in seeing their names on the wall; this increases their sense of ownership, and one side benefit is that people won't mind spending their own time to ensure the excellence of the housekeeping effort, and the safety of the workstation. This way, even if people move around work areas during their shift, they still hold each other accountable to maintain best practices. Why? Because their names were posted on the walls. Accountability partners can emerge in an environment where people are interested in helping each other stay focused on their goals.

When people are given the authority to make higher-level decisions with added responsibility, there is a correspondingly higher risk of making a costly mistake. It's only natural for people to experience an increased fear of failure.

What can help improve team performance and put people's minds at ease when volunteering their ideas needed for decision making? Begin by fostering and supporting leaders who are not afraid to admit their mistakes. It only makes them more human, more relatable in the team's eyes, and provides confidence for other team members to share information regarding their own mistakes.

When you have clearly communicated work objectives in line with your employees' career goals, when you treat your people as experts, talk to them on a regular basis and support them, that's when you have established the foundation for personal accountability. In this kind of structure, you will be able to clearly see who is pulling their weight and who is not. From that point on, any constructive criticism you have for your employees will not be taken as blame, because open, two-way channels of communication have been there all along.

B. UNDERSTANDING THAT OUTPUT QUALITY OR OTHER PROBLEMS AREN'T ALWAYS PEOPLE'S FAULT

Even if leadership puts forth their best efforts to proactively identify and address risks affecting the workplace, things can still go wrong. It could be a customer taking business away from the company for any reason, product non-conforming to requirements, late delivery, a costly workplace injury, or any other unforeseen adversity. When things go wrong, instead of immediately pointing fingers and seeking to assign blame, Caring Organizations carefully investigate the incident through an objective *RCA* process.

RCA is a powerful tool for addressing issues and situations that require resolving. It's never about finding fault; it's about finding facts around an individual case, with the intent to reveal underlying causes contributing to anything from poor design to poor outcome, until the root of the problem is uncovered. A variety of methodologies have been designed specifically to conduct a successful RCA; examples include **8D**, **Fault Tree**, and **PDCA**. (See Chapter 5 for more information.)

The Five Why Method is a foundational tool that supports the PDCA process. This simple tool allows you to ask *Why* after announcing your problem statement. This process allows inquiring minds to peel away layers and layers of superficial causes, such as human errors or faulty oversight by personnel, inviting your team to dig deeper into the underlying causes. The actual number of times the question *Why* is asked does not have to be limited to five. It can be asked as often as needed, until the actual root cause is discovered. To confirm the root cause is in fact the answer to the problem statement, you can test your method by starting at the end and making a series of the *Therefore* statements to see how your answers line up to the original question.

It is advisable to train your team to use these tools regularly, so that they can understand the underlying causes of everyday problems they are facing. Because it is such a simple tool, it can help your team bypass the need to involve a larger group in the problem-solving process. Not every single workplace issue requires a formal investigation. The more autonomy and freedom to investigate their own issue, the stronger your team will grow.

It's also important to teach the team how to investigate issues that may need to be escalated. When the reason for the problem is not clear, there may be a potential for its recurrence. It's also, possibly, an indication of a more serious problem. To allocate resources wisely, the organization will have to decide, on a case-by-case basis, which specific issues qualify for a formal investigation.

Here is a simple example of using the *Five Why Method* correctly. I have demonstrated the concept using this example in my Root Cause Analysis workshops.

PROBLEM STATEMENT: Bob slipped and fell in the plant while performing his regular duties.

1. Why? There was oil on the floor.
2. Why? A nearby machine was leaking oil.
3. Why? A pressure fitting on the machine failed.
4. Why? Inspection of hoses and fittings is not part of the **Preventive Maintenance (PM)** schedule.
5. Why? The PM schedule was not based on equipment manufacturer's recommendations.

CONCLUSION: *An effective corrective action would be reviewing the PM system, revising PM procedures and schedules, retraining PM personnel and other operators, etc.*

If conducted with patience and consistency, the Five Why Approach will reveal the underlying systemic or process issues, often uncovering important understanding that extends beyond the need to blame staff for what looks like a human error. This method is best used face-to-face by the team, not in an automated fashion. It requires a person, or a team of people, to take on responsibility and accountability for resolving the system's error. An impartial approach to dealing with workplace issues can help to build an environment where people feel invited to become a part of the solution, instead of diving down a rabbit hole to avoid punishment.

According to the Quality Management gurus, only a small fraction of workplace issues are caused by people. Depending on which QM guru you follow — Deming, Crosby, or another — anywhere from 80 to 96% of workplace issues are due to management problems; the remaining small fraction is due to human error and other worker problems. Once we understand that the system governs peoples' output, and that management, not workers, are ultimately responsible for the system, choices become much clearer.

The way I explain it is that a majority of working people sincerely want to do a good job. All they need is leadership that supports them and provides systems that allow them to do their job safely and well. The vast majority of problems arise from poor management and ineffective leadership. Even if an RCA shows you that a worker in your organization has a systematic performance or attitude problem, at its root, it's still the problem and responsibility of management that allows the situation to continue in that way.

A famous training tool that illustrates this point is the **Red Bead Experiment**. Created by Dr. Deming in 1982, this experiment introduced a large bowl of beads where white beads (majority) represented good quality material or any desirable things in the workplace. The white beads were mixed with red beads, which represented defective material or problems we experience at work. Participants took on roles: Foreman, Quality Control Inspector, Data Recorder, and **Willing Worker.** The *Willing Worker* represented any worker who wants to do a great job for their employer.

Using a special metal paddle, each Willing Worker drew several beads from the bowl. Each time, they followed the same procedure, but each time they got a significant variation in their results: the undesirable red beads mixed with the good white beads in their paddle. No matter how much the Willing Worker tried, they could not succeed. The system, with its inherent flaws, posed a significant limitation on their performance. A flawed input cannot result in flawless output (redbead.com, 2014).

One of the main lessons this experiment illustrates is that, if the organization does not allow the workers to control the system they are working in, then the workers should not be held responsible for the flawed results they produce. If management expects workers to do a great job, then they must design improvements into the system that people are working with. In other words, when Quality is designed *into* the system and processes, the *outcome* will produce Quality results and performance. This is as good a definition of the QIQO approach as I have found.

In Deming's game, instead of identifying and addressing the root causes behind the presence of the red beads, the employer decided to blame the workers for poor results. Consequentially, the company went out of business. Do you see similarities with this management approach in any of the real-life companies you know? Do you know any teams at your workplace struggling with 'red beads' in their daily operations?

Workers are an essential part of the system. You cannot run your business without people. Well-trained and respected employees can play a critical role in making much-needed improvements. However, it's up to the leadership team to design, establish, and support an open-door policy that encourages people to speak up, try new things, step out from the shadows to improve their own work conditions, learn from their mistakes, ask questions, and share what they have discovered, all without fear of repercussions. This is the inclusive, supportive, intelligent approach Caring Organizations take.

C. HOW TO HELP TURN AROUND UNDER-PERFORMERS

Even if the vast majority of workplace problems do arise from process or system shortcomings, there is always that point in any leader's work life when they must deal with under-performing or flat-out difficult staff members. If problems created by under-performing or difficult people remain unchecked, they will soon affect the rest of the team, and eventually this ongoing difficult situation will lower overall employee morale. Not good for your bottom line or for employee satisfaction.

Let's make it clear upfront that dealing with under-performers and difficult people is different from dealing with mistakes. Anyone can make an honest mistake – it is a natural course of learning and gaining experience. However, if those mistakes become frequent, noticeable, and costly, it's definitely a sign of a situation that needs to be addressed.

No beating around the bush. Other workers who are being affected by the situation will appreciate you dealing with issues in a timely manner.

Let the employee know what you want to talk about, and start by sharing your observations. Ask them what is going on, allow them to explain how they perceive the situation, and listen for their acknowledgment that the issue exists. Create a safe space for them to take responsibility if, in fact, it *is* them. Let them explain what the reasons are, from their perspective.

These are the types of topics you could discuss:

- What is affecting their results?
- Is any other part of the system failing to provide correct and timely input?
- Is there a personal issue that is possibly causing a distraction?

As a Caring Leader, you must ask a lot of questions to understand the underlying cause of the issue. You never know what is going on behind the scenes; you might be surprised by what you learn. If you find yourself making assumptions about the person or digressing into any of their personality issues, ask for support yourself. These are important discussions; having a less-involved witness to hear what you can't might be helpful. Avoid making accusatory 'you' statements – this will only cause the person to shut down or get defensive. Encourage the individual to suggest their own potential solutions to the problem, and offer your support or help.

The root cause could be anything from lack of training or health problems, to unreasonable work expectations and tight schedules. It could also be that a person has outgrown their current position and might be ready to take on new challenges to keep their interest levels up. Then, the responsibility for the next steps ultimately falls on you as a leader, while you do need the employee to be engaged to develop solutions to the problem.

Depending on the situation, solutions will vary too – from offering time off to resolve personal issues, to providing more training in technical or people skills, to expanding or even changing the person's role within the organization. In some cases, accommodating the employee temporarily with flexible work hours or work-from-home options could alleviate stress and raise performance levels. Some roles in organizations are easier to accommodate without requiring the employee's physical presence on the premises.

To me, the best solutions to performance problems are developed when the team member takes part in decision making. Sometimes, you have an otherwise good employee from whom you suddenly start getting an increasing number of errors that cause a waste of organizational resources. This can also lead to a deteriorating relationship with coworkers, who no longer see them as pulling their weight. This may bring down employee morale and affect team performance if not handled correctly.

I once dealt with this exact situation between two employees who were working for me. David felt that the other, Les, was making too many mistakes that jeopardized their project's success. This led to disagreements between the two coworkers. David came to me to complain about Les and share his frustration.

Both were reliable team members and good performers, each offering their own valuable contributions to the company's success, with their own strengths and minor shortcomings. Knowing both of them, I developed a good idea of what the picture looked like. Nevertheless, I brought the two together to discuss the problem in the open, as opposed to having a series of closed-door individual conversations. The three of us went back to the basics of reviewing the project goal, the scope of work, and the original division of responsibilities. We discussed what was working well and what was not. That's when David started listing all the errors Les was making in the final documentation package, an important deliverable at the end of the project that brought together all the material traceability, inspection, and test records.

Knowing our high-end customers, there was no room for error or omissions in the final documentation package. Les did not dispute the argument. Now that everything was in the open, and the end goal of our project was crystal clear, I offered David and Les two options on how we could move forward.

First option: The two of them get together and decide how they want to complete the project, and report back to me.

Second option: I decide for them how to proceed. In proposing this second option, I said I could not guarantee whether or not they would like the decision I made for them.

The team members preferred to come up with their own solution (clearly the best option, the one I hoped they would choose). Given their natural but different strengths — one of them had a better eye for fine detail and the other had more hands-on knowledge of metallurgy and material properties — David and Les decided to reassign their roles in regards to the project, so that each of them could do what they were best at.

End result: Team members solved their own problem, and felt more empowered in taking ownership on properly completing the project they worked on together.

Melrose says that it's hard to see potential in some people, but when we are measuring people, we must measure them right. He reminds us that, even coming from various paths in life, with various professional and educational backgrounds, everyone in the organization, including those who move up the ladder slower than others, have adequate mental aptitude and unique experiences that make their wisdom and perspective valuable. In other words, everyone has something to offer. Melrose calls upon leaders to be more available, spend more time with employees, and learn from them (Melrose, 1995).

Despite the amount of time you spend with your employees, and no matter how carefully you conduct your hiring search, there is a certain percentage of new hires that will inevitably prove to be a managerial mistake. How do you deal with this effectively?

First of all, as a leader, I recommend that you admit to yourself that you made a mistake. The CEO of a Canadian-based international company that I interviewed told me he does not like to resort to firing. He shared how they deal with hiring mistakes: "We like to work with people as much as we can. It's up to the managers to find a better way to work with them. In the first three months of their employment, you can learn a lot about the new hire. We talk to everyone who works with them. If you realize early on that you made a hiring mistake, it's not fair to the person or to the company to keep them aboard. Hopefully, they will find a better fit in the culture of another organization, somewhere else.

However, when it comes to older individuals in your workplace, who you realize do not work well for the company — you should probably have let them go fifteen years ago. When they are in their sixties, they become your responsibility, and you must make it work." So, the conclusion here is:

> ***The earlier we find working solutions for our hiring mistakes, the better it is for all involved parties.***

D. CAN COACHING HELP WITH TOXIC PEOPLE?

Coaching is a great tool to use when addressing workplace issues, including when dealing with toxic people. It can potentially help a toxic person turn around and change their behavior. We must make sure that the message we send is clear. One thing that I personally use in my managerial style is bringing out peoples' better nature. Fortunately, pure evil in people is a rarity. Often enough, the most difficult person has side that is surprisingly human and relatable, and can emerge with the right approach. As soon as I catch a glimpse of that part of someone's personality, I set out to appeal only to that side of their nature and encourage the person to bring it out as much as they can.

One example that personally surprised me was when I had to deal with a Department manager who was a typical My Way or The Highway type. He was known for squashing other people's ideas, for pushing workers to do potentially hazardous tasks, and for displaying vindictive behavior toward anyone who dared to disagree with him. Workers were afraid to confront him. They secretly hated his guts and had no respect for him as a human being. At first glance, there was nothing cooperative or even reasonably relatable about this manager, until I saw him in a situation very different from our everyday work setting. It turned out, he had a soft spot for young children and had a great way of communicating with them! It was eye-opening to observe how he related to our coworkers' children at a company event, how he got them involved in activities in fun and engaging ways, and made them feel appreciated and cared for.

From that point on, whenever I witnessed his back-to-normal, difficult behavior in the workplace setting, I reminded myself of the soft side he had inside him and started appealing to it. Before placing the workers in his crew for their job assignment, I experimented with helping him think of these workers as someone else's children. Would you allow your child to do a task that is less than safe?

This is what I call my One Second test:

Anytime a questionable situation came up — especially when debating whether a task was 100% safe and healthy to perform — I used this test on him. I looked him in the eye and asked "Would you send your child to do this job?" If I saw a momentary hesitation in his eyes, it meant that he had already answered the question without saying a word. However, if he was able to give me a positive answer with zero hesitation, it meant "Yes! We have done our homework – the field is clear." It meant that the job was safe to do for his or anyone else's child.

This might sound too simplistic, but in this case, appealing to someone's better nature did work. I encourage you as workplace leaders to try and find one positive trait in your most difficult people, and see if you can create an environment conducive to bringing it out.

TOXIC CONDUCT

When it comes to dealing with difficult or toxic people, there is no magic pill that works to help everyone rise to expected performance levels. Expanding and changing roles may even lead to the discovery of up-til-now hidden talents and previously unused strengths. It would be great if this was always a successful strategy, but truth be told, coaching does not work in all situations.

Sometimes former superstars have peaked in terms of reaching their potential within your organization. You can tell when they are heading downhill; when you see this, admit to yourself that it's time to acknowledge that they clearly need to move on. There may be those who had been known for doing well, but now are just getting by, resting idly on their previously earned laurels.

Sometimes, there are people who are not interested in getting help to improve their performance. Even though we want to believe that every single person is worthwhile, some are not committed to the goals and values of the team.

Some are not only difficult to manage but also flat-out toxic. They display various types of destructive or negative behavior patterns in the workplace, and all of them are disruptive to the normal course of work, counterproductive to the progress the company intends to make, and, most importantly, they introduce a kind of energy that effectively deteriorates employee morale.

Seeing someone get away with disrespecting or disregarding company values and policies demotivates the rest of the staff, and eventually brings down productivity. However, before calling out a certain behavior as toxic, it is important to proactively define what toxic behavior means in your workplace, so there is no room for subjectivity or bias. How can you accomplish this admittedly delicate task?

Let's say that as a Department manager or a workplace leader, you point out to an employee that they are taking over every discussion, constantly interrupting their coworkers in meetings, asking questions but choosing to neither listen to nor believe the answers provided. You note that, as a result, their peers feel mistrusted and undervalued. In response, the employee does not acknowledge responsibility. Instead, they take a highly defensive and somewhat misguided stance: "Oh, I see! You never want me to bring up safety, then!" The employee persists in declaring that this is exactly what they are getting out of the discussion, and then announces their intention to proceed to spread the word that "Everyone who brings up safety around here will be shown the door."

Pretty much every company has an Employee Handbook that describes the main company policies, including those behaviours that call for zero-tolerance in actions such as bribery or harassment. Leadership has to clearly communicate the consequences of violating those policies. Your organization's criteria for considering someone toxic to your work environment could include such actions as deliberate violation and disregard of company policies. With a step-by-step, progressive disciplinary approach that management follows carefully in case of a breach, the outcome is dictated by the seriousness of a single issue, or the repetitive nature of the violation.

WHEN TOXIC BEHAVIOR TURNS TO THREATS AND BULLYING

Even though there is great benefit to be found by training all managers to be supporting coaches, even the best coach cannot turn around every troublesome situation. Some require a more elevated approach. For handling workplace bullying and harassment cases, it's important to have documented policies and procedures that explain the legal definitions, outline the process for reporting, and identify the parties responsible for investigation and action. The procedures and training materials must be based on and in compliance not only with the company policies but also all applicable local and federal legislation.

To minimize, if not eliminate, the need to rely on those procedures after the fact, workplaces must educate everyone as soon as they come on board as to what constitutes bullying and harassment, emphasizing clearly that this behavior is not welcome. This firm stance has become especially timely in today's culturally diverse workplaces, where people who come from drastically different backgrounds can bring misunderstandings and prejudice into the company environment. What is the norm in one culture can be completely out of the ordinary in others; what is only frowned upon in one jurisdiction could be illegal in another.

Once clear expectations of acceptable and desirable behavior throughout the organization are set, as company leaders you need to reinforce those expectations often. Pay attention, and facilitate in-depth discussions on the concerns of the company as a whole, and team members in particular. The more clarity and consistency in delivering these expectations, the more likely it is that employees consistently honor company values. Your role, and best strategy, is to consistently and regularly recognize those who show their commitment to the values through their daily actions. Leaders themselves should provide an example of practicing the company culture that, above all, values people, appreciates their differences, and honors their intrinsic worth as well as their education, skill, talent, and dedication.

E. WORKPLACE RESPECT IS A TWO-WAY STREET

When you witness toxic behavior from your management team members, address it immediately, with full force. People do catch on, sooner or later, to any double standards.

I worked with a Department manager who completely terrorized her entire team. She controlled every single piece of communication between them; people were 'trained' on when they were allowed to speak, and when they had to remain silent. They were reprimanded for their choice of words when formulating their requests for each other or their manager. They were afraid to ask questions, because she would yell at them for not asking the question correctly. Then, there were times when they were penalized for not asking a question when they should have. There was no way to get anything right on her watch. Yes, the department met their monthly quota, most of the time, but how exactly they got there was completely missed in the process.

This behavior was allowed to continue for too long, because of the perception on behalf of the employer that someone with this manager's skill-set was hard, if not impossible, to replace. This head-in-the-sand approach is not effective, to say the least. After losing more and more of their valued team members, and after a few truly ugly workplace incidents, the company finally recognized who was the common denominator in all of those instances. Only after taking the head-on approach to the root cause of the issue, the company was able to improve the work environment and with it, employee morale.

Your organization must communicate its values with crystal clarity to every team member, starting with those in leadership roles. Stand behind your words, and back them up with your daily decisions and actions. Explain to your management team the benefits of living by your publicly stated values and building together a strong Caring Workplace Culture. Equally important, explain the consequences of knowingly violating the company values. No, the ends do not justify the means, and if those means go against the Workplace Culture, they do much more harm than good.

To remove any room for subjective interpretations when it comes to acceptable behavior norms *vs.* what cannot be tolerated, you can immediately draw a line between the expectations for *negotiable* and *non-negotiable* behaviours. One way to do that is to publish examples of those behaviours in a highly visited area and your Employee Handbook.

Below are some good examples of conflict-causing behaviors as spelled out by authors Jean Blacklock and Evelyn Jacks in their book, ***"Get Your People to Work Like They Mean It!"*** (Blacklock and Jacks, 2006).

NEGOTIABLE BEHAVIOURS	NON-NEGOTIABLE BEHAVIOURS
Failure to Listen	Bullying
Generalizations	Harassment
Inappropriate Assurances	Unscrupulous Behavior to 'Get Ahead'
Defensiveness	Twisting Stories, Blaming Others
Overstatements	Aggressiveness, Need to Control
Ignorance of Cultural Differences	Discrimination
Taking Credit	Stealing and Other Unethical Behaviors

One thing to keep in mind is that while values and guiding principles tend to remain stable for longer periods of time, actual examples of *acceptable* and *unacceptable*, *negotiable* and *non-negotiable behaviour* is a more fluid concept that may change more frequently. Common and acceptable workplace behaviours of the past, in many cases, have become less and less acceptable in more recent times. For example, in the 1990s it was more common for a person in power to start and win most workplace conflicts, regardless of what the actual disagreement was about. In the 2020s, that dominance and control tactic is no longer tolerated, and is now considered quite toxic. Every team member has a much stronger voice to address this type of situation.

Once your workplace has adopted and communicated acceptable norms of behaviour, in support of your company's values and based on your company's guiding principle, it should be easy to call it out when these unacceptable behaviors surface among team members, including the leaders themselves. Allowing toxic behavior to persist, and allowing a toxic person to stay regardless of the issues it is causing in the workplace, is a sign of a backward mentality that sets up your entire workplace for failure. If the toxic behavior has gone too far, it is no longer the toxic person's problem – it's clearly a problem with the management or the system.

The excuses management makes for keeping a toxic person on board can vary widely. One of the most common I have seen in use is the scarcity of skilled labor in the market, and therefore the need for technical skills the toxic employee offers. Usually, this problem is more perceived than real. No matter how depleted the labor market seems to be, one unaddressed toxic person can bring the morale of the entire team down. You are running the risk of losing more of your skilled labor. Besides, as discussed in the previous chapters, technical skills are easier to teach than the so-called soft skills of having the right personality for being a team player and getting along with people.

If a team member is tagged as toxic, it means that management has gone through the entire process, having diligently tried and exhausted its resources to solve the situation. If your team has followed all of the steps prescribed by your company policy, and the toxic situation still has not turned around, it is definitely time to move on and let the difficult employee go. It is always the last resort to terminate employment, but there comes a point when you know that by letting the toxic person go, you are doing a great favor, not only to the company, but also to the person. This must be the wrong place for them.

CHAPTER 9 – THE BENEFITS OF CREATING A CARING WORKPLACE – A PROUD LEGACY TO LEAVE BEHIND

A. REINFORCE AND DISCUSS YOUR COMPANY'S WHY AND ITS VALUES WITH BOTH EMPLOYEES AND CUSTOMERS

Let's go back to the original question we asked at the beginning of this book: What matters most for your company's success? Is it the culture of the organization? Culture includes many things – the environment in which people work, what's considered acceptable behaviour, what drives the action and supports decision making, etc. Every organization's culture is unique, dictated by the varying backgrounds of the people who work there, each of whom contributes elements of their own rich, individual culture. What unites all of those individual cultures, aligns it at all levels, defines it as a whole, and upholds what the company stands for – is the **Mission**. A clearly articulated **Mission Statement** explains to the audience the purpose of the organization, the reason why it exists.

And then there is **Vision**. The *Vision* articulates the desirable future state your organization intends to head towards; it's a roadmap to help your people understand where they are going. Some organizations have one of the two in place, but not both. That's ok. It's not necessary to bog yourself down trying to perfectly nail both, as long as you have crafted and shared a powerful statement that supports your **Purpose** in a way that encourages your people to rally up behind it.

WHAT A CLEARLY DEFINED MISSION AND VISION CAN DO FOR YOUR ORGANIZATION

View your *Mission* and *Vision* in terms of your company's *Why*. Why does your organization do what it does, and why do you care about it? An organization's *Why* usually embodies the strong purpose that motivates its leaders. For every great *Mission Statement*, for every *Vision*, the *Why* contains the *Purpose*, backed by **Core Values**, those inner commitments, touchstones, and beliefs that light your company's path, and that will transcend time. The *Core Values* will remain stable as priorities change to meet new challenges. Change is inevitable, but is usually unexpected and cannot be planned for. The clearly articulated Core Values help everyone who is involved to focus on the way your company plans to navigate uncertain times.

Great visions are described with image-based words. One of the strongest visions in history was painted by Winston Churchill in his famous speech *We Shall Fight on the Beaches,* delivered to the House of Commons of the Parliament of the United Kingdom on 4 June 1940. In this speech, recognized as one of the most powerful speeches of World War II, Churchill effectively used imagery to rally the citizenry behind the cause he was promoting.

> *"We shall go on to the end,*
> *we shall fight in France,*
> *we shall fight on the seas and oceans,*
> *we shall fight with growing confidence and growing strength in the air,*
> *we shall defend our Island, whatever the cost may be,*
> *we shall fight on the beaches,*
> *we shall fight on the landing grounds,*

*we shall fight in the fields and in the streets,
we shall fight in the hills;
we shall never surrender."*

The Vision Churchill shared described the intention of his call to action vividly and in relatable detail, as opposed to using more generic terms description (for example: we will defeat our enemy on all fronts). This made a huge difference in the response of the British people to his **Call To Action.**

Vision Statements that don't remain vividly at the forefront of team members' minds tend to fail; this is due to a lack of clarity and inability to personally relate. The more clearly the Vision is defined, the easier it is for the organization to rally people behind it. If team members understand, relate to, and can 'see' the point of the Vision and the Mission, they are more likely to take needed and appropriate action to bring the Vision into reality, or to accomplish the Mission.

Another well-known example of a crystal-clear *Vision Statement,* one that made it possible to take massive action, supported by the entire country, is the vision that U.S. President John F. Kennedy communicated to a special session of Congress on May 25, 1961:

"To put man on the Moon and safely bring him back home by the end of the decade."

Bold and ambitious, this statement nevertheless described Kennedy's vision in simple, clear words, with a specific deadline – before the decade ended. As with every strong, well-described Vision, *a burning platform* behind it served both as an inspiration and a powerful catalyst for a change in focus for the entire country. In this case, the burning platform was the pressure the American people felt after the Soviet cosmonaut Yuri Gagarin became a global sensation as the first human being to travel to outer space in April 1961.

Kennedy's clearly articulated Vision Statement inspired several NASA missions, one of which, Apollo 11, accomplished the goal of landing Neil Armstrong on the surface of the Moon on July 20, 1969 – just before the decade ended, just as the U.S. president had envisioned. Even though President Kennedy did not live to see the fulfillment of his Vision, his ability to catalyze action was profoundly effective in sparking the project that eventually succeeded so magnificently.

GOALS ARE BORN OF CLEAR MISSION AND VISION

Mission and Vision Statements provide the basis for setting out **Goals**, which help define the current and future course of the organization. The best Mission and Vision Statements describe vividly not only what benefit the people of your organization will receive from their achievement, but also how other peoples' lives will be affected, in positive and appealing ways. I would like to underline again that people like to know what is in it for them.

MAKING DECISIONS BASED ON VALUES AND MISSION

It is not possible to write a company policy or work instructions that cover every scenario employees will face in the course of their work; we rely on people to possess appropriate personal and internal values that will guide them. Leaders of QIQO organizations put focused effort into consistently instilling the organization's values in people, continually communicating those values, and most importantly, publicly and privately serve as the living examples of those values.

Some organizations establish the order of those Values, which can be especially helpful in situations where an employee may encounter a potential conflict of Values. How does the leadership team ensure that all employees know which Value takes priority? For example, what do you do if you must choose between satisfying a customer or upholding a company policy? What if maintaining a production schedule means sacrificing quality? People encounter these choices all the time during the course of their work efforts. Since it is impossible for leadership to explain and manage every preferred choice due to the volume of situations employees encounter, team members can greatly enhance organizational effectiveness and efficiency if they are able to act on their own to resolve questions or conflicting priorities.

In *"Go Team!: Take Your Team to the Next Level"*, Ken Blanchard offered a real-life example of a company that encountered confusion over the order of their organizational values (Ken Blanchard, et al., 2007). As a part of a team training, the CEO of a **Health Maintenance Organization (HMO)** posed a dilemma to his management team; he asked them whether or not they would choose to cover an operation needed to save a life of one of their policy holders, if such an operation was not included in the coverage.

The management team broke into small groups to discuss the dilemma and came up with varying suggestions. Some thought it was the right thing to do to cover the operation to save a life, while others pointed out that the company would go broke if it started covering items outside of its boundaries. The CEO admitted that he was both surprised and saddened by this outcome. He said he had been convinced that the entire management team would know that their company would not allow a person to die under such circumstances. However, he learned a valuable lesson on the importance of ensuring that all team members are crystal clear on **Organizational Values**.

The Walt Disney Company has explicitly established the order of the priorities they believe in. Disney takes pride in providing each guest with unforgettable experiences; this value is instilled in every one of their employees. On stage or backstage, cast members are trained on four key values to creating this experience: **Safety, Courtesy, Show,** and *Efficiency*, in this particular order. I had the privilege of witnessing the results of this training at Disneyland California. A cast member wearing a character costume was being *Courteous*, taking photos with guests, and bringing delight to young children, when he heard a scream from a nearby crowd of visitors. The cast member immediately ran in that direction. This was a display of *Safety* coming before *Courtesy*.

Courtesy is important when it's business as usual, but when there is a risk of someone being hurt or injured, Courtesy takes a back seat, and the priority value of Safety takes precedence. When the order of priority is clearly defined, it's easier for employees to make the right decisions, even when facing tricky or complicated situations, especially when they must act fast.

In their book *"The Real-Life MBA"*, authors Jack and Suzy Welch suggest replacing the word *Values* with the term **Behaviours**, because *Behaviours* seems to pertain more to action, which serves as an organizational mechanism to reinforce the Mission and the Values. It's important to keep in mind what Behaviours we project, ourselves, as leaders, and what Behaviours we promote and reinforce in others in our workplace.

The authors introduced the concept of **Consequences** as another element critical to a company's long-term success. While the Mission pinpoints an organization's destination, and Behaviors describe ways of thinking, feeling, communicating, and acting to fulfill that Mission, *Consequences* are designed to "put some teeth into the system."

Consequences are not necessarily negative repercussions on staff who fail to stick with the Values and Behaviours that lead to fulfilling the Mission. Instead, Consequences can be inserted into standard business practice as positive reinforcements of exemplary behaviors, like promotions and bonus systems, that are clearly offered and described, to encourage employees who embrace and advance the Organizational Mission through their aligned behaviors. I believe in establishing mechanisms with built-in consequences, as the Welches define them, to foster a culture of accountability, reinforcing behaviors consistent with supporting the company mission, while simultaneously keeping the company values alive.

Organizations that operate under the principle of QIQO would ideally establish a system that allows all employees to start out on the right foot. As soon as a new hire joins the organization, they receive documents and training that provide an outline of clearly articulated, desired Goals, Behaviors, and Consequences, ensuring clarity from the start: If expectations are well explained up-front, reinforced periodically through leadership examples and public recognition, and if misaligned actions are dealt with in a timely manner, organizations will find they have reduced mis-hires, misfires, and mistakes. This will adequately support their progress in the right direction.

FINDING INNER AND OUTER ALIGNMENT, WITH OUR WHY

The best alignment is achieved when both the organization and its employees are on the same page with their *Why* statements. Our personal *Why* is the reason behind our actions. As discussed, organizations have their own *Why* as well.

Is it possible for organizations and their employees to align their actions together in terms of their *Why's*? An organizational performance consultant I know worked with a company to help its employees identify their *Why* in life. As an outcome of the consultant's work, a number of employees who discovered their *Why* ended up leaving that workplace. We cannot expect that every employee's personal *Why* will always align with that of the organization. In fact, those with the strongest *Why* of their own will often go on to establish their own company.

Everybody has their own motivations for working where they work. At the end of the day, they are mostly there to make a living. All of us are in different stages of our personal evolution. (See Maslow's Hierarchy of Needs in Chapter 2.) Some clearly have invested more time and effort to develop examined lives than others; these individuals are more determined to find their *Why*. They are the ones who care to be in a career that is not only most closely aligned with their best skills and talents, but who also seek work that is fulfilling on many other levels. These are the people looking for their *calling*, people who don't want to spend their life doing things just because they *can*. To them, that is tantamount to stealing time from what they are born to do.

Start-up companies tend to populate themselves with people who have examined lives. If these people deeply believe in the company's *Why*, and it resonates with their own goals and aspirations, they will not object to the long hours, and they'll willingly bear the brunt of heavy workloads... as long as they feel the work they do is aligned with their *Why*. For example, Elon Musk, founder of the Tesla Company, is someone doing what he loves despite the intensity and complexity of the challenges. At the same time, every organization also has plenty of employees who are there just to earn a living, while their true interests lie outside of work, and many of them are quite happy keeping things that way. Then there are people who show up at work to fill their shift, get paid, go home, have a beer, watch a game, or spend the time with their family. If you push them to find their *Why*, the only effect it will have is to annoy them.

Recognizing that it is a given that most companies employ a wide range of individuals with distinctive lifestyles, preferences, ways of thinking, and personal path, the best employers can do is to locate individuals whose Personal Values are aligned with the Company's Values, to encourage employee growth and development, while doing what is possible to reduce any conflict or effect on their peoples' lives. Employment can be fulfilling and even enjoyable, for a variety of people, if the Company Values don't clash with the employees' Core Values. If there is a clash of values, it's not a good match, and it's best for the employee not to work there.

The possibility exists that there could be a clash with the very products the company manufactures. For example, industries like pharmacology or tobacco might be an unhealthy environment to work in for a person whose personal values do not align with the sale of those products. There isn't one perfect organizational culture nor is there a universal set of values that work harmoniously for all, in every single case.

For example, the Lululemon culture, known for its pursuit of greatness, is not for everyone. However, they've managed to hire mostly the right people who are into that kind of culture, the kind of people who would like to contribute to the company goal and feel good about it. This is an example of what works in corporate hiring strategies.

Caring Organizations encourage people to grow and evolve to the degree they want to rise to. They ensure that their Company Vision and Mission are clearly defined and effectively communicated to all levels inwardly and outwardly. Caring Organizations stay relevant by understanding that priorities change as times change, but Core Values (mostly) maintain that stability, serving as a moral compass. Caring Organizations make sure that as many people as possible understand not only the direction they are headed in, but their Value Chain – their competitive advantage. Everybody needs to know what they, as individuals, and as a company, add as a Value to the product or service, so they can ensure their customers want to continue paying for it and want to continue coming back.

B. BUILDING A CULTURE OF SOCIAL RESPONSIBILITY WHERE PEOPLE ARE PROUD OF THE BRAND THEY REPRESENT

For a long time, showing *Corporate Social Responsibility (CSR)* was considered a sign of a corporate culture that goes above and beyond. In today's world, that's no longer the case. With reports of numerous environmental and human rights violations around the globe, and especially in light of multiple global, financial, economic, and health crises, the line previously drawn between matters of ethics and matters of law has shifted. Actions of powerful world leaders, the mighty organizations they stand behind, and the corporate environment as a whole, prompt us to reconsider our approach towards CSR.

The concept of **Social Responsibility** originated in the late 1880s, when an American industrialist and philanthropist Andrew Carnegie encouraged other wealthy people to support social causes. Inspired by Carnegie, John Rockefeller, another business titan, donated over half a billion dollars, an astronomical sum at that time. One of his projects was the foundation of the Sanitary Commission, with a long-term goal of eradicating hookworm disease across the southern United States (History.com Editors, 2010).

In the early 1900s, a banker from Cleveland, Ohio formed the first Community Foundation to collect donations from multiple sources to support societal causes (clevelandfoundation100.org). In the 1940s, such well-known names as The Hershey Company and Johnson & Johnson stepped forward, and, for the first time, corporations began donating their funds instead of individual business owners setting up private foundations. In 1953, Howard Bowen, an American economist, dubbed the *Father of CSR,* connected the responsibility of businesses to society in his book, **"Social Responsibilities of the Businessman."** In the early 1970s, the *concept of the social contract between businesses and society was declared by the Committee for Economic Development in 1971 (accprof.org).*

The *Social Contract* outlines three essential corporate business responsibilities. These responsibilities are still considered valid today:

- Provide jobs and grow the economy;
- Run the business fairly and honestly towards employees and customers;
- Engage in improving the conditions of the community and environment in which it operates.

An organization can call itself a good corporate citizen by donating to charities that bring positive change to the surrounding community. At the same time there is a problem with limiting CSR to charity. The problem is that a charitable cause, no matter how worthwhile it is, is usually something outside of your business. You donate to it, you believe you have made your contribution, and you go back to minding your own business.

The reasons why a company donates in the first place are also important. Did you donate to feel good about yourself? Did you find yourself under pressure from society? Or maybe, which sadly is the case with some organizations, you donated for tax relief purposes. Sometimes a company donates to charity, but it's unclear whether they care about the cause at hand or even about society at large.

One example is J.C. Penney, a U.S. department store chain. Known for its donations to charities that support children and youth, such as Boys and Girls Clubs of America and America's Military Youth, this company, at the same time, was named in an internationally reported workplace disaster in 2013. Along with clothing manufacturers such as Benetton, Mango, Walmart, J.C. Penney had contracted with a provider for clothing manufacturing at Rana Plaza, located in Dhaka, Bangladesh.

Rana Plaza was an office building illegally converted into an industrial facility to house not one, but five factories. The building collapsed, killing or severely injuring thousands of its workers. A few corporations behind this disaster made a pledge to put their funds together to support the families of those victims; J.C. Penney did not contribute. As reported by Clare O'Connor in Forbes Magazine, instead, the corporate managers focused on finding reasons why they should not be held responsible for what was happening in their supply chain (O'Connor, 2014).

The question that remains to be answered is: How do donations to domestic charitable organizations balance out against disregard to the health, safety, livelihood, and well-being of workers conveniently sequestered out of sight, often overseas where laws and safety measures are easier to circumvent. From a systems perspective we can understand that all of us are parts of a larger system. Made of interconnected and interdependent parts, often located outside of the immediate geographical community as well, this fact can be easily overlooked if we take an 'out of sight, out of mind' attitude.

Caring Organizations aspire to be good corporate citizens, accountable to everyone involved in and affected by their operations, including a vital component – the supply chain. Hard questions must be asked using this perspective. Where are your goods coming from? Maybe there is child labor involved, perhaps human exploitation, a regular violation of building codes or occupational health and safety regulations, or perhaps there is a disregard for the environment? The collapse of that 8-story building in Bangladesh not only killed or injured thousands of people, it affected the environment as well. CSR is not about a good public relations show, it's about truly caring for everyone – from corporate staff to store employees, to the ones laboring to create all the nice things customers want to purchase.

During the two decades of my career in Quality, Occupational Health & Safety, Environmental and Risk Management, in the U.S. and Canada, I witnessed many laws and regulations come into effect that cover most of the issues discussed above. When a new regulation is accepted, the government gives businesses a grace period to prepare for the change and to get into compliance. The tension between governmental regulations and concern for all involved can cost a great deal, and corporations who want to stay in business must tend to their bottom line, as profit is the measure upon which success and viability are based.

However, simply complying with all applicable regulations does not make you a socially responsible organization. Truly Caring Organizations go beyond the bare minimum imposed by the law. They commit to ethical behavior; they seek a healthy balance between their needs and the needs of society. Most definitely, Caring Organizations do not take away from the well-being of future generations.

Businesses engaged in unethical practices run the risk of alienating their customer base. According to Cone Communications & Echo 2017 Research, 88% of Americans said they would boycott companies engaged in irresponsible business practices, and 87% would buy a product with a social or environmental benefit. When price and quality are equal, over 90% of shoppers worldwide are likely to switch to brands that support a good cause. According to a recent study by Nielsen, a global measurement and data analytics company, 66% of customers are willing to pay more for the same products and services to do business with more ethical and responsible companies (McCaskill, 2015).

These numbers speak louder than any words. Simply selling good quality products or services is no longer sufficient. CSR is no longer optional nor is it just a nice thing to do when you feel like doing it. The concept of CSR has evolved into an essential part of doing business.

SERVING CUSTOMERS OR SOCIETY?

When it comes to the outside world, corporations have two main purposes. While the first purpose is to serve customers, the second is the corporation's responsibility to society. Which purpose is more important? There is nothing wrong with putting your customer first – after all, customers are the reason why we are in business today, so long as we also remember and respect our obligations to society at large, including to the environment. How can we successfully balance both of these purposes?

One example of a corporation successfully engaging in this balancing act is Nissan Motors. Nissan's corporate goal is their commitment to their customers to have zero fatalities in Nissan cars. In 2018, Nissan sold 5.65 million vehicles (Tajitsu, 2019). While every year approximately 1.25 million people die around the world in car accidents, Nissan has committed to achieving a goal of zero deaths inside their cars (ASIRT, 2019). That's why they focus on the latest intelligent technologies: to ensure that level of safety for their product. The frequency of car accidents that involve older drivers led to one of the initiatives Nissan has announced: advanced driver assistance technology. At the same time, they are fully aware of the environmental impact of driving vehicles. Nissan's second major goal is to reduce their carbon footprint by focusing on design and manufacturing, aiming to lower exhaust emissions and build more fuel-efficient vehicles (Nissan Motor Corporation, 2015).

Nissan's CSR program is focused on building a zero fatality/zero emissions society. An important ingredient to their program's success is raising employee awareness by keeping them up to date on the latest available knowledge via intranet. Nissan does this by compiling knowledge and building the skills of their frontline employees on CO_2 emission reduction, water conservation, and waste and landfill reduction in best practices manuals shared globally within the corporation. They hold contests to motivate their people to participate in environmental activities, tying participation to annual performance goals. Their people are an important part of their sustainability program. This is the story Nissan is telling the world about their brand.

WHAT CAN YOU DO? SHARING YOUR STORY

Every corporation has a brand story they share with the world. Most frequently, they do so through their marketing departments, PR campaigns, Social Media platforms, or perhaps through messages from the CEO that are shared with the press. With fierce competition vying for the public's eyes and ears, there is a cost to convincing customers that your brand is the best. Besides, it's essential to take into account the skepticism people maintain when it comes to believing marketing campaigns, commercials, and advertisements. If people don't have much trust in official channels that put great effort and expense into communicating their brand story, then who can they trust? As the *2014 Edelman Trust Barometer* shows, people tend to believe your employees' words as opposed to your CEO's message (Edelman, 2014).

Your employees play an important role in what the world gets to hear about your brand. Think about your organization – all of its internal and external stakeholders affected by your business practices. What is your commitment to them, and what kind of story do you want the world to hear about your brand? How can you emphasize your CSR program internally, aiming towards empowering your employees, and building trust with your customers, your suppliers, your audience?

Employees, whether we like it or not, talk to the world all the time. At work they talk to your customers, outside of work they talk to the public, some of whom could become your customers. When employees are confident in the quality of your products, believe in the goodness of your company, and take pride in their job, they speak highly of your brand and share the best story possible! When your employees' words are consistent with your organization's PR message, that's the most winning combination; it's called Branding From the Inside Out.

As business leaders, how do you turn your employees into your brand ambassadors?

For one thing, you need to understand who your prospective employees are and what they are looking for in a workplace. In today's workplaces, the largest cohort consists of the Millennials, who in 2020 made up 50% of the global workforce, according to the *Millennials at Work, Reshaping the Workplace* report published by PWC Global (pwc.com, 2011).

Millennials are looking for more than a paycheck, and they are pretty vocal about their expectations from their prospective employers. According to 2016 research by Cone Communications, three quarters of Millennials consider a company's social and environmental commitment when deciding where to work. They want to know their employer has values they can align with; they expect those values to be reflected in the organization's internal behaviors and to be supported by the leadership team through daily decisions and actions (Cone Communications, 2016).

To attract and retain the types of employees who will help take the company to the next level, Caring Organizations embrace a CSR culture at the heart of their brand as an employer. They seek a solid link between the causes employees care about and what the organization can stand behind. Successfully incorporating social responsibility into the organization's culture is linked to improved sales and operational performance.

In their 2018 book, *"The Purpose Revolution,"* John Izzo and Jeff Vanderwielen highlight an excellent example of a workplace leader who understood this concept and implemented it in practice to transform her workplace. A Body Shop location in Vancouver, B.C. was consistently under-performing, with disengaged staff and low sales. A new store manager was assigned to this location with the task of revitalizing it. She could have tried pushing employees to go after customers, to sell more. Instead, she chose to get to know her team better and to learn what they truly cared about.

Turned out, her employees were concerned with the growing epidemic of AIDS (Izzo & Vanderwielen, 2018). During this time, decades ago, AIDS rates raged seemingly unstoppably around the world, infecting and killing millions.

The store team decided to volunteer together to do something good for society; their own concerns were being addressed in a way that brought camaraderie and meaning to their work. Through this experience, they engaged in learning opportunities and acquired more confidence, while seeing how their actions made a difference. That attitude translated beautifully into enhancing their workplace experience. Engaging with more customers increased the sales numbers, and the store became one of the top performers in the chain. All because one manager cared to learn what her employees valued, and supported the cause they cared about. This is a great example of taking social responsibility and turning it into profit.

BUILDING A CULTURE OF SOCIAL RESPONSIBILITY

The case can be made repeatedly: company leadership plays an important role in building a culture of social responsibility. But how? Start by formulating a CSR strategy that is right for your organization, one that aligns with the core of your business and considers all of the key stakeholders affected by your operation. Start the conversation with the **Triple Bottom Line** in mind. The *Triple Bottom Line* is about People, Economy and Environment. The table below provides examples of causes you and your leadership team might wish to consider.

SOCIAL	ECONOMIC	ENVIRONMENTAL
Gender equality	Send a team of experts to help a struggling NGO	Switch to laptops over desktop; save energy
Embrace acceptance/stand against intolerance (religious or other)	Collect food for victims of natural disasters or poverty	Choose teleconferencing instead of in-person meetings when possible

Creativity and communication are essential to develop a coherent plan around weaving CSR into your operation. It is important to choose a cause that resonates with your leadership team and aligns with your company's vision to sustain the culture you are initiating. Employees are great sources of creative ideas. Set up a survey or use a suggestion program to collect those options. Take a handful of employees who demonstrate the most socially responsible focus, and use their help to generate enthusiasm and excitement in the rest of the team. Recognize efforts and commitment to the right values. Remember about making responsible hiring choices: instead of selecting a candidate based only on their professional and academic achievements, focus on the entire individual. Learn what kind of values they have and how they would fit into your organization's culture of CSR.

Social Responsibility is often linked to large corporations; in fact, most of the examples I used in this book are based on large corporate efforts. The larger the corporation, the more it can afford to invest in CSR, the bigger the impact it makes on the larger society, positive or negative, and the higher its media profile. As a result, we end up hearing more about them. Effective CSR is in no way limited to big name brands though. Small and medium size enterprises are also responsible to those affected by their operations. They too are now being called to build a culture of CSR pertinent to the size, the scope, and the purpose of their business. No one is too big or too small to have a social responsibility program, and to take action in whatever way we can. All of us are compelled to take action, as business leaders, professionals, and individuals.

Investing in CSR is a big part of building a culture of excellence; the QIQO culture is only effective if you commit appropriate resources and strong support to sustain it. Leadership has to live and breathe this culture for it to work. People will buy into this culture only if they believe that their leadership is truthful about it and is trustworthy.

C. WHERE DO WE GO FROM HERE, AND HOW?

As I was writing the last chapter of this book, something unanticipated happened. A global event with severe consequences that has, for now and the foreseeable future, left no aspect our lives untouched – health, social, cultural, economic, political, professional, and personal. As if we are all participating like characters in an apocalyptic movie out of Hollywood, an unfortunately all-too-real pandemic emerged as a virus called COVID-19 rapidly spread to most countries and continents.

It became the top-breaking news in the whole world in March 2020, and has continued to maintain its status as such over a year later; there is no indication that this situation will fade away soon. As the virus unveiled its deadly powers, the world watched in disbelief, first as a news story on a distant outbreak elsewhere in the world. Then, the spread of the virus crept closer and closer, until its repercussions became very personal, affecting nearly everyone's town, local gym, shopping mall, neighbourhood, or family. Even people in remote areas are acquiring this virus. It has been a swiftly evolving experience that everyone on Earth is experiencing somehow.

> **Every few hundred years throughout Western history, a sharp transformation has occurred. In a matter of decades, society altogether rearranges itself — its world view, its basic values, its social and political structures, its arts, its key institutions. Fifty years later a new world exists. And the people born into that world cannot even imagine the world in which their grandparents lived and into which their own parents were born.**
> **Our age is such a period of transformation.**
> **(Drucker, 1992)**

While I see how these words could have applied to the particular time they were spoken in, what we are experiencing today feels like a time of even greater transformation, because the changes have left no aspect of our life untouched. Just over a year ago, no one would have believed it possible. Different challenges have emerged already from the turmoil created by COVID-19 – some polarizing powers found unity in the face of a common enemy; other, previously amicable forces began antagonizing each other while searching for the most expedient measures to deal with this unfolding and ever-expanding crisis.

We witnessed the true colors of people on so many levels: altruism, compassion, and generosity of spirit and action from some, while others exhibited greed, opportunism, ignorance, and unvarnished selfishness. Some rose to the occasion and sacrificed their well-being and even jeopardized their health to serve on the front lines of this intense medical battle, while others came out of the dark with an agenda of dominating the disaster response to meet their own, self-serving needs. The pandemic has swiftly become a test for humanity.

I see this same behavior from the perspective of the corporate response as well. Caught amidst the chaos along with many others, trying to make sense of what was going on, dealing with so many unknowns, and striving to do the right thing, I witnessed how quickly and drastically the circumstances for doing business have changed for everyone in the corporate world.

A list of industries, designated as essential infrastructure, were required to remain functional; they had to ramp up operations to ensure necessities for society's continued operation remain available. The biggest challenge was how to maintain their people's health and safety while running their operations in these new and highly unfamiliar conditions. Other industries, deemed non-essential, had to either close or to move to an online platform, requiring swift and creative solutions to stay functional, operational, financially feasible, and relevant.

The economic crisis imposed on us by the virus brought each company an unprecedented set of challenges. Some industries struggled to stay afloat, cutting costs until they were bleeding red ink, having to quickly let their core people go. Others, driven by the goal of adequately responding to the growing demand on their industry, struggled to keep enough employees at work. Everyone has been stricken with fear, of catching and spreading this insidious disease to their loved ones. The deadly risks are often unpredictable, as this tiny, invisible invader spreads easily from human to human, frequently without displaying signs of infection or even experiencing any symptoms at first. The

COVID-19 crisis has changed our lives in so many ways, from the shocking loss of hundreds of thousands of lives, to a profound and pervasive economic impact around the globe.

Some of the ways people are being affected by the pandemic:

- Losing jobs or forced to go on indefinite leave;
- Working from home – adjusting to this new reality while trying to carry on;
- Forced to remain at work, feeling guilty as the only potential transmitters of the disease from the outside world to a self-isolating family, while children must adapt to online education, and spouses who have left or lost their jobs;
- Helplessly tracking reported exponential infection rates and death toll counts all over the world;
- Saying untimely, heart-wrenching good-byes to loved ones taken by the virus, and adding personal grief to the list of unexpected challenges.
- Experiencing loneliness and depression triggered by the isolation from family and friends due to the mandatory restrictions on social and leisure activities.

Within a few weeks after the pandemic was announced, pretty much everyone knew of someone who had caught the disease, had died from its complications or, in some way, suffering from the underlying conditions that were aggravated by the impact of the virus. Panic and anxiety have gotten the best of many people.

In this extraordinary time, under these extraordinary circumstances, only one thing can make a difference between making or breaking a workplace. It is the workers' attitude towards their job, in particular towards their employer.

Do they feel safe and secure to come to work every day amidst this pandemic? Do they feel their employer cares about their well-being and the well-being of the family members they have left at home?

As I have been writing this book, I have been contemplating the potential impact my conclusions might have on 'business as usual.' Now that the entire world has endured a shock to its system, I believe I have at least one perspective to offer to assist in surviving the aftermath of this major blow to our way of life. My most recent experiences have brought this understanding into crystal clarity to me!

It comes down to a simple question: Are you a manager, owner, business leader, committed to providing a Caring Workplace? I don't mean a workplace that suddenly started caring because it has customer orders to fulfill amidst the crisis, and government regulations to meet to keep its people safe from the virus and its products free from contamination. What I mean is, are you already providing a Caring Workplace? Have you already established a business structure that has been there for your people all along, that has earned your peoples' trust by your ongoing actions and daily decisions, decisions based on essential values such as upholding peoples' worth? Are you dedicated to continuing to provide a Caring Workplace with work conditions that allow your valued team to do their best every day?

When the crisis hit, it became obvious to me that nothing else matters except the long-standing respect you have earned from your employees, who knew that you have their best interests in mind, that they could trust you with their very lives and the lives of their loved ones.

You could be a business savvy organization amply prepared for most emergencies, with a well-thought-out Business Continuity plan that covers all foreseeable emergencies (the keyword here being foreseeable). You may have addressed fire, flood, earthquake, previously known epidemics, and, in some situations, even an active shooter situation. However, the situation we now face is already deeper and more urgent than anything we could have imagined.

Your company may have been one of those few who were not completely caught off guard by this Black Swan event. Were you prepared for most of the world to scale down and go into self-isolation? Were you prepared to deal with the impact of a pandemic of this size and scope, with the added stress of the questionable nature of this perfect biological weapon? This virus is so contagious and so insidious, surrounded by so much mystery and conflicting theories, that it puts paralyzing fear into your people. Due to your work, now you are needing to face the challenges to ramp up your operations amidst the chaos. How can you do that? Were you prepared?

- When your supply chain is global and you have interdependent relationships with multiple partner organizations all over the map, but travel restrictions make it difficult to operate as normal? What will you do now?

- When the virus is on the rise, and there are not enough test kits to identify the true numbers of those infected, and the test results require an agonizing wait period, while it is admitted the testing is not entirely accurate? How do you operate under such conditions as these?

- When you realized the health-care system you have depended upon is ill equipped to care for the growing numbers of patients, while proper treatment and effective prevention methods are not available for the foreseeable future? When the public vaccination efforts cannot keep up with the ever-changing effects of the rapidly mutating virus? How will you handle losing key employees to illness or death?

I have realized, this is the kind of situation that calls forth the manifestation of the QIQO principle – taking responsibility for the Quality of your Inputs so you and your team can expect Quality Outputs. That's the way your leadership qualities will be fully tested.

The true test of the QIQO principle I am proposing is this:

> **When a real emergency hits you and your operation, everyone works as a team, ready to do what needs to be done, knowing you have their backs.**

If you have built trust in your peoples' minds – trust that you've had their backs all along – they will be there for you. Because after all, we are in this situation together. You can't handle the future we all face without your team, and they won't be able to do their job if they don't have faith in you as their leader.

This crisis has become a profound test of leadership – strength of character, commitment to core values, and an ability to be agile and reprioritize on the go. The most innovative and agile organizations knew what to do from the first moment they grasped the scope of what was happening. For example, companies began turning their efforts from a non-essential to an essential industry to save their operation from closing and to keep their people employed. We saw this in many instances with companies and individuals responding to the public outcry for Personal Protective Equipment to save ourselves and our frontline first responders.

These are examples I have seen of how real leaders show that they can be depended upon:

- A Coquitlam, British Columbia based company called Novo Textiles, a pillow and dog bed manufacturer, became one of the first companies in Metro Vancouver to respond to the crisis in this innovative way. They saw their orders dry up pretty quickly as the self-isolation mandates were announced. The immune-compromised CEO knew that either his 20,000-square-foot factory was closing or he had to make a decision to retool quickly. That's when they turned to manufacturing respiratory masks (Ryan, 2020).

- GearHalo, an Edmonton, Alberta based manufacturer of deodorizer pods for sports gear, retooled its production to making masks similar to N95 in as little as eight days, primarily to donate them to frontline workers, and secondly to keep their staff employed. They added value by offering a free mask for every two purchased (Cook, 2020)
- To save jobs and contribute to society, a prosthetics manufacturer, KCK from Kansas City, Missouri USA, also switched gears to making respiratory masks with the goal of producing about 10,000 masks a week, and donating one mask for every mask sold. It also further supported the concept of giving back by encouraging their employees to volunteer. For every hour an employee volunteered, the company gave them eight hours off, to further promote their organizational culture of giving back (Shope, 2020).

Organizations with missions aimed at helping societal problems and supporting those at the greatest risk are now taking the opportunity to stay true to their mission, extending their efforts to alleviate some of the burden. This is done either through product donations, or by virtual or live volunteering to benefit frontline and health-care workers, while showing compassion and understanding to their employees. These are some recent examples of how the decisive behavior of leaders affects trust levels between different groups in an organization, as well as within our society at large. Our collective values are truly being tested. From my perspective, trust is the most important value that comes into play.

At the same time, the crisis helped expose the true colors of other companies, highlighting leaders looking to benefit from the deadly virus and the uncertainty behind it. We have all seen businesses seeking to profit from the misery of others, to make money from compulsory treatments; some legitimate, some not, to take advantage of the fearful and desperate. We have witnessed reports of people behaving as if they are all that matters: from stockpiling and reselling vital products at inflated prices, to the hypocrisy of a high-ranking official of a transnational company captured by building surveillance cameras sanitizing his hands thoroughly before raising his foot to operate the elevators buttons in an attempt to keep himself protected, but carelessly spreading the hazard to everyone else.

The opportunity to grow is right here. From what I have witnessed during the crisis, not every workplace leader has the ability to exude calm, composure, and inner collectedness. When the COVID-19 crisis hit workplaces, many employees even in essential industries relocated their place of employment to their homes. No longer having the luxury of face-to-face interactions with their managers and coworkers, for what seems to be, very likely, a long time, how do leaders keep employees accountable, and help them remain productive during the whole time, when no one is watching what they do? It all comes down to trust, again. I understand: it is a little late to say this, since a crisis is not the time to start building that trust in your remote team, but it must be said. The caring two-way relationships had to be fostered for a consistent amount of time, so you have the necessary assurance, during this crisis and the ones that will inevitably follow, that your team supports your operation in the most effective, whole-hearted manner they can.

Does it help to have a truly Caring Workplace based on QIQO principles when you are facing a *Black Swan Event*? Tremendously! Is it too late to build one now? Not for everyone. If you want to survive and come out stronger on the other end of this challenge, there are actions you can begin to take today. Obviously, one-size-fits-all solutions that apply to every organization don't exist. Meanwhile, a new priority has arisen: to build a more solid foundation on top of your already established structures for further improvement and that most important quality – **caring** for the future.

There are actions a committed leader can take during this time of uncertainty, to rise to their highest potential, and that truly matters. By the time you reach your maximum capacity, more will be required. Your actions can guide your team to push past the anxiety and uncertainty all of us are facing. As a result, we will find ourselves unlocking great innovation and creativity, through the collective power of generating diverse ideas, and acting upon them, in an agile manner, to bring forward the best possible results.

D. CONCLUSION

Should you take the time to measure the principles offered in this book against your own situation, and see how they would apply to serve your needs? If you see the value in what I have shared, you could begin by taking your organization to the next level, while capturing all the best practices you already have in place. Your leadership can help your people shift their mind-frame, from seeing the changes we now face as adversity, to viewing it as an opportunity to tap into their hidden powers, strength, and forward thinking. This will, hopefully, make an enormous difference for themselves and the others whom they love and serve.

Be the role model of the behavior you would like others to display during the crisis. Despite terrifying news reports, externally and perhaps even within your own organization, maintain a positive attitude, a sharp focus on what can be controlled and a powerful message that rises above the white noise. Do not wait until the next crisis. I wish I could confidently say, this is it, this is all you'll have to deal with, but that is not the case. There are many more challenges heading our way, and we must be fully prepared to adapt, adjust, and respond with calm and wisdom. I recommend you spend what time you have right now to build your leadership, your culture, and your team today.

Despite the storm around you, and severe lack of time while dealing with crisis after crisis – show sincere caring to your hardworking people. Take five minutes out of your work discussion to inquire about their well-being, their health, and their family. Appreciate everything they do, and take action to recognize their efforts; even if it's just the effort they put in to showing up to work during a time when most of the people they know are protecting themselves elsewhere from exposure to the virus.

Remain transparent in regards to your expectations; that is such an incredibly important element in your managerial toolkit, something that builds the trust of your team. The focus is on how to continue to operate during the crisis, on what progressive measures to take to keep everyone safe, while staying on top of performance expectations and delivering results. Keep communicating your vision to your team to keep it fresh in their minds. Knowing the goal gives people a chance to meet your expectations without constant instruction and direction.

Delegate tasks as needed to take advantage of your team's collective strengths, and the unique talents each brings to the table. Help your team to step up, so that you can mobilize the best possible technical expertise, intellectual power, strength of character, and moral resources.

> **Most importantly, never delegate and outsource the one thing that matters most: implementing and promoting the QIQO principle to shape the culture of a Caring Workplace that inspires people to do their best every day.**

Whether it's a day of drought with storm clouds of uncertainty looming, or the sunny days we hope to return to, with business-as-usual productivity, cooperation, and achievements, the reward to your efforts will be ample and satisfying.

You've been planting the seeds all along:

- Caring about your people;
- Investing in their growth and development;
- Taking genuine interest in their well-being;
- Teaching accountability;
- Setting an example of high work standards;
- Creating a work environment that inspires your people to do their best every day, so they can find personal meaning while growing to the level they want to.

These are the seeds that grow and provide an ample yield of the bounty you deserve.

It has been my pleasure and honor to share my thoughts, research, and recommendations with you. When I stepped into the journey of writing this book, I had no idea I would be sharing it with a world that is so changed we can't recognize it any more. Perhaps the timing of this book is perfect. The kind of organization that has already taken steps to build a Caring Workspace will have a major advantage moving forward. Now, with the requirements for surviving and thriving in a business environment that has vastly changed, dive into this new way of running your business. You might find that this current crisis is exactly the opportunity you need to find your way into a very different future than you could have ever anticipated. Who knows? It might be way better than you could have ever dreamed.

As children, my siblings and I wanted to build a better future. As we were role-playing and constructing those make-believe cities, we knew something instinctively: working together leads to much more rewarding experiences and much more sustainable results. The support we gave each other was crucial if we wanted to enjoy the long-term success both in our games and our real-life relationships. The benefits of cooperating and looking out for each other's needs were exponential. We had no idea how important this concept of caring for each other would be in the future, but I am pondering: if my siblings and I figured out this simple truth back then, we as business leaders can do it now. We can expand and build on that concept.

I am going to leave you with this:

Now that we are facing a completely different future that no one would have predicted – it's even more important to rely on each other and build each other up. Build true teamwork to take advantage of our collective strengths and wisdom. Think of ways to grow and extend cooperative workplace mentality, so that you can become the leaders of Caring Organizations.

ACKNOWLEDGEMENTS

Years of work and a great deal of inspiration went into writing this book. I feel that I might never be able to properly thank everyone who has been a part of this journey, but I am giving it my best shot.

First and foremost, I would like to thank my mentor, George Verdolaga, the visionary who served as the tipping point in my *Quality In Quality Out* adventure.

I would like to extend a special thank you to my Mother, Valida Isazada. With her endless wisdom and humility, she has been my safe haven, my moral compass, and my sounding board in so many ways.

I thank my siblings and the rest of my incredibly supportive and loving family for always having my back.

I am eternally grateful to my dear father, Oktay Isazada, and my beloved grandparents, who are watching over me from above. They taught me so much with their life examples, and convinced me since my early years that I could accomplish anything. Their values and mine are closely entwined, and I am honored to carry on their tradition.

I thank all the people who helped me learn these incredible life and business lessons, by sharing their valuable industry experience, and real-world stories: Mary Springer, Craig Richmond, Ben Baker, Arc Rajtar, James LeDon Childress, Afshin Asgari, and Lucia Styk, among so many others. I would like to thank my ASQ Vancouver family, especially Santosh Mishra, Mary Duffy, and Sandra Amador, for their direct contributions to this book.

I deeply appreciate the time, energy, and focus my editors - Auz Berger, and especially my developmental editor Ashara Love - devoted to ensuring that my storytelling remained sharp and my message clear. I am also thankful to my book designer, Dragan Bilic, who has developed a beautiful vehicle to help me spread the word of my mission: to reach business leaders to encourage and embrace the concept of Caring Corporations.

I must thank my great friends from all walks of life who were there for me through my own ups and downs. I am grateful to each and every one of them, especially to Feride and Murat Buyuran, who kept believing in me even during the times when not believing seemed more sensible.

I especially wish to honor the many people I met throughout my career, who participated in my research or became the motivation behind the success stories or cautionary tales in this book. And lastly, much gratitude to my blog readers and workshop participants who, over the course of years, inspired me with their insightful comments and unending interest in the concepts and philosophy I honed with their assistance, and the message I have felt compelled to share.

ABOUT THE AUTHOR

Natella Isazada is a Quality, Risk, Health, and Safety Management expert, speaker, and author. She has dedicated herself to promoting and empowering Continual Improvement in organizational performance through personal growth and transformation. With over 15 years of progressive experience, Natella has passionately engaged in helping organizations in the United States and Canada to properly manage risk while maintaining product quality, process excellence, and the highest standards of health and safety for all employees. A long-standing member-leader of American Society for Quality, she chaired the ASQ Vancouver Section in 2020, and is an ASQ Certified Manager of Quality/Organizational Excellence.

Born and raised in Azerbaijan, Natella graduated from Baku State University with a degree in International Journalism. She worked as an investigative journalist, covering larger scale societal issues and human rights stories. To better equip herself with the knowledge needed to further support social justice, she earned a degree in Law from Moscow State Social University. She then moved to the U.S. and proceeded to complete her Master's in Public Administration at the University of Nebraska, Omaha. She began her third career, in corporate management and consulting in the U.S.

After experiencing life in a few diverse places, Natella found a welcoming home in Greater Vancouver, British Columbia, Canada, while continuing to maintain strong ties to her mother country, Azerbaijan.

Natella's extensive world travel, life-long passion for learning, and intention to provide a holistic approach to organizational development, give her fresh perspectives when it comes to effective problem-solving. Natella shares her ideas through professional publications, keynote speeches, and workshops.

She was featured on a TEDx stage in Chilliwack, B.C. in 2019, sharing the roots of her youthful inspiration for global service, encouraging her audience to consider *The Power of Child-Like Innocence*. Her blog, Quality In and Quality Out, and this eponymous book, explain how QIQO is a proven cost-effective business and personal life approach. In this book, Natella is delighted to share her experience, research, and perspective: that a healthy bottom line is more likely when companies create caring workplaces that inspire people to do their best every day.

Natella has plans to teach corporate leaders how to implement the essential foundational tools and structures for Caring Corporations, and she invites you to consider reaping the benefits to you, your company, and the hard-working employees who make it possible to transform work life into a joyful and beneficial enterprise.

REFERENCES

"About", Holacracy, HolacracyOne, LLC, 2016.
www.holacracy.org/holacracyone

American Management Association *"Peter Drucker on The Value of Ignorance"*, Jan. 24, 2019.
https://www.amanet.org/articles/peter-drucker-on-the-value-of-ignorance/

Achor, Shawn, *"The Happiness Advantage: How a Positive Brain Fuels Success in Work and Life"*, Currency, 5 Jun. 2018.

Anthony, Scott D., Trotter, Alasdair & Schwartz, Evan I, *"The Top 20 Business Transformations of the Last Decade"*, Harvard Business Review, 11 Dec. 2019.
hbr.org/2019/09/the-top-20-business-transformations-of-the-last-decade

Association for Safe International Road Travel, *"Annual Global Road Crash Statistics"*, ASIRT 2019.
https://www.asirt.org/safe-travel/road-safety-facts

Association of Corporate Citizenship Professionals.
https://www.accprof.org/ACCP/ACCP/About_the_Field/Blogs/Blog_Pages/Corporate-Social-Responsibility-Brief-History.aspx

Auletta, Ken, *"Googled: The End of the World as We Know It"*, Penguin Press, 3 Nov. 2009.

Baker, Jim, *"Helping People Make Smooth Transitions During Change"*, Sacred Structures, 28 Apr. 2015.
https://sacredstructures.org/movement/helping-people-make-smooth-transitions-during-change/

Beal, Vangie, *"Information Silo"*, Webopedia.
https://www.webopedia.com/TERM/I/information_silo.html

Birkett, Alex., **"Knowledge Management Systems: The Ultimate Guide"**, Hubspot.
https://www.hubspot.com/knowledge-management-systems

Black, Edwin, **"IBM and the Holocaust"**, The New York Times, Oct. 2000.
archive.nytimes.com/www.nytimes.com/books/first/b/black-ibm.html

Blacklock, Jean, & Jacks, Evelyn, **"Get Your People to Work like They Mean It!"**, McGraw-Hill, 14 Sep. 2006.

Blanchard, Ken, Randolph, Alan & Grazier, Peter, **"Go Team!: Take Your Team to the Next Level"**, Berrett-Koehler Publishers, 10 Jun. 2007.

Bloomenthal, Andrew, **"Ringing the Bell Curve"**, Investopedia, 31 Mar. 2020.
www.investopedia.com/terms/b/bell-curve.asp

Bridges, William, **"Managing Transitions: Making the Most of Change"**, Da Capo Lifelong Books, 22 Sept. 2009.

Bulman, May, **"Homeless Man Who Pulled Nails from Faces of Child Terror Victim: I'm Not a Hero'"**, Independent Digital News and Media, 26 May 2017.

www.independent.co.uk/news/uk/home-news/manchester-bombing-homeless-man-helped-victims-says-not-hero-attack-isis-terrorist-salman-abedi-a7757301.html

Cancialosi, C, **"What Is Organizational Culture?"**, Gotham Culture, 17 Jul. 2017.
gothamculture.com/what-is-organizational-culture-definition/

Cappelli, Peter, **"Why Companies Aren't Getting the Employees They Need"**, The Wall Street Journal, 24 Oct. 2011.
https://www.wsj.com/articles/SB10001424052970204422404576596630897409182

Cloud, Henry, **"Boundaries for Leaders: Results, Relationships, and Being Ridiculously in Charge"**, Harper Business, 16 Apr. 2013.

Cohen, William, **"The Practical Drucker: Applying the Wisdom of the World's Greatest Management Thinker"**, AMACOM, 12 Nov. 2013.

Collins, Jim, **"Good to Great: Why Some Companies Make the Leap... And Others Don't"**, Harper Business, 19 Jul. 2001.

Commons, John R, *"The Distribution of Wealth"*, 1893. Creative Media Partners, LLC, 2015.

Cone Communications and Echo 2017 Study.
https://www.conecomm.com/news-blog/2017/5/15/americans-willing-to-buy-or-boycott-companies-based-on-corporate-values-according-to-new-research-by-cone-communications

Cone Communications 2016 Study.
https://www.conecomm.com/research-blog/2016-millennial-employee-engagement-study

Consultant's Mind, *"What Is the Peter Principle?"*, Consultant's Mind, 5 Jul. 2019.
www.consultantsmind.com/2017/06/19/peter-principle/

Cook, Adam, *"Local sports company switches gears to make masks during pandemic"*.

CTV News Edmonton, 14 Apr. 2020.
https://edmonton.ctvnews.ca/local-sports-company-switches-gears-to-make-masks-during-pandemic-1.4896484

Covey, Stephen R, *"7 Habits of Highly Effective People Powerful Lessons in Personal Change"*, Simon & Schuster, 19 Nov. 2013.

Covey, Stephen R, *"Principle Centered Leadership"*, Summit Books, 1 Sep. 1991.

Deming, W. Edwards, *"Lessons From the Red Bead Experiment with Dr. Deming"*, The W. Edwards Deming Institute, 10 Mar. 2014.
blog.deming.org/2014/03/lessons-from-the-red-bead-experiment-with-dr-deming/

"Dilbert", Wikipedia, Wikimedia Foundation, 11 Jun. 2020.
en.wikipedia.org/wiki/Dilbert

Dodson, Eric, director, *"Maslow In Ten Minutes"*, YouTube, 15 Feb. 2014.
www.youtube.com/watch?v=qQJwE6yg6cY

Doke, DeeDee, Bourne, Michael & Hunsaker, Phillip L, *"Building a Team: The Practical Guide to Mastering Management"*, DK Publishing, 20 Dec. 2010.

Doyle, Andy, *"Management and Organization at Medium"*,
Medium, 12 Aug. 2016.
blog.medium.com/management-and-organization-at-medium-2228cc9d93e9

2014 Edelman Trust Barometer.
http://www.edelman.com/Trust2014

Drucker, Peter, *"The New Society of Organizations"*, Harvard Business
Review, Sep-Oct 1992.
https://hbr.org/1992/09/the-new-society-of-organizations

Edmans, Alex, *"28 Years of Stock Market Data Shows a Link Between
Employee Satisfaction and Long-Term Value"*, Harvard Business Review,
24 Mar. 2016.
https://hbr.org/2016/03/28-years-of-stock-market-data-shows-a-link-between-employee-satisfaction-and-long-term-value

"FedEx Attributes Success to People-First Philosophy",
FedEx Newsroom, 7 Apr. 2016.
about.van.fedex.com/newsroom/fedex-attributes-success-people-first-philosophy/

Flade, Peter, Asplund, Jim & Elliot, Gwen, *"Employees Who Use Their
Strengths Outperform Those Who Don't"*, Gallup, 8 Oct. 2015.
https://www.gallup.com/workplace/236561/employees-strengths-outperform-don.aspx#:~:text=Gallup%20analysis%20reveals%20that%20people,likely%20to%20quit%20their%20jobs

Gelles, David, *"The Zappos Exodus Continues After a Radical
Management Experiment"*, The New York Times, 13 Jan. 2016.
bits.blogs.nytimes.com/2016/01/13/after-a-radical-management-experiment-the-zappos-exodus-continues/

Hamel, Gary, *"First, Let's Fire All the Managers"*,
Harvard Business Review, 7 Dec. 2011.
hbr.org/2011/12/first-lets-fire-all-the-managers.

Hamori, Monika, Cao, Jie & Koyuncu, Burak, *"Why Top Young Managers
are in Nonstop Job Hunt"*, Harvard Business Review, July-August 2012.
https://hbr.org/2012/07/why-top-young-managers-are-in-a-nonstop-job-hunt

Harford, Tim, *"The Peter Principle is a joke taken seriously. Is it true?"*,
Needull, 7 Oct. 2018.
https://needull.com/2018/10/07/the-peter-principle-is-a-joke-taken-seriously-is-it-true/

Hemp, Paul, *"Presenteeism: At Work—But Out of It"*,
Harvard Business Review, Oct. 2004.
https://hbr.org/2004/10/presenteeism-at-work-but-out-of-it.

History.com Editors, 2010.
https://www.history.com/topics/early-20th-century-us/john-d-rockefeller

Hunter, G. Shawn, *"Small Acts of Leadership: 12 Intentional Behaviors That Lead to Big Impact"*, Perseus Distribution Services, 19 Dec. 2016.

Isazada, Natella, University of Nebraska, Omaha, School of Public Administration, Capstone Project, May 2001.

Izzo, John & Vanderwielen, Jeff, *"The Purpose Revolution: How Leaders Create Engagement and Competitive Advantage in an Age of Social Good"*, Berrett-Koehler Publishers, 13 Mar. 2018.

Johnson, Michael Arthur, *"What Is the RED BEAD Game?"*, Red Bead Experiment, *Michael Arthur Johnson Company*, 24 Jan. 2014.
www.redbead.com/what/

Kotter, John P, *"A Sense of Urgency"*,
Harvard Business Press, 5 Aug. 2008.

Kruse, Kevin, *"How Employee Engagement Leads to Higher Stock Prices"*, American Express, 27 Mar. 2012.
https://www.americanexpress.com/en-us/business/trends-and-insights/articles/how-employee-engagement-leads-to-higher-stock-prices/

Langton, Nancy, Robbins, Stephen P. & Judge, Timothy A.

"What Is Situational Leadership? How Flexibility Leads to Success", St. Thomas University Online, 25 Nov. 2014.
online.stu.edu/articles/education/what-is-situational-leadership.aspx

Leong, Kathy Chin, *"Google Reveals Its 9 Principles of Innovation"*, Fast Company, 20 Nov. 2013.
www.fastcompany.com/3021956/googles-nine-principles-of-innovation

Lichtenberg, Ronna, *"It's Not Business, It's Personal: the 9 Relationship Principles That Power Your Career"*, Hachette Books, 3 Jan.2001.

Lipman, Victor, *"Surprising, Disturbing Facts From The Mother Of All Employee Engagement Surveys"*, Forbes Magazine, 30 Jul. 2015.
www.forbes.com/sites/victorlipman/2013/09/23/
surprising-disturbing-facts-from-the-mother-of-all-employee-engagement-surveys

Luntz, Frank I, *"Win: The Key Principles to Take Your Business from Ordinary to Extraordinary"*, Hachette Books, 1 Mar. 2011.

May, Matthew E, *"Winning the Brain Game: Fixing the 7 Fatal Flaws of Thinking"*, McGraw-Hill Education, 27 May. 2016.

McCaskill, Andrew, *"Consumer-Goods' Brands That Demonstrate Commitment To Sustainability Outperform Those That Don't"*, Nielson, 12 Oct. 2015.
https://www.nielsen.com/us/en/press-releases/2015/consumer-goods-brands-that-demonstrate-commitment-to-sustainability-outperform/

McGregor, Douglas & Cutcher-Gershenfeld, Joel E, *"The Human Side of Enterprise"*, McGraw-Hill, 11 Jan. 2006.

Mcleod, Saul, *"Maslow's Hierarchy of Needs"*,
Simply Psychology, 20 Mar. 2020.
www.simplypsychology.org/maslow.html

McQuaid, Michelle, *"The 3 Mistakes Companies Make Focusing On People's Strengths"*, Psychology Today, Sussex Publishers, 11 Jan. 2016.
www.psychologytoday.com/us/blog/functioning-flourishing/201601/
the-3-mistakes-companies-make-focusing-people-s-strengths

McIntyre, Douglas A., Hess, Alexander E.M. & Weigley, Samuel, *"Eight Founders Who Ruined Their Companies"*, USA Today, Gannett Satellite Information Network, 10 Feb. 2013.
www.usatoday.com/story/money/business/2013/02/09/
founders-ruin-companies/1905921/

Melrose, Ken, *"Making Grass Greener on Your Side"*, Berrett-Koehler Publisher, 1 Jan. 1995.

NextBigWhat, *" 'The Best Failed Idea'–A Lesson From Ratan Tata's Internal Contest at Tata Group"*, NextBigWhat, 13 Apr. 2011.
https://nextbigwhat.com/the-best-failed-idea-contest-tata/

Nissan Motor Corporation Annual Report 2015.
https://www.nissan-global.com/EN/DOCUMENT/PDF/AR/2015/AR15_E_P10.pdf

Nohria, Nitin & Beer, Michael, *"Cracking the Code of Change"*, Harvard Business Review, May–June 2000.
https://hbr.org/2000/05/cracking-the-code-of-change

O'Connor, Clare, *"These Retailers Involved In Bangladesh Factory Disaster Have Yet To Compensate Victims"*, Forbes, 26 Apr. 2014.
https://www.forbes.com/sites/clareoconnor/2014/04/26/these-retailers-involved-in-bangladesh-factory-disaster-have-yet-to-compensate-victims/#17682f79211b

O'Leary, Kevin, *"Cold Hard Truth: On Business, Money & Life"*, Doubleday Canada, 27 Sept. 2011.

Ottati, Victor, Price, Erika D., Wilson, Chase & Sumaktoyo, Nathanael, *"When Self-Perceptions of Expertise Increase Closed-Minded Cognition: The Earned Dogmatism Effect"*, Journal of Experimental Social Psychology, vol. 61, Aug. 2015, pp. 131–138.,
https://nathanael.id/download/2015-Earned-Dogmatism.pdf

Ovans, Andrea, *"Overcoming the Peter Principle"*, Harvard Business Review, 22 Dec. 2014.
hbr.org/2014/12/overcoming-the-peter-principle

Oxfam America, *"Lives On the Line: The Human Cost of Cheap Chicken"*, © 2015 Oxfam America Inc.

PEST analysis, *Wikipedia*, 27 Jul. 2020.
https://en.wikipedia.org/wiki/PEST_analysis

"Peter Drucker on The Value of Ignorance", American Management Association, 24 Jan. 2019.
https://www.amanet.org/articles/peter-drucker-on-the-value-of-ignorance/

Poznan, Jovana, *"The History of Consulting"*, *Medium*, Brainsfeed, 12 Feb. 2018.
medium.com/brainsfeed/the-history-of-consulting-fdc73d5a10a0

"Millennials at Work, Reshaping the Workplace", PWC.com, 2011.
https://www.pwc.de/de/prozessoptimierung/assets/millennials-at-work-2011.pdf

"What is the ADKAR Model?", The Prosci Adkar Model, Prosci.
https://www.prosci.com/adkar/adkar-model

Proulx, Mike, *"Why We Give Out an 'Epic Fail Award' to Employees"*, *Innovation Leader*, 24 Oct. 2019.
www.innovationleader.com/employee-engagement/why-we-give-out-an-epic-fail-award-to-employees/1193.article

Reh, F. John, *"The Peter Principle and How to Beat It"*, *The Balance Careers*, 15 Nov. 2019.
www.thebalancecareers.com/the-peter-principle-2275684

Rigoni, Brandon & Nelson, Bailey, *"The No-Managers Organizational Approach Doesn't Work"*, *Gallup*, 12 Feb. 2016.
www.gallup.com/workplace/236501/no-managers-organizational-approach-doesn-work.aspx

Robinson, Adam, *"Zappos Pays Employees $2000 to Quit. This Superstar CEO Has a Different Approach"*, *Inc.com*, 12 Jan. 2018.
www.inc.com/adam-robinson/zappos-pays-employees-2000-to-quit-this-superstar-ceo-has-a-different-approach.html

Ryan, Denise, *"COVID-19: Coquitlam company retools, will be first in Canada to produce N95 respirators"*, 08 Apr. 2020.

https://vancouversun-com.cdn.ampproject.org/c/s/vancouversun.com/news/local-news/covid-19-coquitlam-company-retools-will-be-first-in-canada-to-produce-n95-respirators/wcm/fe108057-63db-4dfe-835a-b625afa4aea5/amp/

Savage, Chris, *"Ditching Flat: How Structure Helped Us Move Faster"*, *Wistia*, 15 Oct. 2015.
wistia.com/learn/culture/ditching-flat

Schmidt, Eric & Rosenberg, Jonathan, *"How Google Works"*, Grand Central Publishing, 21 Mar. 2017.

Schroeder, Dean M. & Robinson, Alan, G, *"America's Most Successful Export to Japan: Continuous Improvement Programs"*, *MIT Sloan Management Review Magazine,* 15 Apr. 1991.
https://sloanreview.mit.edu/article/americas-most-successful-export-to-japan-continuous-improvement-programs/

Shelly, Katie, *"Management Buzzwords Decoded: Flat, Holacracy, Lean, Agile, Responsive"*, *Medium*, 15 Aug. 2016.
medium.com/@interkatie/mangement-buzzwords-decoded-flat-holocracy-lean-agile-responsive-936185762493

Shope, Alan, *"KCK company switches gears to make face masks during pandemic"*, KMBC 9 News, 16 Apr. 2020.
https://www.kmbc.com/article/
kck-company-switches-gears-to-make-face-masks-during-pandemic/32178600#

"Silo",Merriam-Webster.
https://www.merriam-webster.com/dictionary/silo.Stevens, Tim. "Dr. Deming: 'Management Today Does Not Know What Its Job Is' (Part 2)." StackPath, 17 Jan. 1994, https://www.industryweek.com/operations/quality/article/21963886/dr-deming-management-today-does-not-know-what-its-job-is-part-2

Tajitsu, Naomi, *"Renault-Nissan group sold most cars last year, but VW's No.1 including trucks"*, 30 Jan. 2019.
https://www.reuters.com/article/us-automakers-sales-japan/renault-nissan-group-sold-most-cars-last-year-but-vws-no-1-including-trucks-idUSKCN1PO0R1

Taylor, Bill, *"Why Zappos Pays New Employees to Quit—And You Should Too"*, Harvard Business Review, 19 May. 2008.
hbr.org/2008/05/why-zappos-pays-new-employees.

The Cleveland Foundation.
https://www.clevelandfoundation100.org/foundation-of-change/invention/goffs-vision/

Turner, Freda, *"An Effective Employee Suggestion Program has a Multiplier Effect"*, Course Hero, 14 Jan. 2003.
https://www.coursehero.com/file/p319qco/
Freda-Turner-An-Effective-Employee-Suggestion-Program-Has-a-Multiplier-Effect/

Valve Software website:
https://www.valvesoftware.com/en/people#:~:text=Boss%2Dfree%20since%20
1996.,simple%20directive%3A%20Collaborate%20and%20create

Vance, Robert J., Ph.D, *"Employee Engagement and Commitment"*, SHRM Foundation, Society for Human Resources Management, 2006.
https://www.shrm.org/hr-today/trends-and-forecasting/special-reports-and-expert-views/Documents/Employee-Engagement-Commitment.pdf

Waterstone Human Capital, Canada's Best Most Admired Workplaces, November 23, 2017.

Watson, Leon, *"Homeless Man Who Rushed to Help Manchester Attack Victims Has Emotional Reunion with His Mother"*, The Telegraph, Telegraph Media Group, 30 May 2017.
www.telegraph.co.uk/news/2017/05/30/
homeless-man-rushed-help-manchester-attack-victims-has-emotional/

Welch, Jack & Welch, Suzy, *"Winning: The Ultimate Business How-To Book"*, Harper Business, 5 Apr. 2005.

Welch, Jack & Welch, Suzy, *"The Real-Life MBA: Your No-BS Guide to Winning the Game, Building a Team, and Growing Your Career"*, Harper Business, 14 Apr. 2015.

Witt, David, *"Servant Leadership: Dealing with Your Ego Requires a Balancing Act"*, Leadership and Management Articles, Videos and Tools, The Ken Blanchard Companies, 1 Feb. 2018.
resources.kenblanchard.com/blanchard-leaderchat/
servant-leadership-dealing-with-your-ego-requires-a-balancing-act

Wooldridge, Adrian, *"Masters of Management: How the Business Gurus and Their Ideas Have Changed the World—for Better and for Worse"*, Harper Business, 11 Nov. 2011.

Zenger, Jack, & Folkman, Joseph, *"The Trickle-Down Effect of Good (and Bad) Leadership"*, Harvard Business Review, 14 Jan. 2016.
hbr.org/2016/01/the-trickle-down-effect-of-good-and-bad-leadership

Zenger, Jack & Folkman, Joseph, *"What Inspiring Leaders Do"*, Harvard Business Review, 20 Jun. 2013.
hbr.org/2013/06/what-inspiring-leaders-do

Manufactured by Amazon.ca
Bolton, ON